NO ROOM FOR COWARDICE

NO ROOM FOR COWARDICE:
A VIEW OF THE LIFE AND TIMES OF
DAMBUDZO MARACHERA

David Pattison

Africa World Press, Inc.

P.O. Box 1892
Trenton, NJ 08607

P.O. Box 48
Asmara, ERITREA

Africa World Press, Inc.

P.O. Box 1892
Trenton, NJ 08607

P.O. Box 48
Asmara, ERITREA

Cover Design: Ashraful Haque

Library of Congress Cataloging-in-Publication Data

Pattison, David, 1941-
  No room for cowardice : a view of the life & times of
Dambudzo Marechera / David Pattison.
       p. cm
  Includes bibliographical references and index.
   ISBN 0-86543-959-1 -- ISBN 0-86543-960-5 (pbk.)
   1. Marachera, Dambudzo 2. Authors, Zimbabwean--20th
   century--Biography. 3. Zimbabwe--In literature. I. Title.
   PR9390.9.M3 Z83 2001
   823'.914--dc21

                                          2001003396

This book is dedicated to the memory
of Dambudzo Marechera,
and to would-be writers everywhere.

Contents

Chapter Three

The House of Hunger

Marechera and the "postcolonial situation"

Chapter Four

The Black Insider and *Black Sunlight*

Neurosis or Art?

Chapter Five

Mindblast

Return to Zimbabwe

A genuine writer must always be prepared to fight for his work. In fact he must expect all kinds of trouble from every quarter. There is no room for cowardice in writing.

(Dambudzo Marechera, "The Journal", *Scrapiron Blues,* p. 134)

INTRODUCTION

An Unsettled Spirit

Listen, that's the song that will forever blow like an unsettled
spirit from the Zambezi – through Harare, Bulawayo,
Mutare, Gweru, down the Limpopo and back again to the
Zambezi – from which it will again turn restlessly back
searching for you and me so that again and again we can
retell their story, which is not our story. Listen to it. How
sad, how profound, and yet so heartbreakingly pitiful.

(Dambudzo Marechera, "The Alley," *Scrapiron
Blues,* p. 47)

Dambudzo Marechera was born on June 4, 1952 in Vengere Township near Rusape in the then-British colony of Southern Rhodesia, the third child of Isaac and Masvotwa Venezia Marechera. Although he was baptized in 1965 with the Christian names Charles William, at birth he was called Tambudzai. Dambudzo is a different version of the same name that means (appropriately enough in view of his short but eventful life) "the troubled one" or "the one who brings trouble." He died from AIDS-related pneumonia on August 18, 1987 in Harare, Zimbabwe, as the former colony had been renamed following the official end of British rule in April 1980.

Some little time after the funeral Michael Marechera, one of Dambudzo's brothers, told an astonishing story which began, "When we buried Dambudzo I was an angry man. For some years I had been aware that there was a family secret that people wanted to keep hidden." That secret concerned the onset of madness in their mother and related to what many considered madness in her son, Dambudzo. Advised by a *n'anga* (a type of traditional healer able to communicate with the spirits of the ancestors) in 1969 that she could only get rid of her madness by passing it on to one of her children, she had chosen Dambudzo (then seventeen years old) as the recipient. As Father Pearce of St Augustine's (the school Marechera attended in Penhalonga) confirmed, evidence of severe psychological disturbance in Dambudzo Marechera emerged in 1971 when he began to suffer from delusions and attacks of extreme paranoia, conditions that persisted throughout his adult life. [1]

During his life Marechera published a collection of short stories, *The House of Hunger* (1978), which won the 1979 Guardian Fiction Prize (shared with the Irish writer Neil Jordan), a novella, *Black Sunlight* (1980), and *Mindblast* (1984), an eclectic mixture of poetry, plays, and poetry. After his death the Dambudzo Marechera Trust was established with two main aims: to collect the unpublished work of Marechera so as to promote its publication, and to honor Marechera's memory by encouraging young writers.[2] By August 1994 the first phase had been completed but the second phase, that of assisting young writers, was still in the very early stages of development. Since its formation in 1988 the trust has published a novella, *The Black Insider* (1990)[3], the collected poetry, *Cemetery of Mind* (1992), and finally to complete the canon of published work, a miscellany of short stories, children's stories and plays under the title *Scrapiron Blues* (1994). The launch of *Scrapiron Blues* (in Harare, July 1994) was greeted enthusiastically by young Zimbabweans to whom Marechera has become something of a cult figure.

Such indications of a sustained and growing interest not only in the work but also in the life of the writer suggests that Dambudzo Marechera will eventually enjoy a more permanent place in Zimbabwean and African literature, and possibly on a wider, international scale, than looked likely in the difficult years that followed his return in 1982 from "exile" in England. Opinions on the quality of his work have polarized between "potential genius" and "pretentious rubbish." One of the aims of this work is to offer an alternative reading, revealing that although Marechera's "fiction" is often autobiographical it is surprisingly accomplished in a variety of genres. As well as a highly talented novelist Marechera was also a fine short story writer, a very effective dramatist, and a perceptive and moving lyric poet. The quality of the writing is reason enough in itself to read Marechera, but in addition to being a rewarding experience, his work also offers a unique and invaluable record of pre- and post-independence Zimbabwe. Having said that it should be conceded that his work can be difficult. The longer works in particular would have benefited from the writer's cooperation with a sensitive program of careful editing. However, as some critics have compared Marechera to Franz Kafka, it is appropriate to quote Albert Camus on Kafka as his comment has a certain relevance to the Zimbabwean writer, "The whole art of Kafka consists in forcing the reader to reread." [4]

Now that it is possible to take an overview of Marechera's literary output, what do we see? I refer to "literary output" rather than *oeuvre* not only because the work has been selectively edited but also because a number of works have been lost. Marechera's lifestyle was so erratic that even the most diligent researcher would be unable to establish the complete *oeuvre* All the posthumous works were edited before publication and the editors also decided that some minor fragments should not be published. Nevertheless the published works offer a guide to the progression and development of the writer. With the exception of *The Black Insider* (1990), the manuscript of which is dated June 1978, the writing of the prose fiction has the same chronology as the publication. (*Black Sunlight* although published ten years before *Black Insider* was in fact written some months afterwards, as an attempt to revise the latter after rejection by Heinemann.[5]) The collected poetry, *The Cemetery of Mind*, covers the period of the writer's adult life.

I intend in this introduction to provide a backcloth against which to view Dambudzo Marechera and his work and to confront the questions of who he was, what he wrote and what influenced that writing.

In 1888 Lobengula, the Ndebele [6]ruler, signed the Rudd Concession giving mineral rights to the representatives of Cecil Rhodes who formed the British South Africa Company. A Royal Charter was obtained in 1889 and the following year 200 pioneer settlers and 500 troops arrived to establish a settlement that they called Salisbury, now renamed Harare. In 1894 the country was given the name of Rhodesia in honor of Rhodes. The Ndebele and the Shona initially put up fierce resistance to the encroachment of the settlers in a series of battles that became known as the First Chimurenga (a Shona word meaning "battle for liberation"). But white supremacy was firmly established by 1897. The British South Africa Company actively encouraged white settlement and ran Rhodesia until 1923 when it became a self-governing colony following the 1922 referendum. A series of legislative acts in the 1920s and 30s increased the social, political and economic dominance of the white minority and weakened the position of black Africans by denying them, among other things, access to the best land and to skilled employment. By the 1940s and 50s, and from a position of absolute power, some moderate white leaders were prepared to make limited concessions to the black Africans to encourage economic growth and to gain some African support.

In October 1953, some sixteen months after Marechera's birth, the British government established the Central African Federation following long and difficult negotiations. This consisted of Southern Rhodesia, Northern Rhodesia and Nyasaland. The declared aims behind the formation of the CAF were to promote economic development and to create a multiracial partnership to ease the path to independence as the movement to disband the British Empire gathered pace with impetus from Westminster. The move to federation was resisted by white supremacists who rejected any notion of power-sharing, and by black leaders who dismissed the arrangement as little more than a sham, due in part at least, to the complete failure of the British government to consult with any black Africans.

It is now a matter of record that the federation never developed meaningful multiracial cooperation, although massive benefits did accrue, principally to whites. Most of the black population in the self-governing colony of Southern Rhodesia was further impoverished as tariffs increased the price of goods, which grew at a faster rate than wages. Against this background black resistance hardened and took shape, generating black nationalism and culminating in the election of nationalist leaders: Hastings Banda in 1961 in Nyasaland, and Kenneth Kaunda the following year in Northern Rhodesia. The Central African Federation was officially disbanded in 1963 and the independent republics of Malawi (Nyasaland) and Zambia (Northern Rhodesia) were recognized in 1964.

Britain refused to grant independence to Southern Rhodesia until the Rhodesian government accepted the principle of majority rule. As the Rhodesian Front Party had successfully contested the 1962 elections on a ticket opposing concessions to the blacks, negotiations were protracted and acrimonious, and inevitably broke down. In November 1965, Rhodesian Prime Minister Ian Smith dispensed with the pretence of further negotiations and proclaimed a Unilateral Declaration of Independence (UDI). Most of the international community (including Britain) regarded the Smith government as illegal, refused to recognize it and imposed sanctions. This tactic was aimed at the country's economy but the resulting isolation had a devastating effect on the intellectual development of black Zimbabweans, who were excluded from the intellectual freedom beginning to be expressed and enjoyed by other black Africans. Not only were black Zimbabweans excluded from international discourse but the initial actions of black leaders had a similar divisive effect within the country. There is evidence to suggest that African Intellectuals split into two groups: radical nationalists, such as Ndabaningi Sithole, Herbert Chitepo and Robert Mugabe; who took militant leadership of the struggle for liberation, and more moderate nationalists including Lawrence Vambe, Stanlake Samkange and Solomon Mutswairo, who went into exile to pursue their academic and literary careers. In this way a split developed between the political and literary movements.

Twelve years of sanctions and increasingly bloody internecine warfare seriously weakened Smith's government and after an ill-judged arrangement with Bishop Muzorewa and other African bishops which led to the short-lived Muzorewa government, Prime Minister Smith renounced UDI and accepted the Lancaster House Agreement in late 1979. Under the supervision of the British Government, represented by Lord Soames, a rapid transition to African majority rule was undertaken. In 1980 ZANU-PF secured a majority in the pre-independence elections and Robert Mugabe was elected Prime Minister. On April 17, 1980 Zimbabwe became independent and gratefully gave up its status as the last colony in Africa.

At this point Dambudzo Marechera was twenty-seven years old, unemployed and living in a squat in London. In view of the turbulent times into which he was born it is not without significance that the first and third sentences in his first published work read, "I got my things and left." and "I couldn't think where to go." (*The House of Hunger*, p. 1), expressing a physical and psychological dislocation that was to become a strand running throughout his writing.

The son of a truck driver, who was killed when Marechera was thirteen years old, and an alcoholic mother who turned to prostitution as a way to support the family on the death of her husband, Marechera nevertheless was able to attend several mission schools, including the prestigious St. Augustine's school at Penhalonga, before entering the University of Rhodesia in 1972 to study English literature. In 1973 he was sent down with other students who were involved in student demonstrations against the Smith government. In 1974, having been awarded a scholarship by the World University Service he went up to New College, Oxford. Unable to settle, or to accept the rigors of academic life, he was sent down in 1976. He then lived precariously as a free-lance writer of no fixed abode in Oxford, Cardiff and London with a brief spell as writer in residence at Sheffield University, before returning to Harare in 1982.

Apparently written on leaving Oxford in 1976 the collection of stories that were to become *The House of Hunger* was submitted to *Drum* magazine in mid-1977. Although there is no reliable record as to when they were actually written it is reasonable to assume that some at least were written in 1976, or even earlier. Certainly the readiness with which Marechera encounters and exposes life in the township and the assurance with which he develops his characters suggests that the experiences described are recent ones.

Neither *Black Sunlight* nor *The Black Insider* show the focussed purpose and certainty of touch and reflect a feature evident in much literature written in exile – an increasing loss of context within which to frame the work. Both works emerged from Marechera's very productive period in 1978/1979. *Black Sunlight* was initially a reworking of the themes and issues first explored in *The Black Insider*, which was itself published (posthumously) only after careful editing removed the more obvious duplicated material. Although an essential piece to consider in approaching an understanding of the complexity that is Dambudzo Marechera, I argue below that the grounds for publishing *Black Sunlight* in the first place were less than convincing and seem to include a large measure of desperation from a beleaguered and Marechera-harassed James Currey (editor of the Heinemann African Writers Series during the period of Marechera's involvement with the publisher). Initially at least, the writer's return to Zimbabwe in 1982 gave a sharper definition to his work and an increased sense of purpose. Unfortunately, he was unable to secure a place for himself in the "new" Zimbabwe and only one work, *Mindblast* (1984), was published before his death in 1987. The final prose collection, *Scrapiron Blues* (1994), and the collected poetry, *Cemetery of Mind* (1992), followed, both volumes offering elegant examples of an incandescent talent.

My first chapter examines the career of the writer and summarizes the critical reception of his work whereas Chapter Two briefly confronts the major issues raised by the writer and his often unique approach to his work and locates the writer's political and intellectual position within those issues. Chapters Three, Four, Five and Six engage directly with the texts and use that material to develop further the issues touched on in Chapter Two. Chapter Seven draws comparisons between Marechera and other Zimbabwean writers. It also considers the development of black Zimbabwean writing and presents an overview of the writer's contribution to that development and to Zimbabwean literature in general.

CHAPTER ONE

An Examination of Marechera's Career and the Critical Reception of his Work

1.1 *The House of Hunger*: A "Premature Success"

As most critical comment has focused on the eponymous story it is common practice to refer to *The House of Hunger* as a novella whereas the work is in fact a collection of short stories with strong thematic links. Inevitable perhaps when so much of the material appears to be biographical: growing up in a divided society; life in the townships; the effect of the guerrilla war on the civilian population, but particularly on young black males; the emasculation of the individual and the family by the pressures of colonization and white minority rule; student life in Salisbury (Harare) and Oxford and the divisive nature of a "European" education.

In an interview with Hans Zell, editor of *A New Reader's Guide to African Literature,* (London: Hans Zell, 1983), the author said of *The House of Hunger* " . . . [it] is about the brutalization of the individual's feelings, instincts, mental processes – the brutalization of all this in such a way that you come to a point where, among ourselves in the black urban areas, that is ordinary reality. . . . I based The *House of Hunger* on fact . . . ." The initial response to publication was muted, but slowly *The House of Hunger* began to attract critical attention, although from the outset opinion on its merits was divided.

In 1980 George Kahari's *The Search for a Zimbabwean Identity* was published by the Mambo Press in Zimbabwe. At that time Kahari was a senior Lecturer in the Department of African Languages at the University of Zimbabwe and his work purported to be the first comprehensive examination of prose fiction written in English by black Zimbabweans. Kahari featured six writers [7] but, surprisingly in view of the attention he had attracted with *The House of Hunger*, Dambudzo Marechera was not included.

This omission was corrected two years later by Musaemura Zimunya in *Those Years of Drought and Hunger* (Mambo Press, Gwelo, 1982). Referring to " . . . strong evidence of serious African fiction in English in Zimbabwe" (p. 2) Zimunya, in his critique found evidence of a "cultural drought" (p. 3), reflecting this in the title of his work; the "hunger" relates directly to the *House of Hunger* which was included by Zimunya along with works by Stanlake Samkange, Geoffrey Ndhlala, Charles Mungoshi and Wilson Katiyo.[8] Zimunya finds some features to admire in *The House of Hunger* but his final analysis is highly critical, even condemnatory. He writes:

> In Marechera Zimbabwe literature achieves confirmation at birth. Unfortunately, the vision is preponderantly private and indulgent. The social and moral undertaking is cynically dismissed at the expense of the aesthetic motive. The artist curries favors and succumbs to the European temptation in a most slatternly exhibition. But, perhaps, the naivete and narcissism will wither and the African become less European. (p. 126)

Here Zimunya is making huge assumptions about the role of the writer, which are challenged below. The comment about "naivete and narcissism" may seem well made, prescient even in the way that Marechera's later writing failed to fulfill the expectations raised by his early work. But the hope that ." . . the African [would] become less European" suggests an unsophisticated view of what constitutes "African" and "European" aesthetics and smacks of the very naivete Zimunya found in Marechera.

Twelve years later Kevin Foster rebutted Zimunya's criticism in a powerful defense of Marechera, claiming "Marechera's treatment of the House of Hunger [Zimbabwe] . . . not only offers a searing critique of the spiritual, moral and cultural starvation imposed on blacks by minority rule, it also nourishes the very ideals of self apprehension and cultural regeneration which Zimunya accused him of rejecting."[9] Foster's argument appeared in 1992 thus demonstrating that interest in *The House of Hunger* remains strong and indicating that it may well hold a permanent place in Zimbabwean literature as a personal record of the turbulent pre-independence years. Of the narrator's development Foster comments:

> . . . Marechera's rejection of the controlling structural norms originates not in an external, ideological impulse, but from the inherent nature of the narrator's development, such as it is, and

Marechera's desire to offer a faithful portrait of it. Had Rhodesia's minority government permitted the narrator anything resembling a complete formative experience, Marechera might have written a more traditionally structured account of his development. (p. 66)

A counter-argument might be that if Marechera had had a "complete formative experience" then he would have written a different book, or perhaps not felt the need to write at all. It is of course difficult to define the nature of a "complete formative experience," or more precisely to define the nature of an "incomplete formative experience." Foster is using a term that does not bear close analysis as it could be argued that any experience is "complete" and "formative" by definition. The argument would be better framed if it was aimed at an understanding of how and why the black experience was manipulated by the white minority so that the socioeconomic and political status of black Zimbabweans remained vastly inferior to that of their white counterparts.

Presumably Foster's point is that the individual was rendered incomplete by his experience. But the term "incomplete" is value-laden and needs a comparative context: "incomplete" compared with what, or whom? It also appears to deny that the intention (of the colonizer towards the indigenous population) may have possessed that limited, and limiting, ambition, and was therefore a complete experience. Whichever argument is followed, an "experience" must be regarded as complete in itself. I am referring to experience as a socio-psychological phenomenon and my aim is to indicate how this phenomenon affects the production and or interpretation of any given text. In that context, it is clear that understanding an experience, or the sum total of any number of experiences, is at the core of interpreting a text. This can be either the totality of experiences of the reader or the author or, more probably, an acceptance of both.

But such experiences must be seen in context. As Frederic Jameson maintains in *The Political Unconscious* (London: Methuen, 1981) when discussing the nature of interpretation, " . . . such semantic enrichment and enlargement of the inert givens and materials of a particular text must take place within three concentric frameworks. . . " (p. 75); it is within those frameworks, which Jameson claims hold the "political unconscious," that we can examine the formative nature of experience. The center circle (according to Jameson) holds the chronicle-like sequence of happenings in time that is political history. Surrounding that are social influences:

> A less diachronic and time bound sense of the tension and struggles between classes, which in its turn is surrounded by a sense of history in its broadest form, holding the "vastest sense of . . . succession and destiny of the various human social formations from pre-historic life to whatever future history has in store for us. (p. 75)

From that great well of history, socializing attitudes, cultural expectations, assumptions and conditioning, political and economic influences plus whatever resides in the collective unconscious (see below), emerges the individual, complete with formative experiences, into what Philip Larkin, perhaps recognizing the infinite possibilities of socio-psychological evolution, called "the million petalled flower of being here" [10] and Marechera recognizing the same random nature of the development of the individual psyche, wrote (with reference to the period following death): "There you will meet all the versions of yourself that did not come out of the womb with you. *It is of them I write.*" (my emphasis) *The Black Insider* (p. 144).

I have referred to the turbulence of the period of Marechera's life in both his external and internal environments. *The House of Hunger* was a largely successful attempt to record those influences and to reflect them within a (probably unintentionally) fragmented form. Later work showed that his ability to enclose that fragmentation did not develop – indeed the discontinuity became more prevalent – leading some critics to form the over-hasty opinion that *Black Sunlight* and *The Black Insider* were incomprehensible. However, despite Zimunya's attack, the consensus of the critics was that *The House of Hunger* was a highly promising and significant work.

The House of Hunger was first submitted to Heinemann in February 1977 under the collective title of "At the Head of the Stream" as a loosely linked collection of short stories. Marechera's letter referred to " . . . a short novel entitled "At the Head of the Stream" and three short stories: "Burning in the Rain," "The Transformation of Harry," and "Black Skin what Mask"; James Currey was impressed and asked for more stories to add substance to the intended publication – Marechera responded with six very short stories ("The Writer's Grain," "The Slow Sound of his Feet," "The Christmas Reunion," "Thought Tracks in the Snow," "Are There People Living There?" and "Characters from the Bergfrith") which Heinemann accepted and regarded as completing the collection.

With some additions (see below) and a change of name the collection was published in December 1978. As Marechera and the truth were often strangers it is no surprise that confusion exists over the genesis of the stories that make up *The House of Hunger*. At times he would claim, romantically if somewhat implausibly, that they were written in a tent pitched by the Isis [11] and at others that he wrote at the kitchen table of some friends called Peter and Shelagh. The eponymous story is the longest in the book, about 37,000 words. All the others are much shorter and their brevity perhaps reflects that it was at the request of his future publisher that more stories were produced, to be "bolted on" in order to produce a total work long enough to publish.

A point of interest here is the role of the Heinemann African Writers Series and particularly the personal involvement of James Currey who, in accepting the six "extra" stories, established a precedent by publishing material from Marechera that had the flavor of hastily worked fragments. Few of the shorter stories match the quality of the title story, with several of the publisher's readers expressing strong misgivings. The relationship thus formed between Currey and Marechera reached an odd climax in 1980 with the publication of the badly received *Black Sunlight* – again published by Currey against the advice of others.

Currey has powerful support from the white Zimbabwean writer, Doris Lessing, who, in her review of *The House of Hunger*, [12] said ." . . it has the consistency and coherence of a novel and I would not disagree if – *pruned a little–* [my emphasis] it had been described as one." She then goes on to concede, "There is difficulty here as if the engine had been fed too powerful a mixture of petrol. One can also make criticisms . . . that the book is bursting at the seams, and uneven." However her comments are best remembered for her observations:

> It is no good pretending this book is an easy or pleasant read. More like overhearing a scream . . .
> The book is an explosion . . . *The House of Hunger* is not polemical writing, far from it: and what a miracle it isn't. But writer and book are both of the nature of miracles. Hard for anyone to become a writer, but to do so against such handicaps? . . . Marechera has in him the stuff and substance that go to make a great writer.

Such praise (Lessing even makes hints of "genius") is perhaps qualified by the faintly patronizing "against such handicaps" and the nagging suspicion that, anxious for the emergence of a Zimbabwean Soyinka, Achebe, or Ngugi, Lessing and others,[13] notably James Currey, became so fulsome in their praise as to give Marechera an inflated view of his status as a writer.

In a more temperate vein, although nevertheless drawing comparisons with Beckett and Kafka, T. O. McLoughlin[14] refers to the breakdown of the narrator (and here in *The House of Hunger* as in Marechera's other works it is impossible to separate

writer and narrator) as "a severance of psyche and language" in
which "The image of home invaded by colonialism deranges the
mind of the narrator. He becomes a victim of spiritual starvation,
of deracination and alienation." No doubt making full use of his
personal knowledge of the writer (McLoughlin taught English
literature at the University of Rhodesia when Marechera was an
undergraduate there) he continues, "Adrift from society, he
communes only with himself, hence the centrality of the interior
monologue and the inclination to write a narrative fragmented by
diffuse memories of the past." "Adrift from society, he
communes only with himself" is a very effective description of
the narrator; it is also a remarkably perspicacious comment on
the Marechera who was to produce *The Black Insider* and *Black
Sunlight*.

Elsewhere, McLoughlin writes of "a double edged
alienation" resulting from exposure to a "new" culture as a
European education attacked the very roots of traditional native
belief and value systems while colonial mores denied black
Africans entry into the world represented by that education.[15]
Although McLoughlin was writing of Mungoshi's Lucifer
(*Waiting for the Rain*) and Samkange's Muchemwa (*The
Mourned One*) he could equally have been referring to
Dambudzo Marechera; but not, apparently, to *The House of
Hunger* which McLoughlin asserts:

> . . . is not about the process of alienation or the
> dynamics of opposing cultures and traditions. . .
> Marechera . . . is so preoccupied with violence
> that the social dimension of his stories fragments
> into a kaleidoscope of personal protestations.
> [Marechera] . . . writes a fiction in which the
> assertion of feelings becomes the substance of the
> narrative. Hence the varied modes of his fiction
> are more obtrusive and telling than those found in
> other Zimbabwean writers. The political
> dimensions of experience in Zimbabwe are taken
> for granted. [16]

McLoughlin is arguing that *The House of Hunger* is existential rather than historical since Marechera eschews the socio-historical and political locating of his narrator's personal difficulties, preferring instead to explore the nature of the psyche. He then argues, "At one level *The House of Hunger* illustrates the devastating effects of growing up in colonial Rhodesia but the vision of that devastation is not presented in social realist terms. Here the black narrator is left almost speechless while in the internal world of his consciousness there is a hyperactive verbal iconoclasm that leaves nothing standing but its fictions about itself" (p. 111). McLoughlin then suggests that future analysts of pre-independence Zimbabwean literature would look to Mungoshi rather that Marechera. But there is powerful argument to support both. Mungoshi bleakly comments on the war and describes the devastating effect on individual and family, unfortunately familiar to a great many. Marechera demonstrates that the mindless brutality of colonialism was itself a form of madness that gave rise to the double alienation: of a people certainly, but also of the individually dislocated psyche. Marechera argued for an acceptance of that state but certainly not a submissive acceptance, but as a point from which to build. In this he is in concert with R. D. Laing who argues that having reached a point of psychological disequilibrium then the way forward is via an understanding and acceptance of the current situation rather than a perpetual examination of the ills and misfortunes that first brought about the disequilibrium.

This is, at once, the strength of *The House of Hunger* and its Achilles heel. Marechera's narrator accepts the excesses of colonialism, accepts in the sense that past events cannot be changed, as determinants in his development and attempts to understand the "here and now" without recourse to a historical cataloguing and condemning of white violence, such violence being an accepted fact of life and something that can be taken for granted in Marechera's world. Implicit in *The House of Hunger* is an acceptance of past excesses and a refusal to indulge in the comfort of a black historicity. Quite obviously, given the nature of Marechera's writing and of the man himself a passive acceptance is not implied – as he remarked in an interview with Veit-Wild, " . . . history is simply a nightmare from which I am trying to wake up" (*SB*, p. 219). Rather he is advocating a redirection, a channeling of energy into the pursuit of self-understanding and self-knowledge, in order to build a "new" individual capable of surviving in a "new" society.

Of course this sanguine view is heavily qualified by the Marecheran conviction that the level of psychological dislocation is so high that recovery is an impossible dream and the best his narrator, and arguably Marechera himself, can hope to achieve is the day-to-day maintenance of a bleak and hopeless existence. (A view he still held towards the end of his life, as he demonstrated in one of his last works, "Rainwords Spit Fire," *Scrapiron Blues*). This nihilism is pounced on by his detractors as anti- African. As Marechera's history indicates, advice or criticism alike merely fueled his sense of paranoia, and the accusations of being anti-African only drew from him the scornful response, "I would question anyone calling me an African writer. Either you are a writer or you are not. If you are a writer for a specific nation or a specific race, then fuck you" (Flora Veit-Wild, *Dambudzo Marechera 1952-1987*, [Harare: Baobab Books, 1988] p. 3).

Despite the urgings of James Currey Marechera's manuscript was received with muted enthusiasm with Ros de Lanorolle suggesting "careful editing would help" and "there may be difficulties of accessibility for readers." Another Heinemann reader, Henry Chavaka, found the stories "most intriguing . . . [reminiscent of] La Guma, Mphalele, Kwei Armah, Kafka, James Joyce" but suggests that "I do not think the three parts sit well. I would suggest that the stories be rearranged so as to reveal a pattern either in setting, chronology or themes-experience" before concluding "A full length novel . . . would have been first rate. If this is Marechera's first effort, then he has a great future as a writer." Ester Kantai was more critical " . . . his [Marechera's] energy and anger, even his bitterness are directed against the wrong targets . . . The unifying force of the story . . . is fatalism and bitterness. What one does not find anywhere is the cause of the fatalism and the resignation." Her conclusion is emphatic as she advised Heinemann against publication, "These stories are damaging to the world bent on liberation. In their present form they are even more damaging to the young writer." Interestingly, Kantai's objections were on entirely political rather than aesthetic grounds. (The above material is from Heinemann's *The House of Hunger* File.)

On Currey's recommendation *The House of Hunger* was published, not on literary merit alone but as an inducement to Marechera to complete a full-length novel. Hindsight shows that this tactic failed miserably. Marechera never produced a full-length novel and continued to experience the greatest difficulty in sustaining coherence and consistency. The sincere and well-intentioned praise and encouragement from Currey and others was received by Marechera not as an incentive to develop his craft but as an unqualified endorsement. Stanley Nyamfukudza, who was with Marechera at Oxford, was to note, "Dambudzo obviously saw the acceptance of his book as a vindication of himself and he wanted everyone to know about it and to celebrate with him in his moment of triumph" (*SB*, p. 179). He (Marechera) was later to consider that that particular moment of triumph heralded a false dawn, as he spoke of the misplaced optimism engendered by the "premature success" of *The House of Hunger* (*SB*, pp. 217-18).

1.2 *The Black Insider* and *Black Sunlight*: The London Works

One of the "conditions" for publishing *The House of Hunger* imposed by Heinemann's James Currey was that Marechera should produce a full-length novel. According to the Heinemann editorial files Marechera did in fact submit three manuscripts during 1978. They were "The Black Insider," "A Bowl for Shadows" and "The Black Heretic." The latter two works have not been seen since their submission to Heinemann and possible return to Marechera who at the time was living in a squat in Tolmers Square, London NW1, so their disappearance, despite extensive searches by, among others, James Currey, David Caute, and Flora Veit-Wild, is not surprising. Paradoxically this very productive period was also the time that Marechera's life was at its most chaotic. However, as I argue below, the chaos of his lived experience is clearly evident in the structure of the London works.

Heinemann reader John Wyllie read all three manuscripts. Of "The Black Insider" and "A Bowl for Shadows" he said " . . . with both manuscripts we are in to R. D. Laing country," a reference to Laing's work on schizophrenia and madness. "The Black Heretic" the sympathetic Wyllie found "a brilliant and fascinating piece of autobiography. . . which goes a very long way to explaining Marechera's perhaps overwhelming, personality problems." He continues his comments with the incisive "I think that he is now incapable of drawing the essence out of the tragic circumstances of being black in a too white world and producing a book." Obviously greatly impressed by Marechera Wyllie goes on to suggest that a selection of material be drawn from the three manuscripts and carefully edited into a new book, claiming " . . . in that form the book would be seen as the most important piece of writing to come out of Black Africa." Currey was still hoping for a strongly cohesive and coherent work from Marechera and did not pass on Wyllie's suggestions. Notifying Wyllie of his views, Currey suggested his idea be held in reserve as "He [Marechera] seems willing to try and produce a developed and structured novel based on "The Black Insider" drawing on these three books. I'm half-afraid he can't do it" (*SB*, pp. 202-06). Unpredictable as ever and in spite of Wyllie's reservations and Currey's fears Marechera submitted the manuscript for *Black Sunlight* to Heinemann in August 1979, contracts were signed in December and the book was published in late 1980. A "black sun" is, of course, a symbol for mental illness, particularly depression as Julia Kristeva explored in her work on depression and melancholia, *Black Sun* (New York: Columbia University Press, 1986). Her despairing "Where does this black sun come from? Out of what eerie galaxy do its invisible, lethargic rays reach me, pinning me down to the ground . . . ," (p. 3) is a cry from the heart which Marechera would certainly have recognized.

In an interview with Veit-Wild in 1986 Marechera claimed "When I wrote *Black Sunlight,* I was staying at what was called the "Tolmers Square Community." This was a squatter community of about 700 people. I was the only black person there" (*SB,* p. 218). No doubt there is some Marecheran exaggeration here but it has been established from the Heinemann files that he was living in a squat at the time of writing *Black Sunlight.* Earlier in the same year Marechera told Alle Lansu "While I was writing *Black Sunlight* I was reading books on intellectual anarchism to reinforce my own sense of protest against everything . . . Intellectual anarchism is full of contradictions in the sense that it can never achieve its goals. If it achieves its goals then it is no longer anarchism." [17] Nevertheless according to Veit-Wild the destiny, if not the stated nor intended goal, of *Black Sunlight* was to become " . . . a manifesto of intellectual anarchism" (*SB,* p. 260).

In a sense, however, this comment confuses an examination of *Black Sunlight* by falling into the "Emperor's new clothes" category. Quite simply, *inter alia,* its lack of a formal structure, the sense of functional disintegration and the inclination to long rambling passages cannot be explained away nor salvaged under the pretext of "intellectual anarchism." The inconsistencies seem to have a personal rather than political significance. Marechera was fighting against a sense of dissolution brought about by the excesses of white minority rule and the double alienation resulting from a colonial European education, his ability to realize his potential as a writer flawed by circumstances beyond his control. Of *Black Sunlight* he concedes "In *The House of Hunger* I had found a voice but that voice ceased to be relevant, because I was now in London in a totally different context" (*SB,* p. 32). It was perhaps his inability to adjust to that new environment, to find a new voice, coupled with the false sense of his standing as an established writer that led to such undisciplined (but certainly not unworthy) writing in *Black*

Sunlight.

Of that writing McLoughlin comments "Marechera's verbal dexterity outstrips that of most African writers but, as . . . *Black Sunlight* indicates, his serious concerns with the metaphysics of creativity and with language itself as a violent instrument take his fiction beyond the accepted bounds of "African" literature." Subsequent remarks from McLoughlin indicate that he felt that *Black Sunlight* had also taken Marechera beyond the pale: "The writing is sometimes obscure and his identity crisis as a black Zimbabwean living in exile has thrown him into the searing problems that surround a writer's relation to reality."[18] In many respects the world he created in *Black Sunlight* was very real to Marechera. In its fragmentation and disintegration, its incohesiveness and sporadic incoherence *Black Sunlight* reflects in no small measure the life the writer was leading at the time of producing the work. In 1979 a disturbed Marechera was virtually penniless, living in a squat, and under enormous pressure, self-imposed and from his publisher, to produce a work delivering the promises of exceptional talent hinted at in *The House of Hunger.* The writer's sometimes slim grasp of everyday reality slipped, and the resulting world of multiple realities, multiple personalities, and paranoia became *Black Sunlight.* In 1986 Marechera said in an interview with Veit-Wild, "Finally I wrote what is now *Black Sunlight. . .* the third version of several efforts to express myself after the great disillusion which came after my premature success. I think I was too successful with my first book, I thought that everything from then on would be heaven" (*SB* p. 218). It was far from heaven as the pressures of fame, the demands of his publisher and living in a state of near destitution were too much for the writer's fragile mental health.

James Currey was a principal observer in this deteriorating behavior, recounting how Marechera would turn up at his offices in various disguises including full hunting pinks on one occasion, as a grey-haired old lady on another, and once festooned with cameras as a *Guardian* photographer. There were also stories of knives being pulled out and at least one fistfight between publisher and writer. Understandably perhaps, there was a hint of expediency about the decision to publish *Black Sunlight.*

The consensus among the Heinemann readers appeared to be that *Black Sunlight* was like the proverbial curate's egg, some parts quite good but others rather less so. Ann Godfrey, alternately "bored" and "impressed," was honestly undecided: "I can't make up my mind whether he is making an extremely bitter, satirical attack on western radicalism, or if it's a load of pretentious rubbish." Wyllie was "very enthusiastic" but suspected that "*Black Sunlight* will not be widely read. . . because it calls for far too much effort." Pantheon, which had published *House of Hunger,* expressed themselves "disappointed" and went on "*Black Sunlight* needs much rethinking and reworking and not even a monumental editing job . . . would be of much use at this point . . . This novel is an exercise in self-destruction. As it progresses . . . there is less and less of a focus for the narrator until we are fully assaulted by a relentless barrage of images and associations cut loose from the outer world and adrift in a void without inherent structure or constraint." The reader from Heinemann Nigeria, Simon Gikandi, suggested " . . . this kind of writing has not had any appeal in this part of the world and can easily go unnoticed . . . there is no single element to suggest that it is written by an African." However, he considers Marechera "an extremely gifted writer" but like Ann Godfrey, he found the style to be of " . . . the *avant-garde* writers of the 1950s. . . placed alongside them he does quite well" (The material in this paragraph was taken from the Heinemann *Black Sunlight* File)

In the final analysis the curate's egg which was *Black Sunlight* was considered too lacking in "good parts" to publish, indeed some readers found very few good parts at all. And yet Currey, against all advice, went ahead with plans to publish. As he explained in a letter to Tom Engelhardt of Pantheon, "I have decided that we ought to accept *Black Sunlight* and have got it formally approved . . . I hope it will remove a psychological block and that he will get down to finishing the Zimbabwean novel." [19] The pattern of publication of *The House of Hunger*: – publishing a work known to be lacking in at least some aspects, to encourage the production of stronger work – was thereby repeated with *Black Sunlight*.

Black Sunlight was, not surprisingly, badly received. Veit-Wild notes: "Public response was less positive than the acclaim that greeted *The House of Hunger*. Most reviewers criticized the lack of structure and conceptual control." (*SB* p. 217). Interestingly, James Lasdun argued, "It is the failure of control that limits what had the makings of an extraordinary piece of fiction, to a disturbing, but ultimately formless document of personal anguish" ("Sunlight and Chaos," *New Statesman and Society*, London: December 12, 1980, p. 46). This observation is probably closer to what the text actually represents than Veit-Wild's "manifesto of intellectual anarchy" or perhaps, Ann Godfrey's ambiguous views of *Black Sunlight* as an "extremely bitter, satirical attack on western radicalism" or "a load of pretentious rubbish." Marechera's "intellectual anarchism" could as easily be interpreted as an absence of discipline and an inability to revise, possibly allied to artistic arrogance. The work is *not* pretentious rubbish: it is an attack on myriad issues across many different fronts which demands a concerted effort from the reader. As well as this, and in addition to typifying his life-style (above), the structure of the book, in its disfunctionality and disintegration, is representative of Marechera's unstable mental condition at the time of writing, and should be seen as that.

The response to *Black Sunlight* disappointed Marechera. He was disheartened, not only by the lack of critical acclaim and literary success but also by his lack of financial success, as he was impoverished and homeless. However worse was to come. On his return to Zimbabwe in 1982 Marechera was greeted at the airport with the news that *Black Sunlight* had been banned on the grounds of obscenity and the rather odd accusation, reminiscent of pre-independence censorship, that "the book imitated negative features of modernist writing" (*SB*, p. 290). But before this, his official connection with Heinemann was severed. In Currey's absence on leave, the managing director, Hamish MacGibbon, was called upon to deal with the barrage of threats and demands for money from Marechera. Eventually he parted with £320 (to which Marechera was almost certainly not entitled, as his advances exceeded his royalties) on " . . . your formal agreement that . . . you will make no further demands for money . . . you will sever all further contact with this firm . . . if you enter the premises again we will call the police . . . We on our part formally waive the option clauses in your current contracts." Marechera thus became the first writer to be banned by Heinemann in their long history as publishers. A few days later days later Marechera completed a bad week (July 1980) by becoming the only person ever to be banned from the Africa Center in King Street. The same pattern of increasingly difficult behavior finally forced Dr Alastair Niven, director of the Center, to exclude him (see Chapter Four).

Black Sunlight was a fourth attempt to provide the novel desperately awaited by James Currey and is less a revision of *Black Insider* than a revisiting of the same issues and themes. Although the text of *The Black Insider* was edited by Flora Veit-Wild several repeated passages remain. Rejected in 1978 and 1984, *The Black Insider* was eventually published in 1990, some three years after the death of the author.

The Black Insider was published as a result of the efforts of Flora Veit-Wild and the Dambudzo Marechera Trust. That the manuscript was recovered at all is thanks to the efforts of David Caute, writer and friend of Marechera. During a search of the files in the Heinemann editorial offices in 1984 Caute discovered photocopies of *The Black Insider* and another Marechera manuscript, *Portrait of a Black Artist in London*.[20] With Marechera's permission both were submitted to Heinemann by Caute. Both were rejected, *Portrait* on the grounds of being "pretty incomprehensible" and *The Black Insider* as "self indulgent," "unstructured," and "not . . . of interest to the general reader" (*The Black Insider*, p. 18).

Caute saw Marechera as a "scandalously gifted writer," a "monomaniac ventriloquist" and strangely as a "baby faced flytrap." The Freudian implications of this peculiar choice of words are underlined by the reference to Marechera as "diminutive and pretty," and the implication that he was not above prostitution. "Marechera went to sleep rough in Cecil Square while keeping a close eye on a parade of white liberal ladies who paid his rent or his price." Caute's review of *The Black Insider* is more an exploration of his relationship with Marechera than a discussion of the novel, of which Caute states, "Civil war rages . . . as a group of refugees discuss the meaning of everything . . . But the scenario is incidental; Marechera's respect for realism had evaporated during his British exile; the here and there of postcolonial terror and (perhaps) atomic war is neither here nor there." He then goes on to suggest, "If his fiction was black hole autobiography, his life was an extended fiction." Caute is suggesting that one of the reasons for reading *The Black Insider* is because of references to the remarkable lifestyle of the author, a suggestion that does have some merit insofar as Marechera's lifestyle reflected his reaction to the strictures of colonialism. Caute comments, "Marechera's respect for realism had evaporated"; in no small measure Marechera lost touch with "reality" because of his illness, which was exacerbated by his environment, and this, in part at least, is reflected in the fractured and fragmented form of *The Black Insider*.

Quite obviously the employment of extravagant language was not limited to Marechera himself, as is indicated above, and in the following from Adewale Maja-Pearce, who at the time of writing the review was editor of the Heinemann African Writers Series: "Dambudzo Marechera's short and violent life has turned out to be a boon for literary necrophiliacs with pseudo-romantic notions concerning the tragic destiny of the misunderstood artist. In this he was at least partly responsible. . . . his writing is directly autobiographical." Understandably, Maja-Pearce conflates the narrator of *The Black Insider* and Marechera himself, supposed fact and supposed fiction, pointing out that "The war is supposed to be a metaphor, which is why the novel fails to convince as anything more than a series of autobiographical investigations dressed up as a continuous narrative." The reviewer recognizes the intensely personal nature of Marechera's prose and the idiosyncratic position of the writer in calling *The Black Insider*, " . . . a more courageous book than almost any other that has come out of the continent in the past 30 years." Issue can be taken with the notion that *The Black Insider* came out of Africa, a limiting verdict that ignores the dual influences of being in England and being away from Zimbabwe. The review closes on a prescient and rueful note, "One can certainly see why Marechera made so many people uncomfortable, and why his death. . . has made it easier to turn this *enfant terrible* of African writing into a romantic legend. The pity of it is that the legend is already in danger of overtaking the work" ("Humbug hater," *New Statesman & Society*, London: January 31, 1992, p. 54).

The substance behind Maja-Pearce's concern is illustrated by Veit-Wild's approach to *The Black Insider*. She finds it " . . . unique in exploring the predicament of the 'lost generation' in exile" (*Teachers* p. 259) bestowing on Marechera the mantle of spokesman which is somewhat at odds with the writer's own highly individual stance. Nevertheless his work is certainly an invaluable record of one person's experience of pre- and post-independence Zimbabwe. Veit-Wild goes further: " *The Black Insider*. . . transcends the concrete political or social situation, taking any condition as a parable of the human predicament as a whole." This comment does get closer to the nub of *The Black Insider*. An argument can be raised to support the view that Marechera's psychological problems did represent a universal condition among black Africans, though *The Black Insider* is also a uniquely personal document. Veit-Wild is well aware of the singular qualities Marechera brought to his work: "*The Black Insider*. . . contextualises the author and dismantles or "deconstructs" the myth of the invisible and infallible literary creator," a technique that many critics accepted, showing no hesitation in acknowledging Marechera's fiction as openly autobiographical. This of course is problematic in a work that " .

. . presents a multitude of voices and disguises, exposing the multitude and diversity of possibilities and views" (*Teachers*, pp. 260-62). If sorting out the "real" Marechera was a problem for the critics, it was one that bedeviled Marechera himself as his work abounds with images of fragmented selves and doppelgangers. As he remarked "I think I am the doppelganger whom, until I appeared, African literature had not yet met" (*Dambudzo Marechera 1952-1987*, p. 3).

Of the Heinemann readers Wyllie was the most enthusiastic although his praise was qualified: "*The Black Insider*. . . [is] full of poetic insights, often superbly written, highly imaginative, magnificently worth reading . . . altogether too frantically, too frenetically "the last desperate ditch of a state of mind." He concluded with the unhappy, " . . . what should be done with *The Black Insider* is . . . a problem . . . I don't believe it is right for . . . the AWS public." Senda wa Kurayera (Heinemann Nairobi) was apparently sanguine but no doubt aware that Marechera was unlikely to heed his advice that, "If the author reduced the vast chunks of quotations and [un]intelligible allusions, inserted a sense of continuity or shortened them to credibility, and made the story end in a convincing manner, it certainly would be interesting reading. . . " (*SB* pp. 200-03).

It should be noted that the Heinemann readers were writing of the unedited, unpublished version. The published version was awarded a Special Commendation from the judges of the 1991 Noma award for Publishing in Africa. One of the supporters was Landeg White who in his presentation to the committee gave an exposition of the work, then added, "This makes *The Black Insider* sound forbiddingly erudite and it is, in fact, hard to describe the book as it is without putting people off." Perhaps because he is unable to take the book quite seriously White describes it as " . . . very good fun. Like all good comedy it is fundamentally serious but there is a dazzling display of verbal wit here in a range of different styles." He goes on, "It is obviously going to be very much more comfortable for us all having Marechera dead and his works issued under the benign

editorship of Flora Veit-Wild than Marechera alive and kicking."
[21]

The published version of *The Black Insider* has a valuable thirty-two page introduction by the editor, which includes a short biography of Marechera, and an exposition and a history of the manuscript; there then follows the novella *The Black Insider*, three previously published short stories, and two poems.

Veit-Wild acknowledges the difficulty of popularizing Marechera when she writes "Yes, it will cost the reader time and effort to read this book. And why not? Should not writer and publisher be proud of that, provided the effort turns out to be worthwhile" (*The Black Insider*, p. 19). As Veit-Wild indicates the general reader would need to be determined in order to discern " . . . a strong inner coherence if the reader is prepared to follow the writer along paths of thought which, though intricate, are an intrinsic part of his work" (*The Black Insider*, p. 20). The reward for the diligent reader will be to " . . . accompany the narrator as he unfolds one reminiscence after another, uncoiling one from the other in the spirals and drifts of Marechera's life and thoughts" (*The Black Insider,* p. 20). Veit-Wild might have added that the reward for completing that journey with the narrator will be an unforgettable insight into a brilliant mind doing battle against the intolerable repercussions of an implacable colonialism.

In the following extract Veit-Wild confronts the accusation that *The Black Insider* lacks a formative structure:

> The writer's desire to strip naked all attitudinizing and to get to the core of things is intrinsically linked to a special, an experimental type of writing. Where logical and straightforward thinking is deemed as oppressive and as leaving no room for the imagination, conventional forms of writing such as prescribed by the distinct and separate literary genres have to be cast aside. (*The Black Insider* p. 29)

In view of his known parlous physical and psychological condition in 1978 it is surely too ambitious to claim that the chaotic form and content of *The Black Insider* were deliberately constructed by Marechera. There may be some truth in Veit-Wild's analysis but it is, however, difficult to distinguish Marechera's "experimentation" from an involuntary reaction to his environment or, indeed, from a simple failure to develop a disciplined approach to his craft. At the time of writing *The Black Insider*, he was not necessarily capable of "logical and straightforward thinking." Such observation is not intended to be a criticism, far from it. The true value of *The Black Insider* is to be found in recognizing the atrocious difficulties the writer was enduring at the time of writing – difficulties that present themselves in various guises throughout the text. That he wrote at all is praiseworthy, that he produced a work with so many passages of breathtaking audacity and brilliance is little short of remarkable.

1.3 *Mindblast*: The Writer Tramp

The image of the writer tramp inspired by Marechera's lifestyle in Britain was confirmed as he established himself in Harare on his return to Zimbabwe:

> . . . the last section of *Mindblast*. . . is simply a factual record of what was happening to me each day while I was homeless. In it I recorded even anything that walked by as I was typing, how I had slept the night before etc. I did that precisely because the idea, that someone can actually write a book while being a tramp, is not accepted here. But I did it.
>
> Kirsten Holst Petersen, *An Articulate Anger* (Sydney: Dangaroo Press, 1988), p. 37

This interview reveals a typical Marecheran reinterpretation of events. In actual fact he wrote in the park because he was a compulsive writer who was homeless, he was not conducting an experiment.

The park bench diary is an appendix to the book *Mindblast or The Definitive Buddy* (hereafter *Mindblast*) that Marechera began submitting to publishers within a year of his return. A collection of material gathered over the year, *Mindblast* is a mixture of plays, prose, and poetry, in which, according to the back cover blurb "Award winner Dambudzo Marechera turns the full blast of his formidable powers on Zimbabwe in transition." Marechera told Fiona Lloyd in an interview recorded in 1986:

> *Mindblast* is based on contemporary Harare . . . it has to do with those states of mind now prevailing in the new Zimbabwe, the new Harare . . . Those states of mind are contradictory. They tend to be eccentric or tend to be downright shallow. (*SB*, p. 311)

One of the criticisms made of *Black Sunlight* and *The Black Insider* was that they reflected the dilemma of the writer in exile, – that is the absence of a framework within which to place his work in context. Back in Harare Marechera was able to overcome this difficulty and the existentialist approach of *Black Sunlight* and *The Black Insider* is replaced in *Mindblast* with a more direct political involvement that is observant and critical of the postcolonial state. This was a brave stance to take in the euphoria that was the immediate aftermath of the achievement of independence.

Not surprisingly, prospective publishers were cautious in their approach. Charles Mungoshi, who in his role as editor with the Zimbabwe Publishing House (ZPH) had rejected the manuscript, said later in his obituary to Marechera which took the form of an open letter:

> . . . you brought me *Mindblast* . . . I knew I couldn't persuade my publishers to publish it. One, because of the well-known reputation you had made for yourself which my colleagues in the

publishing house did not feel was commercially profitable. Two, I thought if the book was difficult or if it was difficult for me to understand – who is going to buy it? Dambudzo, I felt you were not communicating to the people.

This professional judgement did not extend to their personal relationship it seems as he adds:

> . . . one day you said "You aren't an artist." I felt bad. But when I saw you next, already, I had begun to miss you. That's all. Dambudzo, you had a way with me that made me question my own sincerity in my job, my life-style and most things I took for granted. You actually were asking me: who am I? *Dambudzo Marechera 1952-1987*, pp. 13-14

Rejected by ZPH, Marechera approached the College Press (part of the British Macmillan Group) for whom his fellow student from Oxford, Stanley Nyamfukudza, was an editor. Like Mungoshi, Nyamfukudza found the book had merit, but felt it needed careful editing: " The prose sections in particular were very uneven and also occasionally libelous." Eventually Marechera agreed to cuts but after that "there was another battle with the management at College Press. They felt that the book was anti-government (which in those days was not the done thing), that it was obscene and liable to be banned." Nyamfukudza then adds an interesting comment, which not only reflects Mungoshi's experience but also goes some way to explaining the Marechera/Currey/Heinemann relationship:

> One curious aspect of my relationship with him when I worked as a publisher is that while I myself found him to be quite philosophical and easy to deal with, within the establishment of the publishing house he had a reputation as wild and dangerous, even as a bit of a madman, and no one would deal with him. He was also equally despising of them. So I ended up having to deal

with him on everyone else's behalf. (*SB*, p. 339)

Mindblast was eventually published in August 1984 during the Book Fair and, as Nyamfukudza told me (June 1998), became a College Press best seller. At the time of publication Marechera was in detention having been arrested for causing a disturbance at the fair. He was detained without charge under emergency regulations until the fair was over. Eccentric behavior from Marechera was now common and even his detention aroused little comment. David Caute deals with the episode in his essay "Marechera and the Colonel." Referring in his opening to the actual arrest he writes, "Clearly Marechera's fate was of little concern to the Zimbabwean writers, academics and politicians lazily circulating among the bookstands," adding scornfully "exchanging greetings prefaced by the triple revolutionary hand-shake: thumb-palm-thumb. An urgent clasp already grown lethargic and decadent with ritual use," (*The Espionage of the Saints* [London: Hamish Hamilton, 1986], p. 3).

Although Caute's essay quotes extensively from *Mindblast,* the (at that time) unpublished *The Black Insider*, and also *The House of Hunger*, it is not a critical work. It is a record of their relationship, and to some extent a commentary on Marechera's attempts to locate himself in the "new" Zimbabwe. But chiefly it is an examination of an alleged incident that occurred shortly after the first review of *Mindblast* appeared. Apparently Marechera was accosted in a toilet in the Harare Holiday Inn hotel and severely beaten by a colonel of the Zimbabwean Army who accused him of writing filth that would defame the reputation of Zimbabwe and its government. Caute's investigation found witnesses, named the Colonel and concluded that the allegations were substantially true. However, as he points out in an early passage " . . . in this essay we shall learn more about Marechera . . . though we may remain uncertain as to whether his life owes more to his art than the reverse" (p. 9). In identifying this age-old dilemma of life imitating art or art imitating life, Caute is making a distinction that would, perhaps, have been lost on Marechera to whom writing – his art – was his life.

Mindblast was not distributed internationally and, apart from those with a professional interest in Marechera, like Caute and Veit-Wild, critical comment has been largely confined to Zimbabwe. Attracted by the "here-and-now" stance of *Mindblast* as the antithesis of the obsessive interest in the past history of the struggle, young Zimbabweans identified with the prominent themes of corruption and the need for social change. Oliver Nyika, then aged twenty-one, wrote in *Mahogany* magazine (August/September 1984, p. 46) "*Mindblast* is mind-boggling . . . as it is prophetic, and horrifyingly honest." Another undergraduate from the same time, Munoda Mararike told Veit-Wild (*SB*, pp. 390-91) "I purchased . . . *Mindblast*, and that was when I began to understand a lot more about him, his political standpoint. He would write things that happened within society, within the people." Despite wanting to like Marechera, even to identify with him, Mararike cannot ignore the familiar problem of accessibility and of implicitly asking who Marechera was writing for: recognizing that although Marechera was writing about what he saw as a sick society he "would use excessively difficult language to project these issues, so it was rather difficult for the general reader to understand what he meant."

I referred earlier to a Marechera cult among young Zimbabweans and Mararike confirms this in his reference to his generation as the "*Mindblast* generation." He also unwittingly highlights the paradox of a writer ostensibly writing for the people but whose work is not generally available except (apparently) for academic purposes. As Mararike explains:

> While we were at the University, we used to do practical criticisms of Dambudzo Marechera's texts . . . while Marechera consistently denied that he was writing for a socialist government, on the other hand he was, in fact, writing for the povo [a Shona word meaning proletariat], for the peasant farmer in Buhera, he was writing for the blind person at Kapota School, he was writing for the

ghetto, he was writing for the township, he was a
writer who penetrated all strata of society.

These extravagant claims sit very uneasily with Mararike's
earlier comments on the difficult language of *Mindblast* and have
the flavor of the seminar room rather the street or the peasant
farm. However, it is beyond dispute that, to a certain era of
university undergraduate and others, *Mindblast* was an important
text and the romantic writer tramp, haunting the parks and
shebeens of Harare, a cult figure. Mararike's interview
concludes:

> . . . we don't have any writer to take up the
> concerns of what I would call the *Mindblast*
> generation, people who are prepared to take up
> from where Marechera left. As a result we are not
> progressing very much in terms of analyzing
> things that are happening directly in our society at
> this very moment.

Whether there is much difference between the lifestyles of
the penniless London squatter and the destitute Harare writer
tramp is doubtful, although Veit-Wild comments, "Marechera's
writings after his return to Zimbabwe in 1982 – published and
unpublished – tend to suffer from an overly self-centered and
self-indulgent viewpoint: they reflect the egocentric existence of
the bohemian and generally miserable poet acted out in bars and
shebeens" (*Teachers* p. 308). Any criticism of *Mindblast* implied
in her comments is qualified as she continues, "However by
focussing on the city Marechera contributed substantially to the
development of a new urban literature" (*SB*, p. 309) and
nominates the book as "the manifesto of his satiric indictment"
(*SB*, p. 281). Again, it has to be said, the desire to label
Marechera's work with such over-close, perhaps even over-
intellectual, definitions heralds the danger that the essence of the
writer is not engaged.

As for the accusations that *Mindblast* is "self-centered and
self-indulgent," yes, in parts, it is. But then to at least the same

degree so were *Black Sunlight* and *The Black Insider.* No doubt
the role of the returning writer rebel, and his struggle to find a
place in building the "new" Zimbabwe, had its effect on
Marechera as the concern with self shifted emphasis to an
obsession with his role as perceived by others (*Mindblast* and
Scrapiron Blues) rather than the earlier relentless examination of
self as perceived by self (*Black Sunlight* and *The Black Insider*).
Recognition of that personal and political engagement takes the
reader closer to the essential Marechera who was struggling for a
sense of identity in a country facing the same dilemma.

1.4 *Scrapiron Blues*: "A sad and lonely figure"

From the introduction to *Scrapiron Blues,* the third and
final volume in a series of posthumously published Marechera
works:

> At a lecture in Harare in 1986, Dambudzo
> Marechera said: "My whole life has been an
> attempt to make myself the skeleton in my own
> cupboard." When he died less than a year later, he
> left behind a large number of unpublished literary
> skeletons. Since then, on behalf of the Dambudzo
> Marechera Trust, I have tried to assemble as
> many of them as possible and so ensure that the
> contents of his cupboard can, as he wrote in a
> 1985 book review, "send a mad look to the end of
> time." (*Scrapiron Blues* p. ix.)

It is tempting to see this volume as the last sweepings of
the cupboard. But the pejorative implications of such an
observation should be resisted. *Scrapiron Blues* is important,
not simply for its varied literary content which, I suspect, will
not lose Marechera any friends nor – despite Soyinka's praise
(see below) – convert his detractors. Critical analysis has yet to
emerge but it is safe to assume that opinion will remain divided.
Quite probably those who saw genius in Marechera will find
evidence of it here and those who saw rather less than that will

not be persuaded otherwise. However, if that case does prevail then an opportunity will have been lost. *Scrapiron Blues* ties up some "loose ends" but it does more than that. There is evidence here (and in *Mindblast*) that the writer felt keenly the dilemma of his role as "artist" *versus* his role as "good citizen." The works published in Harare indicate that, although he experimented with both standpoints, it was a dilemma he never resolved. In choosing *Scrapiron Blues* as his "book of the year"[22] Wole Soyinka reflected some of the frustrations imposed by the tormenting brevity of some of the pieces as well as his sadness at the writer's death:

> . . . most of the prose, playlets, and verses appeal to this reader much more like fragments of stained glass, scintillating, multi-textured and tantalizing. The world of literature, and African literature in particular, has lost an authentic brush in the sphere of creative evocation.

After *Mindblast* in 1984 Marechera had no more work accepted for publication. Longman had rejected *Killwatch* in 1983 and College Press, Harare, and Heinemann (UK) rejected *Depth of Diamonds* in 1985. (*Killwatch* is included in *Scrapiron Blues*, but *Depth of Diamonds* was omitted and there are no plans for its publication) His poetry was constantly rejected or published and poorly received. Veit-Wild, who was in daily contact with Marechera at this time writes how his situation – anxiety over his role as a writer, his increasing physical and psychological isolation, and his deteriorating health – depressed him deeply. He completed very little of the work begun in 1986 and 1987 and submitted nothing to publishers in that period.

Although Veit-Wild writes of *Scrapiron Blues* with sympathy and enthusiasm for the "literature of urbanization" enriched by Marechera who recorded life in Harare "quietly scribbling notes amid all the noise and commotion of public bars," the picture she presents is of a sad and lonely figure, who " . . . divided his time between writing at his flat and drinking in the hotel bars and shebeens of the city center." *Scrapiron Blues,* a miscellany of prose, poems, and plays, reveals a writer running out of time and one who no longer burned with the fire that produced *House of Hunger*, had lost the fierce, manic drive of *Black Sunlight* and *The Black Insider*, and had neither the energy nor the stomach for the political confrontation of *Mindblast*. Veit -Wild finds in *Scrapiron Blues* a "new subtlety and a gentle descriptive lucidity" that combine to offer "perceptive insights into Harare life in the 1980s." *Scrapiron Blues* also offers insight into the development of Marechera the writer, providing a postscript to his career as a writer and also to his life.

1.5 An Overview

The majority of Marechera's published output was written in the period 1976 to 1979 and there is little argument that his first publication, *The House of Hunger*, remains his best work. As it was praised largely on the grounds of the potential ability of the writer ("genius" was a word used by, among others, Currey, Wyllie and Lessing) an overview of the Marechera corpus concludes that that potential was only partially realized. The quality of the writing took a different hue as the eccentricities of *Black Sunlight* and *The Black Insider* presented themselves, to be labeled intellectual anarchy in some quarters and pretentious rubbish in others. Both books were written in the direst of conditions with the writer homeless and suffering from a chronic behavior disorder brought on by extreme paranoia. The nature of Marechera's work is openly auto-biographical and these points must be given consideration as they informed both the form and content of his work, as the writer himself commented: "The thing I remember most about it [becoming a writer] is that I always tried to reduce everything into a sort of autobiographical record. As though I needed to stamp myself with the evidence of my own existence" (*The Black Insider* p. 109).

In the years 1976 to 1979 Marechera wrote, in addition to the published work listed above, the unpublished and subsequently lost *Black Heretic* and *Bowl for Shadows*. The frantic activity of these years was inspired by the critical acclaim given to *The House of Hunger* as Marechera tried desperately to fulfill the extravagant predictions of his future as a writer and to satisfy the demands of his publisher. Unfortunately, the flaws critics had identified in *The House of Hunger* remained and the later work, unless it is very short, suffers from structural problems of coherence and continuity, as Marechera's apparent inability (or reluctance) to revise his work became a major drawback.

The 1984 publication of *Mindblast* avoided the problems of structure to a certain extent by comprising three plays, two short stories, forty-two poems and the park bench diary as an appendix. Nevertheless, although some of the pieces are among his best, some of the writing has the flavor of a first draft and would have benefited from editing and rewriting. However, the very lack of revision may be felt on occasion to give the works a kind of honesty, true to the moment of creation, in which the writer's influences are more easily discerned.

There is a certain sadness about the final collection of work, *Scrapiron Blues*, not only because the writer continues to circle irresolutely around the familiar themes and issues first raised in *The House of Hunger*, but also due to the extreme shortness of some of the pieces which seem to indicate Marechera's failure to sustain his undoubted ability as a writer. If there is sadness, there is also joy as the collection contains one of his finest works, the short story "First Street Tumult" and confirms his exceptional talent as a dramatist, which was first revealed in *Mindblast*.

The final work to be published, *Scrapiron Blues*, in itself does not fully answer the question why Marechera's considerable though incandescent talent did not become a lasting flame, but it does complete the picture. My subsequent chapters will examine in detail each of the individual works that make up that picture.

Before doing that it will be helpful to locate Marechera's position *vis-à-vis* the major critical issues raised by his work. Thus my next chapter briefly confronts the major issues raised by the writer and his often unique approach to his work and locates the writer's position within those issues while considering, *inter alia*: the validity of a psychological approach: the use of biographical material: his rejection of nationalism for universalism: his determined espousal of individualism rather than the role of communal spokesman; and, the effect on the writing, not only of his illness but also of the liberal consumption of alcohol and the use of drugs.

CHAPTER TWO

The Writer and his Work: Some Critical Perspectives

On March 30, 1979, in response to a letter from Tom Engelhardt of Pantheon Books, asking whether he could communicate directly with Marechera, James Currey replied, "I'd be quite happy for you to correspond directly with him though I must repeat my professional warning. THIS MAN IS DANGEROUS! Not to you! Not to me! But to himself!"

In addition to the pattern of disturbed behavior, Marechera's courage in striking unpopular poses attracted as much attention as his unique, and ultimately self-destructive, approach to his work. In the course of this chapter I will investigate the extent to which the prose fiction reflected Marechera's disconnected lifestyle, and consider the effect, if any, of his drinking habits and the use of drugs. I will examine how his writing was affected by his illness and explore the relevance of psychoanalytical interpretations to what are, in the final analysis, works of art. I will also explore the influence of his mental instability on his writing and indicate how his literary development reflects the tenor and conduct of his life on his journey from Rhodesia, through Oxford and London, to Zimbabwe. Such a profile offers an extended mind map of the writer as he moved from the apparent heights of the *Guardian* Prize for Fiction through rejection and the banning of his work to lonely unfulfillment while living through the most turbulent period in Zimbabwe's history.

I will also review Marechera's position in the "artist as communal spokesman" *versus* "artist as Romantic individualist" debate, and his repudiation of the notion of the writer as teacher, guide, or mentor. This will lead to an examination of the dispute between national commitment and literary universalism, and his rejection of the "Africanist" label.

2.1 Art and the Psyche

"The rotting corpses within" (*The Black Insider*, p. 35)

In concentrating on a psychoanalytical approach I aim to establish more clearly how Marechera's illness, his life history and his reaction to the various environments he encountered informed his writing. In taking this approach I also have in mind Max Friedlander's argument: "Art being a thing of the mind, it follows that any scientific study of art will be psychology. It may be other things as well, but psychology it will always be." [23]

As Jung argued " . . . the human psyche is the womb of all

the sciences and arts," [24] it follows that a psychoanalytical examination of works of art enables inferences to be drawn about the individual psyche responsible for their creation. Jung goes on to suggest that there is a two-fold purpose to psychological research of this nature: one is to explain the formation of a work of art and the other is to reveal the factors that make a person artistically creative. My intention is to concentrate largely on the former but the two inquiries are inextricably linked and some speculation on why Marechera wrote is inevitable.

Freud suggested that all works of art are created out of the personal experiences of the artist, and that the component parts of a work of art can be traced back to complexes, in the sense of interconnected conscious and unconscious ideas and feelings usually gathered in early childhood, within the artist's psyche. As Lionel Trilling points out, Freud was known to some as the "discoverer of the unconscious" a title he refused with the words, "The poets and philosophers before me discovered the unconscious; what I discovered was the scientific method by which the unconscious can be studied." Trilling goes on to maintain that " . . . the human nature of the Freudian psychology is exactly the stuff upon which the poet has always exercised his art." [25]

According to R. D. Laing, in the sense that we all experience life as taking place in "our world," "our world" and our idiosyncratic view of it will die with us, while "the world," which provided the stage for our experiences, will continue. [26] This is not true for everyone. The creative artist leaves behind poems, novels, paintings, and so forth that can offer a permanence in "the world" to the artist's "own world" view. But any exploration of a work that called only on Freud's theories of the id, the ego and the super-ego to the exclusion of others, the Jungian collective unconscious, for example, would be dangerously one-sided. These factors – id, ego, super-ego, collective unconscious – are revealed in readings of *The House of Hunger, Mindblast* and *Scrapiron Blues*; and although these works will be treated separately they are to be seen as points on the same continuum. The apparent stylistic excesses of *The Black Insider* and *Black Sunlight* call for a slightly different approach. While also drawing on the works of Jung and Freud these readings must recognize the existential nature of the works and the way their construction more obviously reflects the physical and psychological condition of the author at the time of writing.

It is commonly held that works of art are an enduring legacy in which aesthetic appeal is complemented by psychological interpretation. This is a view with which Marechera may well have been sympathetic. The following appears to acknowledge the psychological significance of paintings, poems, and stories: " . . . I agreed that there was nothing left of us except . . . the paintings we painted on the painted walls; nothing left except the poems and the stories I sweated blood to bleed out of me" (*Black Insider* p. 144). Sartre expressed similar sentiments, though in bleaker terms: "In life, man commits himself, draws his portrait and there is nothing but that portrait." [27] But of course that portrait, however and wherever it exists, those poems and stories, are themselves rich sources of information about the artist, even while it remains precisely true to say that "there is nothing but that portrait." As Marechera implies, after the death of the artist there is nothing left to interpret except the work. Ironically, in Marechera's case, stories of his behavior are assessed and reassessed as frequently as his writing. However, taking a wider interpretation of Sartre's "portrait," that is perhaps inevitable.

Although there are differing views on the influences forming the psyche there is broad agreement that elements of the psyche that created the work reside within the work, in its contours, its shades, and its tones. The manifest content is available to everyone but the latent content is available only after very careful examination. The latent content is not immediately available to the artist. As Freud argued, psychologically we are not masters in our own house. The origin of emotions and motives for action is held in the unconscious and is therefore inaccessible under normal conditions. It is of course possible to take a psychoanalytical approach, among many others, to the reading of any work of prose or poetry. But in view of the complexity of Marechera's work and the way his life-style was inextricably linked with his work, a psychoanalytical approach seems particularly appropriate. Such an analysis is not without a certain irony in view of Marechera's well known views on psychology as "a way of justifying insanity" (*Scrapiron Blues*, p. 204). However, the fear and mistrust expressed by Marechera are themselves symptoms of a particular mind set, where, perhaps " . . . human consciousness and human striving instills in me fears of something radically missing from my own make-up" (*Black Sunlight*, p. 116).

In the following piece from *The Black Insider* that same fear and mistrust is linked to bitter condemnation of psychiatry in general, and probably of Dr. Hoare and Professor Gelder [28] of the Warneford Mental Hospital in Oxford, in particular (*SB*, p. 160):

> Some psychiatrists today diagnose
> disenchantment with social structures as a disease
> and proceed to inflict a cure on the patient. Some
> of our greatest writing comes from writers in a
> state of disillusion, disenchantment and dismay.
> (*The Black Insider* p. 128)

Marechera felt that a "cure" for his illness would destroy his muse. Anthony Storr maintains in *The Dynamics of Creation* that "successful" psycho-analysis may remove permanently a writer's reasons for writing and undoubtedly some weight can be attached to Marechera's comments. But if the "disenchantment" is so severe that it leads to, or exacerbates, a neurosis, or psychosis, then the writing begins to reflect more accurately the mental ills of the writer, rather than the social ills to which Marechera alludes. Nevertheless, as the social ills are "responsible," at least in part, for the mental ills, then the writing is still capable of reflecting the social structure.

The image of the mind, or psyche, as a complex arrangement of rooms and tunnels became an obsession with Marechera and the House of Hunger can be interpreted as a metaphor for the Marecheran psyche. The Arts Faculty in *The Black Insider* and Devil's End in *Black Sunlight* in addition to being central organizing devices within the novels, are similarly representations of Marechera's psyche. The Arts Faculty is "stupendously labyrinthine with its infinite ramifications of little nooks of rooms, some of which are bricked up forever to isolate forever the rotting corpses within" (p. 35), and the Devil's End is a "network of caves and interlocking tunnels" (p. 52). Devil's End is at the center of *Black Sunlight* and *The Black Insider* is located entirely within the Arts Faculty.

The use of such metaphors to represent the psyche brings to mind Lacan: " . . . the formation of the I is symbolized in dreams by a fortress, or a stadium – its inner area and enclosure, surrounded by marshes and rubbish dumps, dividing it into two opposed fields of contest where the subject flounders in quest of the lofty, remote inner castle whose form . . . symbolizes the id in a quite startling way." [29] The symbolism of caves is, according to Jung, equally important: "The dark cave corresponds to the vessel containing the warring opposites. The self is made manifest in the opposites and in the conflict between them . . . Hence the way to the self begins with conflict." [30]

The three works are dominated by two things, *The House of Hunger* perhaps less obviously but no less significantly than *Black Sunlight* and *The Black Insider*. The first is a journey back to the beginnings, the search for the primordial I; and the second is a building or complex of rooms, which is a central feature of the journey, and which, in both Lacanian and Jungian terms, represents the formation of the I. Marechera's fictional or philosophical journey could also be described in Hegelian terms as "the moment of indetermination," [31] in which the writer withdraws psychically from his surroundings as, by a psychical negation, he is able to remove himself from involvement with finite things. To do so offers an interesting perspective on Marechera's psychological predicament in which it can be seen that the Hegelian dialectical logic is incomplete, as Marechera moved between thesis and antithesis but did not achieve synthesis and, as a consequence of that, remained psychologically out of balance.

Mindblast and *Scrapiron Blues* are both collections of short works that demonstrate the writer's dilemma of being a "good citizen" (writing in uncritical support of the socialist government), or of remaining true to his individualism and the freedom of his art to express his views without fear or favor. As we will see in Chapters Five and Six, Marechera never resolved that dilemma and became physically and psychologically isolated from the nation builders. His return to Zimbabwe became notable for his failure to establish his role as an artist in a culture too new, too disorganized, and too preoccupied with the demands of material survival to be concerned with could be seen as more ephemeral issues.

2.2 Biography into Art

"Sunlit memories?"

The stereotype of the "tortured genius" or "two minds in one body" kind has been readily attached to Marechera. And it is tempting to avoid the limiting tendency of this stereotype by refusing to cast him in the role of the outcast, the loner, the young and very sensitive artist, at odds with the brutality and horror of the townships and the desperate predicament of his family, the grinding poverty and extreme hardship. But, in actual fact, this *was* his inevitable role. For the adolescent Marechera the effect of his immediate environment, which owed much to the cumulative effect of seventy years of white minority rule, was devastating. The effect of his wider environment – the illegal Smith government declared UDI in 1966, further worsening conditions for black Zimbabweans – was no less so.

Although David Buuck [32] argues that The *House of Hunger* and the journal section of *Mindblast* are "His [Marechera's] most autobiographical works," he goes on to concede that " . . . in *The*

Black Insider and *Black Sunlight,* the schizophrenic self and text seem to become one; though clearly constructed as "fictions," these books in many ways present a more telling portrait of the author than any conventional autobiography could." Buuck is referring to the standard autobiographical method of a sequential engagement of a series of events. In *The Black Insider* and *Black Sunlight* the sequence of events – his father's death, life in Rhodesia, life in Oxford, for example – are clearly biography. The problem with the biographical explanation is that it sheds a good deal more light on the life than the art. To combat this Raymond Williams argued that biography was inevitably enclosed within a "structure of feeling" representing "the most delicate and least tangible parts" of "the particular living result of all the elements in the general organization [of everyday life]. To get away from the "biography" and closer to the "art" it is necessary to deconstruct the reported event to determine the "structure of feeling" supporting it. [33]

Thus it can be argued that in *The Black Insider* and *Black Sunlight* the fragmented form that encloses those biographical events represents the "structure of feeling," the tenor of his life, as he experienced it at the time of writing. Williams' hypothesis has relevance for this study in that it seeks to establish evidence of the influence of external forces on the formation of individual experience. Silvano Arieti developed a similar hypothesis, basing his views on the examination of written work produced by schizophrenics (although his theory is not necessarily exclusive to schizophrenics). According to Arieti, such examination revealed that the writers were operating within a "sphere of meaning" wherein "The meaning is conveyed not by logical progression of thought but by the totality of the thoughts. No matter how disconnected, the [written work] conveys a tone, an atmosphere, what at times is called a *sphere of meaning."* [34] The "tone" or "atmosphere" is captured within the structure of the piece; so it is that the clues to Marechera's lived experiences are to be found in the formal presentation of the works as well as in the content.

Subsequently I will explore further the notion of sphere of meaning by suggesting that the changing form of his works can be seen to represent the changing circumstances of the writer's lived experience. But, first, taking one example of a "live event" (his father's death), I will examine how Marechera used that biographical material.

Although at various times Marechera claimed that his father was murdered by the police or by the army, it seems likely that the official report of the drunken Marechera senior being the hapless victim of a hit and run driver is probably accurate. It is perhaps too facile to accept Marechera's revision as an unsophisticated attempt to make sense of his father's death by inventing a reason for it, but that possibility does exist. However his claim that he personally viewed the bloodstained corpse is imaginatively embellished and most probably untrue:

> I was thirteen. My father had been killed, rather
> mysteriously. We still don't know which army
> officer did it . . . the police were knocking on the
> door asking mother to come and identify father's
> body because he had been killed . . . My two
> older brothers were away and so mother took me
> alone. It was really horrible in the mortuary; you
> could see that he had been riddled with bullets,
> the heavy automatic bullets which had almost cut
> off a part of his body, because they had sewn it
> back, you could see the stitches." (*SB*, p.11)

Another version claims:

> . . . you could see where the car had hit him, his
> body had been broken into two from there and the
> head and one arm had been flung to one side and
> the rest had been flung to the other. . . and his
> head had been smashed. . . and I was seeing this
> at eleven years of age. (*SB*, p. 47)

It is evident from the various interviews on record that Marechera could vary the content of a familiar story, even perhaps to present himself in tragic pose. For example, although there are many witnesses to the fact that he stammered from very early childhood, he was inclined to blame his bad stammer on the trauma of seeing his father's mutilated body, claiming he was unable to speak for several days and when his speech did return it was with a severe impediment.

The many different versions Marechera presented of his experiences became a kind of truth in themselves as he merged imagined reality with the actual events of his life. Such fictionalizing allowed Marechera to explore a more complete and complex imaginative vision of human action. His tendency to revisit and to rewrite his experiences can be seen as a constant search for different levels of meaning from a particular experience. In a work of art, after all, exact and literal truth is not a fundamental requirement. Sylvia Plath's father was not a Nazi, but that does not matter to an appreciation of her poem "Daddy." In reply to Audrey's, "I do not know what poetical is. Is it honest in deed and word? Is it a true thing?" Touchstone responds "No truly: for the truest poetry is the most feigning" (*As You Like It*, Act 3, scene 3). By exaggerating the circumstances of his father's death Marechera is able to examine his own traumatic responses with a greater degree of honesty. Whether Marechera saw his father in the mortuary or not is, to a degree, immaterial. The depth of his anguish was real, painfully honest, and clear to see.

The experience, real or imagined, was used to vivid and moving effect in "Throne of Bayonets" as he mused on the lasting effects on him of his father's death:

Did I mistake the corridor
And the doorway (each step
Irrefutable, irreversible)
Now the Room endless black rain
And the blood distant vistas
Of photogenic Falls?
    Sunlit memories?
  Rather My butchered father
On a mortuary slab, and I
All of eleven years old, refusing

But forced to look. I know now: Learn
Mortality early and you are doomed
To walk forever alone.
                    (*Cemetery of Mind*, p. 36)

Dramatic and highly effective though this account is it was
not Dambudzo, but his brother Michael Marechera, who in fact
was the one who visited the mortuary with his mother,
Dambudzo Marechera being away at boarding school at the time
of the accident. In terms of a psychoanalytical study that sets out
to discern the influences that determined his behavior and
affected his development as a writer such detail is important.
Worthy of note in the sense that distortions and rewritings of his
personal history have important implications for an attempt to
develop a better understanding of the writer and his work, though
in terms of a literary appreciation of the work such detail is of
lesser importance.

2.3 The Effect of Drink and Drugs

"A fight in Bedford Square"

Although it seems unlikely and perhaps more by good
fortune than good judgement, Marechera did avoid hard drugs
but "drunk and smoked dope more or less continuously while
consciousness and money permitted and also experimented with
LSD" (*SB*, p. 157), in *Mindblast* he refers to the London squat;
reminiscencing about ." . . our experiences of cannabis,
belladonna, LSD, cocaine" (p. 156). During our conversation in
January 1995 James Currey recalled that the period after leaving
Oxford and before returning to Harare (October 1977 – January
1982) was one when Marechera was "Often in a desperate state,
rambling and incoherent, whether from drink, drugs or illness, it
was impossible to tell." Currey describes a "fight in Bedford
Square" outside the offices of Heinemann International: "One
great occasion that was much remembered by a lot of people
when he was particularly obnoxious and drunk I finished up

wrestling with him in this lovely square with plane trees. I was wrestling with Dambudzo on the pavement with everybody hanging out of the windows" (see also *SB*, p. 225). The Reverend R. D. de Berry, who knew Marechera during his brief time in Sheffield wrote, with some sympathy, "I would doubt if Mr. Marechera will be alive for very much longer – he hardly eats and only drinks" (*SB*, p. 227).

Marechera was a heavy drinker throughout his adult life. During his brief period in Sheffield the residential Secretary of the YMCA, G. Lawrence, commented on Marechera's " . . . totally undisciplined and drunken state of existence" (*SB*, p. 227). At Oxford "He disturbed college life through frequent bouts of drunken behavior," "running amok when drunk" and was " . . . arrested for being drunk and disorderly" (*SB*, pp. 159-75). When back in Harare Veit-Wild reports "He refused to be "cured" of his excessive, unhealthy life style or his heavy drinking" (*SB*, p. 313), although how capable he was of exercising such a choice is a moot point. The "chicken and egg" question of whether the "excessive, unhealthy life style" and the "heavy drinking" were symptom or cause of his illness is difficult to answer, though it should be observed that while Marechera's illness dated back to his childhood, his self-destructive lifestyle was an adult development. In adulthood, it can be observed, the one exacerbated the other, no doubt contributing to his early death. It can also be observed that, however it was acquired, the "heavy baggage" of problems, both real and imagined, that Marechera carried was central to his writing. No "heavy baggage" would have meant no Dambudzo Marechera, writer.

Aware that some readers and critics considered that his development – or lack of it – as a writer was attributable to the excessive use of alcohol and other mind – expanding stimulants, Marechera told Alle Lansu in an interview recorded in February 1986: ." . . I would never write when I was drunk, I never write when I am drunk or smoking dope. Most people think I do, but I don't" (*SB*, p. 26). Nevertheless, he was well aware of the creative possibilities of such stimulants, as this lucid reference to the effects of drugs makes clear:

> Offering the mind-blowing cigarette. Behind which glowing point my mind thought; refusing to focus on anything but the concussing effects of space and time. The thousand separate perspectives from which to view the point of a needle. The making of a story. (*Black Sunlight* p. 101)

Although expressed in more poetic language there is an understanding here of Huxley's description of the effects on the mind of taking the drug mescaline: "Place and distance cease to be of much interest. The mind does its perceiving in terms of intensity of experience, profundity of significance, relationships within a pattern."[35] If Marechera was sympathetic to the use of drugs then it was tinged with a bitter appreciation of their emasculating effect, as he observed with a typically vivid simile: "The dope helped at first. And then it began to hurt, splitting my head systematically, like a housewife calmly slicing cucumber" (*House of Hunger*, p. 105). Huxley may well have been one of the "gurus" to whom Marechera makes sarcastic reference: "Nowadays we have a thousand gurus to teach us to stand on our heads ...to blast our minds with mescaline ...to escape the horrible boredom that makes us bite our hands and neither fear the final day nor wish for it" (*Black Sunlight*, p. 116). If one "neither fear[s] the final day nor wish[es] for it" then there is no incentive to change the *status quo*, and that for Marechera was a highly unlikely and undesirable condition. More than one reviewer suggested that Marechera had an affinity with the beat poets of the sixties and his life-style was certainly similar. A major difference is that unlike, *inter alia*, the poets Ginsberg or Ferlinghetti, the writers Huxley or Castenada, Marechera, apparently, did not use drugs for their alleged creative effect. Any impact of drink or drugs on his writing was not intentional.

The following short extract shows the complexity of the writer's thought processes as ideas tumble out at a frantic pace. An initial reading might suggest that the apparent obscurities in the text were the result of mind-influencing stimulants, but on analysis a more controlled engagement with issues is revealed:

> Fucking Allah! And there was Hitler at the Olympic games turning his backside on our finest athlete ...Motherfucking Buddha! I've spent my life running from one bit of earth to another. Carrying my smashed peace of mind into the oddest gangs of peoples. Take this one for instance. I bring them music and laughter and poetry and they throw me into a pitlatrine. By now Blanche can smell my inglorious flight, covered in humanshit, chickenshit and prickling all over with ghastly spears. Stanley meets Mutesa. Blanche Goodfather I presume. I am a bit of alright, Blanche, just a slight case of black wasps I trod on. You know. A nip into the pool will quickly restore me to my old self. Fucking military arse! Another spear just shaved of my right sideboard. The persistent bastards. I'm only a fucking court jester, Chief, not a dissident like Sakharov. Shit. The spears are still flying. I wonder if Walter Mitty ever daydreamed anything like this? (*Black Sunlight* p. 9)

The kaleidoscopic tumult of ideas suggests a very creative mind in overdrive. There is the strange adoption of the black American athlete, Jesse Owens, as "*our* finest athlete" followed by reference to Marechera's physical ("running from one bit of earth to another") and psychological ("smashed peace of mind") dislocation. Reference to the personal rejection he feels and the rejection of his work ("I bring them music and laughter and poetry and they throw me into a pitlatrine") and the humiliation of his "inglorious" flight, arguably from Rhodesia *and* New College, is followed by the unconvincing attempts at self reassurance "I am a bit of alright," and at belittling his problems "just a slight case of black wasps I trod on." His sense of equanimity will, it seems, be restored by intercourse, "a nip into the pool," with Blanche Goodfather (the name is obviously an unsubtle pun on the role of the colonizer) as he gleefully declares "Fucking military arse!"

Marechera's self-doubts about his role as a writer resurface immediately, he is only a "fucking court jester" not a "dissident like Sakharov." The writer then undermines his serious pretensions by making comparisons of his work to that of the American humorist, James Thurber: "I wonder if Walter Mitty ever daydreamed anything like this." This passage then can be seen to be tightly controlled examination of his predicament.

However, there are passages that are not so thematically lucid:

> That's when the chill from beyond fades into warm doorways and crams descriptions of Africa into a confined room. That's when the rain out of the empty air pulls down a victim tense and white. What is it pounding at my door like brain and tongue red-hot to speak? The fist is clenched around Golgotha-red flowers to crack the stony heart with hammers of human knuckles. Not a shred of emotion lingers; the wind has scoured it all. A frail and tattered grace outlines the continent in the round moonlight. Oh, black insider! (*The Black Insider*, p. 101)

This beautiful and imaginative prose is highly charged emotionally and the despairing tone is heavy with meaning. However, the literal meaning, the sense of the passage, is not immediately apparent. Whether that suggests a conscious attempt at the surreal, rather than the darker inspiration of drink or drugs, is difficult to determine. Regardless of the inspiration, such passages probably led Marechera's critics to comment unfavorably on the accessibility of his prose.

2.4 Marechera's "sphere of meaning."

"Voices in the gritty trumpet"

The above extracts are not dissimilar to many others in *Black Sunlight* and *The Black Insider*. It can be argued that the rapidity with which the writer moves between diverse and complex issues reflects the fragmented nature of Marechera's "sphere of meaning" (his lived experience in London), as well as confirming his obsessive pursuit of those issues.

House of Hunger is more recognisably conventional in structure than either *Black Sunlight* or *The Black Insider* in that there is a chronologically sequential coherency to the story line. In no small measure this pattern suggests a sphere of meaning that reflects the remnants of the semblance of order imposed on his life by the requirements of being a student at New College. Perhaps it is unwise to refer to any part of Marechera's adult life history as orderly, but the Oxford experience did establish some sort of discipline and a framing of activities, which was to dissolve completely as he struggled to find a role for himself after leaving New College and student life. On his move to London the framework of Marechera's life began to disintegrate and his "sphere of meaning" became increasingly precarious and fragmentary. Evidence of this is to be found in *Black Sunlight* and *The Black Insider* as, in comparison with *The House of Hunger*, the form collapses and the use of violent imagery increases with an emphasis on gore and disgorgement, the scatological, the profane and the sexual.

> The ugly fact. Erect. Oozing a black light. Plunged. Heaved. Up down. Up down. Smiling and unsmiling authority. Fucking the ugly fact of the street. Controlled jets of moonwhite water spurted from the desolation's wrenched-open mouth. Thoughts that crack like nuts in the explosion of a raindrop...The utmost and edge. Struck the ear. With bestial fact...Fucking and

> sucking the air with speech ...Spreading the
> thighs across my groin...Heaving. Up down.
> Squelching spittled words into the many eared
> cunt. (*Black Sunlight*, p. 97)

The short sentences, as well as the descriptive "Plunged.
Heaved. Up down. Up down.," represent the rhythm of sexual
intercourse, which is portrayed, not as an act of love, but as a
violent act of possession. The violence of the language and
fragmented sentences are themselves symptomatic of his life in
London.

Although there is a coherency in *The House of Hunger*, the
progression through the plot is not a smooth one, as the writer
intertwines a basic story line with sudden insertions of apparently
unconnected material. Because the interjections are not clearly
signaled the sudden shifts are initially disconcerting until it is
realized that one strand is in the "here and now" and the other
strands are recollections that feed into and complement the main
thrust of the story. These "recollections" vary thematically but are
plainly autobiographical references as Marechera began the
"painstaking exploration of the effect of poverty and destitution
on the psyche" (*The House of Hunger*, p. 61) and which
continued in *Black Sunlight* and *The Black Insider*.

The question of the relationship between Marechera's
psychological illness and his writing brings up even more
complex issues than that of his heavy drinking and drug taking.
My concern is not only with the relationship of the meaning of
an image within the context of a specific literary text, but also
with the larger psychological context that imposes its meanings
on the image.

I am also concerned with the very issue of madness itself,
which is more often defined in terms of social attitudes towards
deviant behavior than a clinical diagnosis. Marechera was mad
only in the Foucauldian sense, that is, by the manner in which the
depths of his passions revealed themselves: "The savage danger

of madness is related to the danger of the passions and to their fatal concatenation."[36] Although he could behave in a dilettantish fashion, as he was very self-aware , "I was enjoying playing the part of the unfathomable black intellectual mind. I still do" (*The Black Insider*, p. 87), he was demonstrably passionate in his beliefs. Issues of sanity and madness are often difficult to resolve and although Marechera was not "mad," neither was he "sane." He was suffering from a personality disorder and was certainly, in Dostoyevsky's words, an "oddity":

> For not only is an oddity not always a detail and an isolated instance – on the contrary, it may occasionally transpire that he it is who bears within him, perhaps, the very heartwood of the whole, while, for some reason, the other men of his epoch have all of them been wrenched loose from it for a time as by some tidal gale. [37]

A "tidal gale" such as colonialism or neo-colonialism, perhaps, arousing such passions as Foucault recognized in his comment "The possibility of madness is …implicit in the very phenomenon of passion"?[38]

At one extreme Marechera's psychopathology could be seen simply to undermine the coherence of his writing. The following is from a long piece in which the narrator struggles to describe the lasting affects of colonialism (or neocolonialism):

> Having smashed the boot through the glass veneer of the state. Of our nerves. And minds. That sheer blatant austerity. Is wealth. In our wake, smashed institutions. Smashed minds. Smashed traffic signs. Smashed courtrooms. Smashed armouries. Eyeballs whirring. Their red veins sticking out to encapsulate the black sunlight up there down here. Right here in our heritage. Fucked. Leaving nothing but Bull Shit Organs. Screwed. The assholes. Those ugly facts. My trial. (*Black Sunlight* p. 103)

There is an overwhelming sense here of the writer's barely controlled rage at the parlous state of the human condition, and one can take that potent meaning from the passage. The very short staccato sentences, the violent language, the discontinuities and the obfuscatory "red veins sticking out to encapsulate the black sunlight up there down here" are an effective portrayal of utter disillusionment. However, although Marechera's anger is very clear, the literal meaning is obscured by the manic pace of his writing and thought processes. One reading of the passage suggests that Marechera is writing of "the people." Another reading suggests that the incoherent presentation of the piece reflects the disarray of Marechera's own lived experience, a reading that may well be confirmed by the otherwise obscure reference to "My trial."

At another extreme the brilliant surrealism of his sentences could be seen as plumbing depths unavailable to the more rational and "sane" among us. For example, again from *Black Sunlight*:

> Ants, tulips, and anacondas, are the voices in the gritty trumpet. Cigarettes and whisky, artichokes and popstars; are the beads strung round Nick and Nicola's frail shoulders. There are pink crabs at the shallow end of the pool"
> (p. 114).

Here, although even the primary meaning is not immediately apparent, there is a gentle beauty about this rhythmic prose which offers an enjoyable, if somewhat daunting, challenge to the reader.

This issue of the relationship between his psychological illness and his writing is interestingly complicated by Wilson Harris's idea that schizophrenia is a creative, imaginative response to the strictures of colonization. This involves the notion of "creative schizophrenia," which is (according to Wilson Harris):

> . . . a complex threshold into a cross-cultural

medium that breaks the mould of a one-sided,
conquistadorial realism, . . . bringing into play
parallels and alternatives through which to revision the complicated global legacies of the
past as those become active in original and
profoundly intuitive ways within the present and
the future. [39]

Schizophrenia is then, in Harris's view, a form of anti-
colonial psychological adjustment. The implications of this
hypothesis for Marechera's prose fiction are explored in Chapter
Four.

An alternative source for Marechera's mental disorder lies
deep in the cultural traditions of his African heritage. Michael
Marechera, Dambudzo's elder brother, told the story that their
mother got rid of her madness by passing it on to her unfortunate
son Dambudzo (see appendix, p. 257). Michael Marechera
recounts that one of their ancestors had been killed as a witch,
but that her evil influence had been passed on to his mother. The
consequences were that:

. . . Towards the end of 1969, Mother
became mad. She went to consult a *n'anga* who
told her she could only get rid of the problem by
passing it on to one of her children. She did not
choose Lovemore because he was her favorite.
She did not choose me because I was named
after a powerful ancestor whose spirit would
protect me from such things. She chose
Dambudzo.

In 1971 he began to suffer delusions. He
was sure two men were following him
everywhere. Only he could see them. He was
then writing his "A" levels and I don't know
how he managed because he was taking so many
tranquilizers.

Subsequently I felt he must have known what Mother had done. When later he left for England my bones told me he was running away from something. When he returned to Zimbabwe he refused to see Mother – I now understand why.

It is difficult to explain such matters to those who do not know our culture. But I feel this story explains why Dambudzo always said he had no family and why he saw himself as an outcast. (*SB*, pp. 53/ 54)

If, as Michael Marechera suggests, Dambudzo was aware that his own mother had betrayed him, this would have placed yet another pressure on his precarious grasp on his mental well-being; his burgeoning paranoia would have been given sharp focus and his fragile hold on reality would have been further threatened. There is no doubt that Dambudzo Marechera began to experience mental problems from around the age of 13, probably induced or at least precipitated by the traumas of his father's death and a subsequent deterioration of a life style that was already harsh and demanding.

One childhood friend recalled how Marechera's behavior changed " . . . when his father died and when they were forced to move out of their house and when his mother started to go out with men (*SB*, p. 52). That Dambudzo Marechera was aware of his mother's visit to the *n'anga* was confirmed in a letter from Dr Anthony Chennells to me dated August 29,1995. (Dr Anthony Chennells is Associate Professor of English at the University of Zimbabwe. He was one of Marechera's tutors during his time at what was then the University of Rhodesia.) Chennells recalls discussing with Marechera the story about Marechera and his mother, apparently in the context of "being caught between European and African culture." Chennells writes "You can imagine my horror when instead of the usual details with which students illustrate their cultural confusion, Marechera produced a

story very similar to the one Michael Marechera told. He used it
to show that Shona culture had rejected him." It is significant that
Dambudzo Marechera expressed the view that his culture, rather
than simply his family, had rejected him.

None of Marechera's works could be accurately described as
a *roman a clef*. But, as issues around his illness are recurring
themes in all of his writing, some background to that illness is
important. not simply in biographical terms, but also as a key to a
deeper understanding of the text. He writes of his time at
Penhalonga:

> It was at this time I began to write poetry, each
> thickly affected by whatever English or American
> poet I was reading at the time. I would take an
> easy chair onto the edge of the cliff on which the
> school was built and nibble at the landscape
> sprawling beneath me, scratch at the soul
> irritation that was beginning to make me suspect
> that all was not what it seemed, that all inside me
> would never be echoed by what was outside. I
> was beginning to grow up. I was on my way to
> the Hararean mazes of Skidrow. I was not going
> to be whatever the whites and the blacks expected
> of me. (*Mindblast*, p. 122)

The image of the young Marechera, realizing he is
"different," and at the start of what was to become a compulsive
search-for-self, is brilliantly evoked as he regards his
philosophical journey from the rural idyll of Penhalonga to "the
Hararean mazes of Skidrow."

There are reports that Marechera began suffering attacks of
paranoia and hallucinations while at primary school, which he
attended from age 6 to age 13 and his years at St. Augustine's
Mission school at Penhalonga were marked by developing signs
of a psychological illness. As the principal at the time, Father
Pearce commented, "He showed a number of signs of clinical
mental sickness, including hearing voices threatening him, and

so forth. Also repeated hypochondria, requiring us to motor him into the hospital at Umtali for treatment of supposed "heart attacks" which were shown not to have happened. Hypochondria is in itself an illness and it seems likely that the "heart attacks" were in fact panic attacks brought on by a state of acute anxiety, a corollary of paranoia. However as Father Prosser, one of the staff at St Augustine's, explains," . . . of course we have never given anybody psychiatric treatment, being far too rough and ready a place for that." (*SB*, pp. 68-69) The fact that the young Marechera was an exceptionally gifted student may well have been a factor there is little doubt that his exceptional talents would have placed him outside the usual experience of the African schoolboy, leading to his isolation and exacerbating his paranoia.

In *The House of Hunger* Marechera describes with a Lawrentian passion a violent storm at Penhalonga: "That rain, it drummed the drum until the drum burst, stitching the mind with thongs of lightning. It was like a madman talking incessantly; whispering rapidly into the ear of the sky" (p. 32). Confronting the elements like "Pauline travelers on the road to Damascus" has the result of curing Marechera of his hallucinations:

> *They* had gone! I could feel it. They had erased
> themselves into the invisible airs of the storm.
> The daemon had been exorcised and gone into the
> Gadarene swine. For the first time in my life I felt
> completely alone. Totally alone. It is as if a storm
> could rage in one's mind and no one else has the
> experience of it. It frightened me a little. (p. 34)

The key to this very dramatic passage (which covers three and a half pages, 31-34) is in the introduction of the parable of the Gadarene (Mark 5: 1-13). The storm can be seen as a metaphor for Marechera's illness, it can also be seen as an illness (the daemon) that (as colonialism) is endemic among black Africans. In this latter reading Marechera, like the Gadarene, was not alone in his difficulties: "My name is Legion, for we are many" (v. 9). As the Gadarene's madness was "cured" by being transferred to the swine who, thus driven mad, dash headlong into the sea, so the "ills" of Africa will disappear when the colonizer is banished.

I argued above that, in sections of *Black Sunlight* and *The Black Insider* particularly, Marechera engages in a search-for-self, the primordial I, that involves being free of all prior influences. In this passage, with the imaginative exorcising of his personal daemons, he achieves that: "For the first time in my life I felt completely alone." Marechera's personality problems tended to destroy friendships but he could be, by all accounts, a friendly and sociable man. It seems likely that he was not naturally a solitary being and the prospect of being alone and misunderstood, "no one else had the experience of it," was "frightening." A possible explanation of that fear is offered by R D Laing. Quoting William James, Laing wrote: "No more fiendish punishment could be devised ...than that one should be turned loose in society and remain absolutely unnoticed by all the members thereof." [40]

Although Father Pearce attached a note to his recommendation form on behalf of Marechera to the University College of Rhodesia qualifying his comments: "On the day I write this he [Marechera] is going to the doctor suffering from what appears to be a serious mental disorder" (*SB*, p. 92), the only extant medical report on Marechera appears to be the one produced following his examination by psychiatrists Dr. Hoare and Professor Gelder at Warneford Mental Hospital, Oxford. The actual medical record is not available, and the following information is taken from an exchange of correspondence between Sir William Hayter, warden of New College, Oxford, and Len Rix, lecturer at the English Department of the University of Rhodesia. Hayter quotes the psychiatrists as offering the view that "he [Marechera] was not in their sense mentally ill" but that he was "psychopathic and had a personality disorder for which there was no treatment" (*SB*, p. 175).

As psychopathy is not untreatable – indeed it requires or is susceptible to medical treatment, whereas psychosis is inaccessible to psychoanalytical treatment – it seems likely that there is a confusion of terminology in Hayter's account, and that Marechera was diagnosed as psychotic rather than psychopathic. It seems that he suffered from a schizoid state aggravated by paranoia. The importance of this distinction is emphasized by R. D. Laing who argued that a psychotic breakdown was more in the nature of a breakthrough, an existential crisis from which an individual could reach a more authentic way of being, rather than a physical illness treatable with drugs.[41] Anthony Storr had this to say about the schizoid character:

> Schizoid people . . . very often fail to develop any realistic sense of their position in the human hierarchy . . . Thus they often continue to feel themselves to be unrealistically weak and incompetent on the one hand, and to have equally unrealistic phantasies of power on the other. Moreover, the less satisfaction a person gains by interacting with people and things in the external world, the more will he be preoccupied with his own inner world of phantasy. This is a notable characteristic of schizoid people, who are essentially introverted: preoccupied with inner, rather than outer, reality.[42]

As Fanon pointed out a recurring condition of colonial occupation was the powerful sense of displacement experienced by the indigenous population; taking this "inheritance" to Oxford could well have exacerbated Marechera's uncertainty about his place in the "human hierarchy" and hastened his retreat into phantasy and a preoccupation with "inner reality," bearing in mind his already fragile mental state.

Both psychiatry and psychoanalysis recognize three functional psychoses: schizophrenia, manic-depressive psychosis, and paranoia. Evidence of schizophrenia and paranoia abound in the writings of Dambudzo Marechera. According to Dr. David MacSweeney, a member of the Royal College of

Psychiatry:

> When we are young we interject bits and pieces
> of key figures in our lives: a good father, a good
> mother, or a good teacher. In his *Republic,* Plato
> suggests that work is needed to integrate the
> diverse parts of the inner self. He says: "Only
> when man has linked these parts together in a
> well-tempered harmony and has made himself
> one man instead of many, will he be ready to go
> about whatever he may have to do." [43]

Quite clearly the adult Marechera never achieved the "well-tempered harmony" and, as he demonstrated throughout his writing, never became "one man instead of many." As a consequence of this he struggled to do "whatever he may have to do," which was of course to write and possibly through that writing discover "a more authentic way of being":

> I am the luggage no one will claim:
> The out-of-place turd all deny
> Responsibility:
> The incredulous sneer all tuck away
>   Beneath bland smiles;
> The loud fart all silently agree never
>   Happened;
> The sheer bad breath you politely confront
>   with mouthwashed platitudes: "After all its
>   POETRY."
> I am the rat every cat secretly admires;
> The cat every dog secretly fears;
> The pervert every honest citizen surprises
>   in his own mirror: POET.
>   ("Identify   the   Identity   Parade,"
> *Cemetery of Mind*, p. 199)

The title hints at an ambiguity along the lines of "Will the real Zimbabwean please stand up?" Exactly which identity is being sought in the identity parade? Marechera's own identity is under attack: he is "the luggage" no one wants; the "out-of-place-turd"; the "loud fart" and "bad breath" greeted with hypocrisy, platitudes and a patronizing excusing of his "faults," "After all it's poetry." And yet, the writer maintains in an affirmation of his self-image that he is what others secretly want to be. Reference to the "honest citizen" is an ironic reversal of values. Marechera the "pervert" and "poet," is honest, and the "honest citizen" is a hypocrite who publicly denies Marechera's "truth" but secretly recognizes the validity of the writer's stance (arguably, his identity) and, if he had the courage, would adapt it for himself.

A series of misdemeanors had led to the university-initiated psychiatric examination held in early 1976. Marechera had (selecting from a lengthy catalog of disasters) assaulted various people, threatened to murder named people, set fire to the college, stolen property to fund his drinking and been arrested and fined for being drunk and disorderly. Marechera had agreed to the examination when presented with the ultimatum of psychiatric treatment or expulsion; it is little wonder then that the university viewed the diagnosis of "untreatable" with some apprehension. In February 1976 the College informed Marechera that unless his behavior improved he would be sent down. His behavior did not improve. There were more violent incidents, and on March 15, 1976 he was expelled.

Typically Marechera rewrote the history of his expulsion, claiming "I very much resented the implied accusation from Oxford of insanity. They demanded that I either sign myself voluntarily into their psychiatric hospital or I would be sent down. That choice really freaked me out" (*SB*, p. 160). The period following his expulsion marked the beginning of Marechera's career as a writer. Quite obviously he had been writing while at Oxford and before that, but the works that were published were written very substantially in the post-Oxford era. In subsequent chapters the framework of the development of the writer becomes the texts themselves, which, as the Heinemann reader John Wyllie in his report on *The Black Heretic* (circa November 1979) commented, clearly reflect that Marechera's intention was to say, "Look, here is the way I am and here is the reason for it." In every single text the perturbation, the instability and insecurity is personal and all pervasive. This approach to the writing of what purports to be fiction is not simply an imposition of art on life but rather reflects the fact that the art-to-life relationship is a two-way street – the one is not discredited by association with the other.

2.5 A Question of Political Commitment

A Writer for a Specific Nation?

I shall now turn to the question of Marechera's rejection of the almost obligatory roles for the African writer of his generation, as spokesman for "the struggle" or "teacher" of his people. Marechera's views on the "commitment" of the writer were vigorous: "If you are a writer for a specific nation or a specific race, then fuck you" (*Dambudzo Marechera 1952-1987*, p. 3, see also above). A more temperate version emerged from a paper Marechera presented to the Zimbabwe German Society, on October 29, 1986. His topic was "The African Writer's Experience of European Literature." He said "From early in my life I have viewed literature as a unique universe that has no internal divisions. I do not pigeon hole it by race or language or nation" (*SB*, p. 362). This deliberately syncretic approach to literature is confirmed later in the same article when he claims " . . . Mikhail Bakhtin has offered a category of narrative whose unifying factor is a "carnival" attitude to the world. This category includes writers from different backgrounds . . . Heaven and hell are close and may be visited. Madness, dreams and day-dreams, abnormal states of mind and all kinds of erratic inclinations are explored." [44] There are echoes here of Marechera's own work, of course. It can be argued that " . . . carnivalized writing . . . reproduces within its own structures and within its own practices, the characteristic inversions , parodies, discrownings of carnival proper." [45] Undoubtedly, Marechera's work shows some of those qualities

But what of Marechera's clear vision of the writer existing simply as a writer in a "unique universe," with no barriers and, therefore, with no limiting expectations? Is this anything more than an impossible dream? This is something of a rhetorical question. But what does matter, certainly in Marecheran terms, is that the writer should be free to operate without prior expectations informing either the form or content of his work. Such a view is not unique, of course, either to Marechera or Africa; as Louis MacNeice bitterly observed, in *An Eclogue for Christmas*:

> I have not been allowed to be
> Myself in flesh or face, but abstracting and
> dissecting me
> They have made of me pure form, a symbol
or a
> pastiche
> Stylized profile, anything but soul and
flesh.[46]

In trying to escape from that "stylized profile" Marechera was seeking a sense of his own unique identity, but (as I argue below) the first step was to become disentangled from the influence of the notion of identity created for the writer by sundry others. The escape was through writing, as Barthes argues: "Writing is that neutral, composite, oblique space where our subject slips away, the negative where all identity is lost, starting with the very identity of the body writing."[47] Of course Barthes" argument was concerned with the primacy of the reader but the significance of the death of the author had, perhaps, a different resonance for Marechera in that such death could lead, not to obscurity, but to a rebirth from which the "pure" individual could emerge having purged himself of pernicious influences.

Such individualism did not sit easily in newly independent countries where it seemed that the initial task of black African writers was not to write about their own experiences but to record a sense of history and culture to replace that ignored by colonial writers and historians. The role of the writer was typified as " . . . teacher or guide, lending his skill to the education and direction of the masses."[48] As Achebe remarked, "The writer cannot expect to be excused from the task of re-education and regeneration that must be done. In fact he should march right in front." [49] Ngugi argued, "An African writer should write in a language that will allow him to communicate effectively with peasants and workers in Africa."[50] He was referring specifically to writing in an African language rather than a European language, but the notion of accessibility, regardless of the African language/European language debate, was one to which Marechera paid little heed. He was in any event under no pressure to write in Shona as a means of protest, since the activities of the Southern Rhodesia Literary Bureau ensured that more African language books were published in Rhodesia than in any other African country. Writing in *The Search for Zimbabwean Identity* (p. 15), George Kahari claimed that following the establishment of the Southern Rhodesia Literature Bureau in 1953 "to encourage, assist and advise local authors in Shona," more than 60 such novels had been published up to 1980. What is now the Zimbabwe Literature Bureau is still very active – albeit with a very different political agenda.

Marechera had his own perception of the activities of the Bureau: "In Zimbabwe we have these two great indigenous languages, ChiShona and Sindebele. Who wants us to keep writing these ShitShona and ShitNdebele languages, this missionary chickenshit? Who else but the imperialists." [51] This stance is opposed to that of Ngugi for whom the fact that his language had been hijacked by missionaries and imperialists would have been a very powerful reason for writing in it, to set the record straight. (Subsequently Marechera did, nevertheless, write in Shona. The one-act play "The Servant's Ball" was published in *Scrapiron Blues* in English and Shona language versions.) As for his own use of English Marechera explained:

> Shona was part of the ghetto daemon I was trying
> to escape. Shona had been placed within the
> context of a degraded mindwrenching experience
> from which apparently the only escape was into

the English language and education. . . . English language was automatically connected with the plush and seeming splendor of the white side of town. . . (*Dambudzo Marechera 1952-1987*, p. 7)

This is followed by the bleak observation "I was therefore a keen accomplice and student in my own mental colonization."

A counter to the argument that the use of English is a political statement and indicates mental colonization is that Marechera's use of English is rather an indication of a continually regenerative hybridization.[52] As he argued with typical extravagance when explaining his "experimental" use of English:

> . . . you have to have harrowing fights and hair-raising panga duals (*sic*) with the language before you can make it do all that you want it to do . . . this may mean discarding grammar, throwing syntax out, subverting images from within, beating the drum and cymbals of rhythm, developing torture chambers of irony and sarcasm, gas ovens of limitless black resonance. (*Dambudzo Marechera 1952-1987*, pp. 7-8)

A similar theme – that of a "new culture" emerging from the clash of the "old cultures" – is explored by Dash who argues (of colonized people), "The only thing they could possess (and which could not be tampered with) was their imagination and this became the source of their struggle against the cruelty of their conditions." He attributes the notion of such a "counter-culture of the imagination" to Wilson Harris who claimed that "the imagination of the folk involved a crucial inner re-creative response to the violations of slavery and indenture and conquest." [53] Dambudzo Marechera rejected the idea of a black historicity to recreate "his" lost culture and which attempted to disown the European culture transplanted to Africa. His "inner creative response" to this vacuum was to offer a portrait of an individual adrift in a culture in permanent transition, lost in a world of hybridity and incompleteness. Marechera is too unforgiving of himself with his accusations against himself of being an accomplice in his own "mental colonization." He experienced a dynamic and powerful process of socialization in which any degree of choice was not a realistic option.

As for the role of teacher preferred by Ngugi and Achebe, Marechera rejected the argument, saying, "I don't know that the writer can offer the emerging nation anything . . . Writing can always turn into cheap propaganda . . . As soon as one talks about a writer's role in society . . . you are already into censorship" (*Dambudzo Marechera 1952-1987*, p. 19). Of the reader, he comments: "Those who do not understand my work are simply illiterate. One must learn" (*Black Sunlight*, p. 110). Marechera's points on the role of the writer are well made and to an extent echo the criticism leveled at the activities of the Southern Rhodesia Literary Bureau, which ensured, by very strict censorship, that no politically sensitive material was published. His comments on the reader, however, may seem arrogant and dismissive. They have the air of rationalization as the writer attempted to answer his critics, especially those who accused him of being difficult to read.

The following extract from *The Black Insider* is extracted from a polemic on the nature and use of language, sustained over several pages (pp. 47-52) in which Marechera entertains the notion of language, among other things, as a corrupting agency and as tool of individual freedom:

> Language is like water. You can drink it. You can swim in it. You can drown in it. You can wear a snorkel in it. You can evaporate and become invisible with it . . . The way you take your water is supposed to say a lot about you. It is supposed to reflect your history, your culture, your breeding etc. It is supposed to show the extent to which you and your nation have developed or degenerated. The word "primitive" is applied to all those who take their alphabet neat from rivers,

sewers, and natural scenery – sometimes this may
be described as the romantic imagination. The
height of sophistication is actually to channel
your water through a system of pipes into your
very own lavatory where you shake the hand of
the machine and your shit and filthy manners
disappear in a roaring of water. Being water you
can spread diseases like bilharzia. And if you
want to write a book you cannot think unless your
thoughts are contagious.

The latter half of the above is a thinly disguised attack on
the notion of the writer as communal spokesman, comparing that
activity to the spreading of a disease. It is also a lament for the
individual who is not "allowed" to think unless his "thoughts"
are contagious, that is, unless he can be understood and accepted
by everyone. As I demonstrate in Chapters Five and Six there is
abundant evidence available that he remained true to those ideals
in the work he produced on his return to Zimbabwe.

2.6 An African Writer?

"The worst kind of hypocrite"

I shall now move on to consider the dangers and difficulties
of writers attempting, or being encouraged to attempt, the
creation of an "African identity" or a "sense of nationhood,"
leading to the question of Marechera's rejection of the label
"African writer." In the scramble for Africa in the late nineteenth
and early twentieth centuries, "new" nations were created by the
English, the French, the Germans, the Dutch, the Belgians, and
the Portuguese, and with these new nations "new" identities were
established indistinguishable from the "home" country of the
colonizer and settler. Wole Soyinka commented: "One hundred
years ago . . . the colonial powers that ruled Africa met to divvy
up their interests into states, lumping various peoples and tribes
together in some places and hacking them apart in others like

some demented tailor who paid no attention to the fabric, color or pattern of the quilt he was patching together." [54] When Southern Rhodesia became the independent republic of Zimbabwe in April 1980 it signaled the end of colonial rule in Africa. The process of recapturing an "African identity," which had begun decades earlier elsewhere in Africa, began to gather force in Rhodesia/Zimbabwe. And it is impossible to understand this process without specific reference to the local factor of the Rhodesia Literature Bureau, which largely informed or deformed it during the final years of colonization.

The Rhodesia Literature Bureau was established in 1953 under the auspices of the Native Affairs Department with the express intention of encouraging the publication of black African writing in Shona and Ndebele, the languages of the indigenous peoples of Zimbabwe. The Literature Bureau functioned as a literary agency; among other things it organized writer's workshops to teach writing skills, assessed manuscripts, and recommended and prepared them for publication. But the Literature Bureau always had a double function.[55] On the one hand, it played a very important role in promoting vernacular writing and providing the means for its development. On the other hand, it had been established in order to prevent the emergence of critical political literature. All submissions to the Literature Bureau were closely vetted by the Native Commissioners who rejected all political or religious subject matter, both one would imagine appropriate topics for a country that had been colonized by British entrepreneurs accompanied by proselytizing missionaries.

This censorship ensured that indigenous writing was unable to tackle serious issues and followed a completely separate development to black writing in English. The national identity constructed by the writers working to the orders of the Literature Bureau portrayed an apolitical, one-dimensional, folklorist people very difficult to reconcile with the soldiers who eventually overcame the Smith regime and bearing no resemblance at all to the worlds depicted by, say, Charles

Mungoshi in *Waiting for the Rain*, or Stanley Nyamfukudza in *The Non Believer's Journey*, or in Marechera's *House of Hunger, Black Sunlight*, or *The Black Insider*. The efforts of the Literature Bureau ensured that the work of the black Zimbabwean writing in Shona or Ndebele was heavily censored, severely limited in subject matter and became part of a literature branded in pejorative terms as "native." If a national image was being prepared and presented for consumption by the black Zimbabwean then it was one cynically manipulated by the white government.

Preben Kaarsholm writes of the struggle for the "hearts and minds of the people" that was "an integral part of the process of decolonization in Rhodesia from the Unilateral Declaration of Independence in 1965 and the first initiatives of guerilla warfare on the part of the nationalist movements from March 1966 onwards . . . to the independence of Zimbabwe . . . in 1980." [56] She continues, "The struggle has been maintained since then in the attempts by Zimbabwean writers, poets and artists . . . to consolidate and develop the foundations of a new, autonomous culture that were established during the war." I argue later that such a "new" culture is in fact a hybrid of what had gone before; here I wish merely to illustrate the dangers inherent in trying to recreate a national identity or sense of nationhood.

But there were attempts to escape the interference of the Literature Bureau and some black Zimbabweans writing in English, often from exile, did take on politically sensitive matters. However, even for these brave political writers, there were problems in recreating history and they did not necessarily get it right. In 1980 the Mambo Press published *The Search for Zimbabwean Identity* by George Kahari, at that time a senior lecturer in the Department of African Languages at the University of Zimbabwe. Kahari examined the first novels written in English by black Zimbabweans. One of the novels was the previously mentioned *Waiting for the Rain* by Mungoshi which Kahari calls " . . . a novel of bleak social realism charting the disintegration of the family unit" (p. 134). He also refers to

Year of the Uprising by Stanlake Samkange, " . . . another historical novel which shows how the African spirit media influenced the people in resisting the Charter Company Administration . . . and the reasons which led to the rebellion of 1893-1897" (p. 19). Musaemura Zimunya in *Those Years of Drought and Hunger* examines the emergence of "serious African fiction in English in Zimbabwe" (p. 2). Of *Year of the Uprising* he notes the central role of the spirit mediums and refers to the "documental-historical significance" (p. 16) of Samkange's work. Obviously *Year of the Uprising* contained vital information for those searching for clues to the Zimbabwean identity.

Terence Ranger's book *Revolt in Southern Rhodesia: 1896-1897*, first published in 1967, was hailed (in the blurb to the second edition [1979]) as ." . . [a] classic of Rhodesian historiography" and ." . . one of the most intelligent analyses yet produced . . . an engrossing and meaningful study of the nature of the Shona and Ndebele fight against the rule of the British South Africa Company." This is not the place to enter into the detail of Ranger's claims about the socio-economic and political organizations of the Shona and Ndebele peoples or to examine his interpretations of the events that preceded the wars of 1896-1897. But Ranger emphasized, among other things, the importance of the Mutapa and Rozwi empires, suggesting that the structures and memories of those empires were significant in 1896 in achieving combined action against the whites. He also stressed that the spirit mediums played the most important role in bringing about unity in the risings. The Shona, he suggested, were imperialists and the Ndebele warriors were dependent on the Shona for agriculture and technology. Suffice it to say that these conclusions, and others, were subsequently questioned and the validity and accuracy of his text brought into serious doubt by, for example, David Beach in *A History of the Shona,* [57] and Julian Cobbing in *The Ndebele Under the Khumalos: 1820-1896.* [58] In the preface to the second edition of *Revolt*, published in 1979, Ranger accepted many of the criticisms, adding the comment, "It is now ten years since *Revolt in Southern Rhodesia* was published and ten years is a long time in Africa and in African historiography . . . If I were writing about the risings today, I would certainly do so very differently" (p. xi).

Such withdrawals do not come easily and only after long and arduous examination of the available facts. Of his search for evidence with which to support his own findings and to contest Beach and Cobbing, Ranger comments, "Often in the past ten years I have read a book which seemed at first sight to confirm the argument about . . . leadership in 1896 only to realize that the book itself was drawing heavily upon the interpretations set out in my own book. This is true, I think, for Lawrence Vambe's book *An Ill Fated People* and Stanlake Samkange's *Year of the Uprising*" (pp. xiv-xv). Samkange acknowledged his debt to Ranger, and of Vambe's *Ill Fated People*, which stresses the central role played by the spirit mediums in the risings, Ranger comments, " . . . the overall account of mediums and revolt . . . is [drawn from *Revolt*]."

Samkange's novel was used by Kahari in his search for a Zimbabwean identity as validating certain characteristics of the Shona and Ndebele identities but Samkange's novel was based on neither primary research nor specialist knowledge. As Samkange acknowledges in the preface to his novel he relied on the evidence appearing in Ranger's book, evidence that was subsequently disputed and found to be in error. It would seem that the construction (or reconstruction) of a national identity is a task that is fraught with the difficulties of censorship, false notions of history, and the personal, often idiosyncratic intentions of the writer. The Zimbabwean experience has been repeated elsewhere: writing in *Tasks and Masks* of Ngugi's *A Grain of Wheat*, Lewis Nkosi claims " . . . so strong is this historical sense, so pervasive the influence of the Mau Mau uprising, that by comparison the characters seem to me not as important: it is possible to argue that history itself, as it unfolded in the Kenya struggle for freedom and independence, becomes the true "hero" of the novel."[59] This raises the issues of whose sense of history is being recorded and what is the provenance of that "history," if it is to be taken as more than fiction, as Nkosi implies.

Marechera had a keen sense of history but only insofar as it offered the key to understanding the present. Flora Veit-Wild wrote, "Marechera refuses to identify himself with any particular race, culture or nation; he is an anarchistic thinker. . . the freedom of the individual is of the utmost importance. In this he is uncompromising, and this is how he tries to live" (*Dambudzo Marechera 1952-1987*, p34-36). This is an uncompromising approach certainly, but Marechera was not without humor, stating in *The Black Insider* "Writing has made me the worst kind of hypocrite – an honest one," and referring disparagingly to the African exiles as "those dogs in London" (p. 79) and their talk of "cabbages and kings of racist phenomena and the onions and inkwells of the African image in diaspora" (p. 61). As for nationalism, "National culture," he scoffed in *Scrapiron Blues*, (p. 26) " . . . seems to mean a lot of fat women dressed in the Leader's colors and a crowd of half-naked traditional dancers leaping in clouds of dust."

Clearly Marechera can himself be felt to exhibit the two-minds-in-one-body syndrome. He can be seen as exemplifying the identity crisis of the African exiled in Europe, in physical and psychological exile. Kristeva says; "Writing is impossible without some kind of exile." In Kristevan terms one becomes a writer "by becoming a stranger to one's own country, language, sex and identity."[60] Moreover, in addition to physical exile the sense of alienation induced by the excesses of colonization meant that many Africans were, in effect, exiled in their own country.

Certainly his own acute awareness of the two-minds-in-one-body condition is evident in the following passage, which has added relevance in that Marechera questions the ability of the novel to contain something as complex as a national identity. On the emergence of the "black writer" the narrator comments:
Suddenly it seemed all our best minds were

accessible, had experienced the same anguish as ourselves, had felt the same anger and humiliation at the hands of the whites and were writing about it to let every brother know. And then, of course, the African image which we ourselves were constructing in our novels and poems was as limited and as false as in the white novelists and poets descriptions. Perhaps the limitation and falseness are inbuilt within the novel as a genre which has . . . never fully accommodated the multitude and psyche of whole continents." (*The Black Insider* p. 109-10)

Here I suggest Marechera is referring to the Jungian collective unconscious, " . . . a certain psychic disposition shaped by the forces of heredity." He is asking how the novel can hope to accommodate something so intangible as an identity when the roots of that identity go back thousands of years and spread over a whole continent.

2.7 Approaching a Universal Audience

"Literacy is the surgeon's needle"

Despairing of the many and various attempts to create an "African image" Marechera was particularly scathing in his attack on the government of the newly independent Zimbabwe dismissing it as a "machine-like state" with a desire to " . . . give the citizen a prefabricated identity and consciousness made up of the rouge and lipstick of the struggle and the revolution" (*Black Insider*, p142). Not that he had any answers himself as he followed that particular attack with the bemused "Had we lost the African image or had the African image lost us?" (*Black Insider*, p142). Undermining the certainty of his readers with such rhetorical questions is a common Marechera device. Of course it could also mask the writer's own uncertainty as a writer.

The following passage suggests that although writing helped Marechera as an individual he considered that much African writing was actually damaging to the African:

> Literacy is the surgeon's needle with which I bind my wounds. I would do a better job of it if I had an anaesthetic. I suffer from insomnia. And wear Gogol's overcoat at nights and seek out the secret of his genius. Africa needs him desperately, otherwise we will choke in self disgust. I have found in nineteenth-century Russian literature an empathy with the breath and experience of Africa which I have not found in literature . . . We have done such a good advertising and public relations stunt with our African image that all the horrors committed under its lips merely reinforce our admiration for the new clothes we acquired with independence. (*Black Insider*, p.113-114)

No doubt it is the Emperor's new clothes to which Marechera makes reference.

In "The African Writer's Experience of European Literature" Marechera identified two types of writer: "There are those who write while working in the service of the state, or some religion or ideology. There are writers who can only write while they are free to develop their own personality, to be true to themselves" (p. 104). Marechera was of course in the latter category and the journey to become a writer was a painful one "The writer is no longer a person; he has to die in order to become a writer" (p. 103). It was a journey that Marechera did not see inhibited by borders or territories " . . . the direct international experience of every single living entity is for me, the inspiration to write" (*Dambudzo Marechera 1952-1987*, p3).

This sentiment is problematic as it seems to suggest that experience itself can be shared. It cannot of course be shared. Experience is unique in itself. It can be imperfectly explained, but not shared. However this is not to argue that because the only certainty is our own experience that we should always look inward; not only because of the dangers expressed by Kristeva ("Depression is the hidden face of Narcissus, the face that is to bear him away into death, but of which he is unaware while he admires himself in a mirage") [61] but also because, as the poet Sylvia Plath suggested, " . . . personal experience is very important but shouldn't be a kind of shut box and mirror looking narcissistic experience. I believe it should be relevant to the larger things, the bigger things, such as Hiroshima and Dachau and so on." [62] This would seem to me an obvious truth. To relate our experiences to the world at large is a way of understanding them, of placing them in a context in which they can be measured. But, although I can relate them, place them, measure them, my experiences remain stubbornly mine. However much I as a writer or social commentator may want it, I cannot see through your eyes, nor stand in your shoes. This, I suggest, leaves the writer able only to represent himself or herself and notions of speaking "for and on behalf of a people" become, in practice, illusory and impossible to realize.

"Speaking for and on behalf of a people" is a battle cry for the black African writer introduced by the Kenyan writer Ngugi wa Thiong'o. This leads immediately to problems of definition and self identity as Marechera demonstrates in *The Black Insider*: " . . . "I've never met any black writers. Are you angry and polemic or are you grim and nocturnal or are you realistic and quavering or are you indifferent and European. Those are the categories, I think." she said . . . "I write as best I can." I replied, at a loss for words" (p. 68). There is little doubt that the black writer, the respondent, is Marechera himself, the sentiment is certainly his, though I doubt that he was ever at a loss for words.

Dambudzo Marechera was a complex individual, deeply affected by the excesses of the circumstances of his internal and external environments. As a writer his work is often obscure as he muddles his way through a fog of reminiscences, impressions, and imaginings toward a sort of clarity of personal vision and purpose. Until the physical illness of his last years drained his strength it was a quest in which he was indefatigable. Undoubtedly his psychological illness informed his work but is his work diminished by his illness? It may be too much to argue that the work was enhanced by it, but as his traumas were part nature, part nurture, they do offer valuable insights into the sufferings of an individual caught between two cultures, as he moved from Rhodesia to Oxford and London and back to Zimbabwe. The obsessive search for a sense of his own identity and purpose caused him to reject any idea that he could, or should, act as spokesman for anyone but himself, and the fruitless nature of that search led him to reject the notion of writing for a specific nation or race as he saw himself – as a writer – approaching a universal audience.

This endless circling around the nature of existence led to accusations of obscurantism and irrelevance, and it is true that some of the work is not an easy read. But if he is unread on the grounds of obscurity or difficulty, then the blame, such as it is, should be shared between writer and reader. On reading an unpublished novel Philip Larkin wrote to the author "For you . . . the events speak for themselves . . . the reader wants that impure thing, literature – plots, suspense, characters, ups, downs, laughter, tears. . . Your narrative isn't a story, it's a frieze of misery . . . this is the most difficult thing to make a book of." [63] Difficult, but not impossible, he might have added. More often than not the reader does want the finished article, polished and in readily recognizable form. But the occasional excursion into the difficult and less familiar world of Dambudzo Marechera may extend the reader and ultimately provide an experience against which to measure other experiences.

In his rejection of nationalism for universalism; his determined espousal of individualism rather than the role of communal spokesman; and his determination to continue writing although often in a debilitated state, physically and mentally, Dambudzo Marechera traveled a lonely road. It was a combination of these qualities that led to his unique contribution to African literature: perhaps reflecting Robert Frost's sentiments on the nature of choice in "The Road Not Taken," "I took the one less traveled by, / And that has made all the difference." [64]

CHAPTER THREE

The House of Hunger: Marechera and the "postcolonial situation"

3.1 "Havoc in the College" [65]

Dambudzo Marechera arrived in England on October 3, 1974 to read English literature at New College, Oxford. Starting his life in England as he was to continue it, he took a taxi from Heathrow Airport to Oxford, which was paid for by the college as he had arrived with no money, no possessions, and only the clothes he was wearing. Oxford was unlike anything he had ever experienced and, on one level at least, he responded with traditional romantic enthusiasm to its characteristic ambience:

> A few rusty spears of sunlight had pierced through the overhead drizzling clouds. Behind the gloom of rain and mist, I could see a wizened but fearfully blood-shot sun. And everywhere, the sweet clangor of bells pushed in clear tones what secret rites had evolved with this city. Narrow cobbled streets, ancient warren of diverse architecture all backed up into itself, with here there and everywhere the massive masonry of college after college. ("Oxford, Black Oxford," *The Black Insider*, p. 158)

A less romantic view comes from the Alle Lansu interview. Lansu had asked whether he felt at home in Oxford:

> I knew the United Kingdom only through its authors, its poets, its playwrights. I was now actually on the soil where all these writers I'd been studying for years and years had lived and died, and the reality was so disappointing. Oxford has got one of the highest unemployment figures in England. And Oxford is also segregated, though I thought I had left segregation behind. On the one side there are the students, the aristocracy of Oxford. On the other side, there is a whole army of thousands and thousands of ordinary workers who live and work there. I mean, Jesus Christ, for the first time at Oxford I had a white servant. She had to come every day to my house, sweep up everything, clean my empty beer bottles, clean up everything. Thousands are unemployed and live on social security. . . . Their residential areas are totally cut off from the university, and so you have the same kind of segregation as at Rusape. And if you tried to cross the boundaries, if you as a student tried to drink in pubs where the workers drink, you

would get beaten up. I got beaten up myself when
I got tired of the student pubs and wanted to drink
in pubs where there were some other black
people. (*SB*, pp. 23-24)

Recorded eight years after the event and bearing in mind
Marechera's capacity to distort past experiences the above
comments nevertheless retain a powerful sense of alienation.
Despite the efforts of many, he never settled at Oxford and left
in March 1976. In a subsequent rationalization of this episode he
expressed a passionate (though probably unreasonable) distaste
for his time at New College: "I discovered they were trying to
make me into an intellectual Uncle Tom. I was being mentally
raped" (*SB*, p. 152).

Sir William Hayter, warden of New College, had the
unenviable task of dealing with Marechera on a daily basis. In
February 1976 he began an exchange of letters with Len Rix, a
lecturer in the English Department at the University of Rhodesia
and one of Marechera's referees, exploring the possibility of
Marechera returning to Rhodesia. On being asked for details of
Marechera's "bad behavior; Hayter replied:

He has found adjustment here very difficult. He
consistently overspends his allowance and is
always borrowing money from everyone; he is
being sued by a local bookseller for non-payment
of a very large debt. He has been drinking much
too much and has been arrested by the police for
being drunk and disorderly. He is offensively
rude to, and on occasion physically assaulted,
other students and members of the domestic staff.
He has threatened to kill various people and to set
fire to the College (he did start one fire, which
luckily did no damage). His behavior to an
American School here last year was so
unbearable that their supervisor threatened to
cancel the course unless he left the College. (*SB*,
p. 175)

To claim that Marechera was merely a poor student is obviously an understatement. In a letter to me (July 5, 1997), Professor Ann Barton, one of his tutors at New College, remembers a colleague's view towards the end of Marechera's time at New College that "...he [Marechera] had probably cost the college more in trouble and expense than any undergraduate in its 600 year history." Using similar language to Hayter, Professor Barton mentions Marechera's behavior and refers to tutorial difficulties "...not only because he simply wasn't interested in doing the English course, but because he was likely to convert complaints about his failure to do much academic work into accusations of racial prejudice on the part of those teaching him." Suggesting that Marechera was unable to accept the consequences of his own actions she adds "These were wholly unfounded but Charles obviously needed to fall back on them." Robert Fraser, who first met Marechera at the Africa Center, which he (Fraser) described as "the best club in London," confirmed (June 1997) that "he [Marechera] was more interested in his artistic development then getting an English degree." Alastair Niven, who was director of the Africa Center to which Marechera was a regular visitor at this time, adds to that view with his recollection (July 1997) that "Dambudzo enjoyed intellectual debate almost in a dilettante way. He would take an opposite view just for the sake of a debate."

Typically, Professor Barton's memories of Marechera are tinged with frustration and sadness. On being asked for her view on the "unfulfilled promise" or "wayward genius" dilemma, she replied, "Promise unfulfilled sounds more like the truth to me than wayward genius. Whichever way you look at it, though, it is a very sad story. One wishes it had ended differently." In similar vein, Sir William Hayter, in spite of the terrible problems he was caused by Marechera, was able to say to Rix, "Oddly enough, I rather like him; there is something there, and he is certainly intelligent" (*SB*, p. 175). Sir William died in 1995, and his widow, Lady Iris Hayter, who was too ill to be interviewed, wrote to me (June 1997); "I am glad to have known DM and wish his life had been easier" and this despite the fact that she had herself suffered grave difficulties with him, as her diaries indicate (*SB*, p. 162-4).

Professor Norman Vance, now of Sussex University was also a tutor in Marechera's first year. When interviewed in July 1997 he recounted the story of going to Marechera's room: "I could hardly breathe because it was incredibly steamy. What had happened was that he had washed all his clothes in the washbasin in the room and hung them up on a piece of string across the room and then turned on the electric fire and closed the windows." Professor Vance recalled he had told Marechera about washing machines and tumble driers in the college but on reflection felt that Marechera probably didn't know how to operate them and was too proud to ask. He continued, "I actually knew nothing about Charles Marechera other than he was on a JCR scholarship. I didn't even know whether he was from a rural area or an urban area." He shared the view of others that Marechera was unable to cope with the formal demands of studying English at Oxford. Vance suggested that Marechera might have found the interwar years Oxford more to his liking:

> Charles had a completely non-academic frame of mind. He just wanted to read as widely as possible, and, magpie-like, pick up whatever appealed to him. The Oxford of the Twenties and Thirties with its acceptance of "being what you wanted to be" and a much less disciplined set of expectations may well have suited him better than the exam driven environment he found himself in.

Vance saw little of Marechera once his stint as his tutor had finished. After his first term Marechera attended very few seminars and became nocturnal (*SB*, p. 153), sleeping during the day and only appearing at night, to the great aggravation of those who were trying to sleep. Vance remained interested in his erstwhile student but did not initiate contact, as he explained, "Charles had a harsh and cruel tongue and I saw no reason to expose myself to it."

In the next part of this chapter I will examine the work produced immediately following his departure from New College, the award-winning collection, *The House of Hunger* followed by a discussion on Marechera's status as a postcolonial writer.

3.2 *The House of Hunger*:

"I got my things and left."

The House of Hunger was probably written in Oxford in mid to late 1976 following Marechera's abrupt departure from New College. His relatively recent involvement with the academic world possibly accounts for the more substantial plot and character development than that evident in later works where, as Wyllie also observed in his comments on *The Black Heretic*, he presents himself as a spiritual and intellectual wreck. The collection of stories also benefited from the writer's ability to draw on the still fresh experiences of his life in Rhodesia, providing a grounding of gritty urban realism and, at times, an assured narrative voice. The element of autobiography is immediately apparent in the opening sentences: "I got my things and left. The sun was coming up. I couldn't think where to go" (p. 1). In view of his subsequent life history the prescience of these opening sentences, in which the writer offers three things – a departure, a new beginning, and uncertainty – is particularly telling.

Although set in a Rhodesian township and in part dealing with the events leading up to and beyond his expulsion from the University of Rhodesia it also reflects the dilemma Marechera experienced on leaving New College and finding himself, possibly for the first time in his life, with nowhere to go. All of his life had been directed towards obtaining access to formal education and now that this goal was no longer valid other goals had to be established. As part of that process Marechera engaged in an examination of his current situation and how it arose: " . . . I was reviewing all the details of the foul turd which my life had been and was even at that moment" (p. 1). The subsequent examination of the influences on his psyche is much more extensive in *Black Sunlight* and *The Black Insider* where he searches for the primordial I. But it begins as a cry for the integrity, the sanctity almost, of the individual in *The House of Hunger*, where "One's mind became the grimy rooms, the dusty cobwebs in which the minute skeletons of one's childhood were forever in the spidery grip that stretched out to include not only the very stones upon which one walked but also the stars which glittered vaguely upon the stench of our lives" (pp. 3-4). The pathetically grotesque image of the "minute skeletons" is poignant recollection of the lost innocence and unfulfilled hopes of childhood, which are recurring themes in Marechera's work.

Evidence of Marechera's paranoia is offered in the first paragraph, "I couldn't have stayed on in that House of Hunger where every morsel of sanity was snatched from you the way some kinds of birds snatch food from the very mouths of babes. And the eyes of the House of Hunger lingered upon you as though some indefinable beast was about to pounce on you" (p. 1). There is an argument that the House of Hunger of the title signifies Rhodesia and that may well be the manifest meaning, but the latent signification is Marechera's psyche. This becomes clear as the story unfolds and the writer – almost as if he is working it out for himself as he progresses – comes to realize that the only way to be free of a colonized mind is to go back to a time before those influences held sway. Erich Fromm argues that by becoming "self aware" an individual "can gain insight into the fictitious character of his conscious ideas; if he can grasp the reality behind these ideas, if he can make the unconscious conscious, he will attain the strength to rid himself of his irrationalities and *to transform himself*" [66] (my emphasis). This is not in the way of reinventing or developing a tradition as Chinweizu advocates (see later in this chapter), but is rather a freeing of the mind to become the "one true self" in a Rogerian sense.[67] The search for the reality of self is often a painful and troubling one. It is also an ultimately impossible quest to complete, as the journey itself is the destination. R. D. Laing argued that being born into an alien world hinders the Rogerian search for the reality of self:

> We are bemused and crazed creatures . . . born into a world where alienation awaits us. We are potentially men, but are in an alienated state, and this state is not simply a natural system. Alienation as our present destiny is achieved only by outrageous violence perpetrated by human beings on human beings. [68]

Marechera confronts that outrageous violence. His conflation of psychological and physical starvation is an attack on the excesses of white minority rule in the allegorical reference to the "theft" of the land by the colonizers and the subsequent disenfranchisement of the people which led to "political tyranny and psychological emasculation."[69] The allusion to the theft of sanity can also be seen as a reference to the ultimatum he received from New College when he was asked either to accept psychiatric treatment or to leave. However, it could also be a thinly disguised reference to the actions of his mother, whose "transference" of her madness to Dambudzo was itself an assault on, or theft of, his sanity.

In *On Becoming a Person* [70] Carl Rogers refers to Soren Kierkegaard as suggesting that the most common despair is to be in despair at not choosing or willing to be oneself. Ignoring the implications of Laing's "outrageous violence" he goes on to argue that "To will to be that self which one truly is, is indeed the opposite of despair." As far as Dambudzo Marechera was concerned that statement simply isn't true. He had that will, but it did not bring him happiness, nor did it stave off despair. Quite possibly, on his return to Zimbabwe, if circumstances had been different he could have achieved self-fulfillment, and through that, happiness. But, unable to become established in the new country, this did not happen.

As is common throughout Marechera's work the passage from *The House of Hunger* is ambiguous and lends itself to alternative interpretations. In typically extravagant form he claimed, "I spread my fingers outstretched and played a tune without listening to the sound I was playing. It has always been like that" (*SB*, p. 205). Although it would be unwise to accept Marechera's contention without reservation, an inspection of his typed manuscripts reveals a compulsive writer whose typing occasionally runs off the edge of the page and who could not stop writing long enough to order his work into paragraphs. In her report to Heinemann (September 8, 1978), Senda Wa Kwayera commented on *A Bowl For Shadows,* "The first striking thing about this novel is that it is written in one paragraph of seventy one pages!" On the other hand, Marechera's implication that his writing was free flowing and spontaneous is, perhaps, more nearly a justification of his indiscipline and reluctance to revise.

It was at the suggestion of James Currey that the title of the longest story in the collection, which was to give the title to the volume, was changed from Marechera's original "At the Head of the Stream" to "The House of Hunger." In a memo of April 28, 1977 introducing Marechera's work to Akin Thomas of Heinemann Africa, Currey writes, "I detect a searing talent here. This is some of the most powerful slum writing and reminiscences I have ever seen. It still needs more work and a far more powerful title. (I suggested The House of Hunger to him.)" The title was changed and with the change a subtle but important shift of emphasis was introduced. "At the Head of the Stream,," Marechera's original title, makes reference to a source, a place of beginnings. The primary level of the work concerns the day to day life of a particular individual living in a township, but the secondary level suggests that the path to recovery from the excesses of white minority rule is to go back to the beginning. The title "At the Head of the Stream" reflects the secondary level and matches more closely the tone of Marechera's musings on his origins and subsequent direction. It is also a more accurate representation both of Marechera's individualism and the themes and issues of the later work.

On the other hand, the title "The House of Hunger" implies that the work has a broader ambition. Given his background and circumstances it is inevitable that Marechera's writing has political undertones. In choosing "The House of Hunger" as a title for the book Currey foregrounded the political content and effectively placed the writer into the position of speaking on behalf of those who have been oppressed – a position Marechera did not seek, and one with which he was not comfortable. However, when the House of Hunger is seen as a representation of the psyche then the sheer individualism of the work emerges.

Currey's agenda was of course to encourage Marechera to write "the Zimbabwean novel" and he expended a great deal of time and energy on that ultimately frustrated quest. Unfortunately, Currey's well-intentioned efforts in promoting *The House of Hunger* and the subsequent publicity, which concentrated on historical and political angles, may well have led to an undervaluing of some of the unique features of *The House of Hunger*, which concern the development of the individual. Such publicity also conditioned others to anticipate Marechera's eventual emergence as the Zimbabwean Achebe or Soyinka. In the event the writer's later works were deemed failures because, in part at least, they did not fulfill these over-optimistic forecasts, which mistakenly lauded Marechera as a political commentator.

Indirectly, such promotional hyperbole may have caused the subsequent London works to be written in such a manner that Marechera's "message" concerning the alienated individual was made abundantly clear. He rejected attempts to control the direction of his work and followed his own inclinations with increasing determination. The "Zimbabwean novel" did not emerge as, despite the publicity (and advice) he had received, the writer ignored matters of "national interest" in his obsessive pursuit of his own identity. On his return to Harare he briefly engaged with wider issues and adopted a more overtly political stance in his writing, as I discuss in Chapter Five. But it was a position in which he was ill-at-ease, and one he did not accept when based in London. Certainly *The House of Hunger* is a more coherent and cohesive whole than the works that followed it, but if Marechera had been encouraged to develop the search for "self as self" which begins in *The House of Hunger*, rather than to engage with socio-political, historical issues, then his personal history, and perhaps the development of writing in Zimbabwe, might have been different.

One of the first people to read the manuscript "At the Head of the Stream" was Heinemann reader Ester Kantai whose generally unfavorable report commented that "The unifying force of the story is fatalism and bitterness." That is fair comment but the organic unity of the text is a journey through the psyche. How Marechera came by her report is unclear (the Heinemann file indicates that Currey tried to keep reader's critical remarks away from the writer) but that he did is strikingly evident as he uses her exact words in *The Black Insider*:

> But there I was . . . oblivious of the unusual eye watching me, as I tore at my hairs because a critic had, in passing, written this about my short stories: "It is clear that the writer does not have a high opinion of the black man. He is pompous and a bore, trying to fight liberation from western capitals while all the time wishing he was white. But the black man cannot really hide his identity, however hard he tries. By admiring the whiteman so much he is also accepting the whiteman's image of him. . . These stories are damaging to the morale of the world bent on liberation. In their present form they are even more damaging to the young writer. He should be given the chance to represent these stories on a more rational plane. Furthermore, they should be experiences which can be shared by people who want to know what it means to be in Southern Africa today. (pp. 146-7)

Taitz and Levin argue that for Marechera writing was "a way of stitching together the fragments [of his] life. [71] As Marechera himself puts it: "Afterwards they came to take out the stitches from the wound of it. And I was whole again. The stitches were published. The reviewers made obscene noises" (*The House of Hunger*, p. 39). The agony Marechera must have felt at Kantai's offensive and ill-informed remarks, and the isolation he may well have felt at such a misreading, is indicated in *The Black Insider*, when immediately following the above extract his best friend leaves him to return to Africa and his wife asks for a divorce and leaves for America.

With a subtlety he later abandoned in *Black Sunlight* and *The Black Insider*, Marechera plots a journey of death and rebirth in *The House of Hunger*. In the closing section of the story an old man, a storyteller, talks to the central character, the young Marechera:

>A man to whom everything under the sun had really happened was walking home when he met a green dwarf who looked up at him scornfully, sneeringly.
>
>"Why do you walk with a crutch?" the dwarf asked with contempt. The man held out his hands and stamped his legs on the gravel road and said:
>
>"Can't you see I have no crutch? Indeed I have no need of it."
>
>But the dwarf spat on a passing chameleon and said to the man:
>
>"You have the biggest crutch I have ever seen a cripple use."
>
>"What crutch?"
>
>And the dwarf, spitting again at the skulking chameleon, said:
>
>"Why, your mind."
>
>And with that they parted. Now the road is between the water and the earth and many have grown old and died journeying upon it. (p. 82)

Marechera uses images of the sky and the sun obsessively and in this case it is not clear whether "everything under the sun" is good or bad. What does seem clear is the unquestioning acceptance of his experiences by the man who demonstrates that he is not crippled by walking on the "gravel road." At the risk of overliteral allegorization it might be noted that graveled roads were laid at the order of the colonial powers and were not always to the benefit of the indigenous population, often heralding the end of a traditional way of life and a speeding up of the colonizing process, as Joyce Cary demonstrated so effectively in *Mr. Johnson*. Therefore, the actions of the man could be seen to signify that others control his direction in life. The fact that the roads were often built with forced labor would imply a subtle irony in the use of a symbol of colonial exploitation to deny that he has been marginalized. Consequently the dwarf, an ancient magical earth figure, tells him he is crippled in his mind. This could be seen as, on one level, an attack on colonial exploitation, the usurping nature of colonial education and its alienating effects on the minds of black Africans and the resulting psychological damage, of which, claims Marechera, many are unaware. The reference to the chameleon [72] can be seen as a pointed comment on the survival techniques adopted by many of absorbing the cultural requirements of the colonizers in order to merge into the background, hence the contempt for the creature. The road that leads between "the water and the earth" leads to the "head of the stream," hence Marechera's choice of title, is the road to the vagina and the birth canal. In short, the experience of the man to whom "everything under the sun had really happened" is useless, and worse than that, it is dangerous. The only escape is to go back to the birth experience and to start again.

That much is implicit in the following from an "old man" who "simply wandered into the House one day out of the rain," in a monologue which closes the story and emphasizes the need for a spiritual and psychological cleansing:
That's when he said ""I will live at the heart of a

grain of sand."" And he also said ""I will light a
match: when it flares I will jump straight in to the
dark heart of its flame seed."" But as he listened
to himself, to the thirst and to the hunger, he
suddenly said in words of gold: "" I will live at
the head of the stream where all of men's
questions begin."" (p. 80)

The monologue is addressed to the narrator who, in view of
the wealth of autobiographical material, is clearly Marechera
himself. That he did not always take himself seriously is
indicated in the narrator's comment on the old man, "What he
loved best was for me to listen attentively while he told stories
that were oblique, rambling and fragmentary" (p. 79). (Perhaps
there is a rare example of the writer's gentle, self-deprecating
humor here.) As Marechera chooses to close his story with the
"old man" the character does assume some significance. He may
well represent the ancestors and their ancient wisdom or be the
father Marechera would have preferred, learned, wise and
philosophical. And then again he may just be a vehicle for
Marechera's ideas.

As was demonstrated in Chapter One some of the readers
and critics of *The House of Hunger* would consider the criticism,
"oblique, rambling and fragmentary," to be an appropriate one.
The initial structure locates the narrator in a bar in conversation
with two others. Occasionally, and without warning, the
narrative shifts in time and place and autobiographical material is
introduced. Just as suddenly the narrative shifts again, back to
the bar. Although disorientating this is an effective device
demonstrating the unreliable and fragmentary nature of township
life, as is the loss of the locating device in the later stages as the
story becomes increasingly fragmented.

That such fragmentation reflects the condition Marechera
experienced for himself is indicated throughout the text. In this
instance he is talking, through the narrator, to Edmund, a school
friend who "lived out his tortured dreams in humiliation" and

was "the only one in the class who knew that Yevtushenko really existed. Dostoevsky, Chekhov, Turgenev, Pushkin, Gorky – he read them all" (p. 61). This is a thinly disguised portrait of the young Marechera of course: "He [Edmund] had actually written dozens of novels (all unfinished) and short stories (all unfinished) whose plots alternated between the painstaking exploration of the effects of poverty and destitution on the psyche" (p. 61). This can also be seen as an apposite summary of the driving force behind Marechera's compulsion to write.

In the London works, *Black Sunlight* and *The Black Insider*, the use of other characters to represent the multiple selves of the writer is much more apparent. However, Edmund, who is not only a writer but becomes a guerilla, is the Marechera who stayed to fight, as is Nick in *Black Sunlight* and Owen in *The Black Insider*. In an obsessive reworking of themes and ideas Marechera desperately tries to come to terms with the concept that his life from birth has been little more than a series of intersecting influences over which he had little, if any, control. Thus, what became central to the London works, the exploration of the psyche, and the psyche represented as a series of rooms or tunnels, is also central to *The House of Hunger*, but is less compulsively worked through.

The "rooms" motif is introduced in *The House of Hunger* with typical Marecheran uncertainty "I did not quite know what happened next. Something seemed to split my mind open . . . And the mind slowly became the room. And the room – floor, roof, walls – was boxed in by other rooms. . . And they were all contained within each other, papering over the cracks" (p. 37). The reference to splitting suggests the formation or emergence of other personalities and recognizes the schizoid tendencies, which had been tentatively diagnosed. The intricacy of the mind is pictured by an infinite series of rooms, each room representative of an influential force and each room is responsible for "papering over the cracks." That is, each one contributed in some way to Marechera's mental colonization, and each one is complicit in the disguising of incipient insanity, itself an inevitable result of the actions of those forces. "My mind felt like nothing. . . . A doorway yawned blankly into me: . . . I could not bring myself to touch the walls to prove that they were really there. . . . For some reason I began to wonder if *I* was really in there: perhaps I was a mere creation of the rooms themselves" (p. 76).

This is the key to *The House of Hunger* – the narrator is a creation of sundry others. As a person unto himself he does not exist. As I explore below, recognition of the influence of "others" is taken further in *Black Sunlight* and *The Black Insider* where Marechera argues that all the "other selves" must die in order that the essential self can be realized. The reaction of the narrator of *The House of Hunger* is not so drastic, the terror is so overwhelming it precludes any action but flight: "I ran from that house like a madman who has seen the inside of his own ravings" (p. 77). The lack of help from others and the acute loneliness of his individual path through life are implicit in the following: ." . . the picture of my skull has since blended into the memory of that empty but strangely terrifying house which – when I called – merely maintained an indistinct silence" (p. 77). Blaming his predicament of double alienation on his mental conditioning he continues, "It was the House of Hunger that first made me discontented with things" (p. 77).

In the circumstances it seems reasonable to place this increased awareness around the time that his illness became more severe. In *The House of Hunger* the narrator recalls a conversation with his sister-in-law: "I . . . told her about my nervous breakdown when I became aware of persons around me whom no one else could see. . . . This had happened a few weeks before my sixth form examinations – which I then had to write with a massive dose of white tranquilizers" (p. 28). Leaving aside the obvious connotations of "white tranquilizers" the autobiographical content is confirmed by Michael Marechera's letter (see above and appendix, p. 257), "In 1971 he [Dambudzo Marechera] began to suffer delusions. He was sure two men were following him everywhere. He was then writing his 'A' levels and I don't know how he managed because he was taking so many tranquilizers."

Michael Marechera then gives details of the "passing on" of the family mental problems to Dambudzo from his Mother – which he dates around 1969: "I felt he must have known what Mother had done." This suspicion seems to be confirmed as the passage from *The House of Hunger* continues, "Meanwhile the voices continued to torment me: . . . I never told the psychiatrist the whole truth about what they were *saying*; but I did send off a series of hysterical missives to Peter [the narrator's elder brother] demanding "the truth of the matter." . . . What the voices said was something quite obscene about my mother's morals." The remark about his mother's morals is, perhaps, a distraction, a denial to himself of "the truth of the matter" – that she had given him a form of madness. He gives graphic descriptions of her as an adulteress (p. 48), as a whore (p. 77), and as a foul-mouthed harridan. She chastises him for soiling his bedsheets by masturbating and exhorts him to get a girl, demanding:

> "Why don't you get on with laying one or two?" or three. Or four. Or five. . . . "You stick it in the hole between the water and the earth, it's easy. She splays out her legs and you bunch your pelvis between her thighs and Strike! right there between her water and her earth. You strike like a fire and she'll take you and your balls all in. Right? Up to your neck. When you come you'll see it misting her eyes." (p. 78)

This is probably the passage David Caute was referring to when, in comments on *The House of Hunger*, he claimed that Marechera " . . . stuffed painful obscenities in the mouth of his loyal mother." [73] Whether Marechera's mother was "loyal" is a matter of some debate but it is true that he did portray her as a drunken, adulterous whore.

Initially, Mrs. Marechera is portrayed sympathetically, "Her face long and haggard, scarred by the many sacrifices she had taken on our behalf" (p. 8). The sympathy with her suffering on her children's behalf is, however, "spoiled" since the sacrifice is depicted as worse than useless. "I sent you to University," she says pathetically to the protagonist:

> There must be big jobs waiting for you out there.
> "Tell that to Ian Smith," Peter butted in maliciously. "All you did was starve yourself to send this shit [the narrator] to school while Smith made sure that the kind of education he got was exactly what has made him like this" (p. 9).

His education alienated him from his people and equipped him for the "white" world from which his color barred him entry. Ultimately his parents are to blame, as Larkin said, "They fuck you up, your Mum and Dad." [74] Two Marechera themes are reflected here: the effects of education and perhaps less obviously but more radically, the passing on of inhibitions, complexes, and attitudes from one generation to another. Again as Larkin said of "Mum and Dad," "But *they* were fucked up in their turn/ By fools in old-style hats and coats" (my emphasis).

There is a subtext in *The House of Hunger* in which the writer constantly circles the subject of his mental instability, blaming it on everything around him. For example, his education: "My parents starved themselves to give me an education and make me what I am now . . . Usually that means they have decided to sell you mind and soul to the bloody whites" (p. 112); or the actions of Ian Smith's Government: " . . . Smith made sure that the kind of education he got was exactly what has made him like this" (p. 9). There were also the far-reaching effects of colonialism: "An iron net had been thrown over the skies, quietly. Now it, tightening, bit sharply into the tenderer meat of our brains. . . we were whores: eaten to the core by the syphilis of the white man's coming" (p. 75); and the influence of his environment: ." . . cast out of village, town and country. Cast out of womb, home and family. A veritable desert" (p. 79).

But beneath this political version lies a more simply human

complexity. However superstitious and insubstantial he may have regarded the ancient curse imposed on him by his mother, its existence could not but embitter his relations with her. Certainly, Michael Marechera is at pains to stress the magnitude of the situation: "It is difficult to explain such matters to those who do not know our culture. But I feel this story explains why Dambudzo always said he had no family and why he saw himself as an outcast." The violent emotions raised in him by the contradictions and competing expectations caused by, among other things, the meeting of ancient beliefs and traditions and his European education at Mission School and the University of Rhodesia, followed by the cloistered calm of New College, Oxford, were obviously enough to disturb the balance of his fragile mental health. *The House of Hunger* was his first and most nearly successful attempt to reconcile those internalized contradictions.

3.3 The Other Stories:

"Like the eye in the painting"

I have thus far concentrated my comments on the eponymous story from *The House of Hunger*. The other nine stories were either submitted by Marechera with *At the Head of the Stream* ("Burning in the Rain," "The Transformation of Harry" and "Black Skin What Mask") or were written to fill out the proposed book at the specific request of James Currey ("The Writer's Grain," "The Slow Sound of his Feet," "The Christmas Reunion," "Thought-tracks in the Snow," "Are There People Living There?" and "Characters from the Bergfrith"). Ester Kantai, Heinemann reader, in her undated report, offered this view: "Marechera's short stories are confusing in many points because he crams very many events or incidents into a short space. As one event is getting interesting one is transferred to something totally different. In fact this style is comparable to the modern art of circles and shades etc., with a weird eye looking out of each circle. The unifying force of the story, like the eye in the painting, is fatalism and bitterness." She continues, "What one does not find anywhere is the cause of the fatalism and bitterness." Kantai, it seems, was looking for something less obvious than " . . . the tragic circumstances of being black in a too white world."[75]

"Burning in the Rain" confronts the problems of identity ("The mirror said it all and in it he knew his kinsman; the ape, lumbering awkwardly into his intimacy" (p. 85)) and of colonization (" . . . he woke up to find that he had painted himself with whitewash and was wearing a European wig. It took him hours to get rid of the paint and for days afterwards he reeked of nothing else" (p. 86)). "The Transformation of Harry" brings up issues of personal loyalty ("I see you're still using your friends to make up improbable stories" [p. 91]) and national identity ("and there we were; in an uncertain country, ourselves uncertain" [p. 92]), and "Black Skin What Mask," the title a casual pun on Fanon's popular work, takes as its central point Marechera's expulsion from Oxford. Typically the narrator (Marechera) is telling the story to a black friend who "was always washing himself. . . He did not so much wash as scrub himself until he bled. He tried to purge his tongue too, by improving his English and getting rid of any accent from the speaking of it" (p. 93). Marechera himself had an incredible accent that had no trace of Africa and appeared to be pitched somewhere between Oxbridge and the World Service of the BBC. Robert Fraser described Marechera as having a " . . . very marked Oxford accent, far more exaggerated than most English Oxonians would have. It had a very marked roll to it and he used to speak in what we would call a very lah-di-dah way, rather like an Edwardian Oxonian than a late 20th century Oxonian."

This could be attributed to simple affectation, or be seen as part of an elaborate game with the nature of meaning. It is interesting that in Chris Austin's film *House of Hunger,* shot for Channel 4, Marechera appears in the London scenes wearing a kurta, which he has changed for a sober three-piece suit when filming in Harare, being African in Europe and European in

Africa. However as "The Writer's Grain," one of the stories written at Currey's request, indicates, a profound obsession with his own identity was beginning to emerge and his writing became more clearly autobiographical and revealing of his paranoid tendencies: "At college they had all been hell bent on making life intolerable for me but I had somehow kept my end up and of course when I became worth knowing they occasionally invited me out for a glass of grape poison" (p. 104). The story also explores the theme of the alternative self or doppelgänger (later pursued in *Black Sunlight* and *The Black Insider*), as "elemental twin" (p. 102), "my phantom double" or as a "twin brother" who takes over his life until the confusion of identity is total and the double alienation made obvious in the following Laingian questioning, "Am I him or is he me or am I myself and is he himself? (p. 112).

Themes of false identity also arise in "The Slow Sound of his Feet" linked to the suggestion of possession by others, "the feeling of the silent but desperate voices inside me" (p. 136). He also links the death of his father with his stuttering, which in turn becomes a dumbness symbolic of the inability to direct his own affairs. Perhaps the most unusual story, because of its apparently stereotypical approach to the "problems" of colonization, is "A Christmas Reunion." A straightforward story of how African traditions were replaced by the actions of the colonial powers and the missionary societies, it is also an allegory of the battle between the white minority government and the black "terrorists" and a superficial justification, made on intellectual grounds, for Marechera not joining the struggle.

The shorter stories in *The House of Hunger* are notable for the identification of the theme of "other selves" that achieved prominence in later works and for containing what could well be Marechera's philosophy of life. In "The Writer's Grain" shortly after "Mr. Warthog," a black warthog, has eaten a "fine old violin" followed by a "gigantic cello" he lectures "the boy" (arguably Marechera):

> . . . to insist upon your right to go off at a tangent.

> Your right to put a spanner into the works. Your
> right to refuse to be labeled and to insist on your
> right to behave like anything other than anyone
> expects. Your right to simply say no for the
> pleasure of it. To insist on your right to confound
> all who insist on regimenting human impulses
> according to theories psychological, religious,
> historical, philosophical, political, etc. . . . Insist
> upon your right to insist on the importance, the very
> great importance, of whim. There is no greater
> pleasure than throwing or not throwing the spanner
> into the works simply on the basis of one's whims.
> (p. 122)

This implacable insistence on the rights of the individual
and the autonomy of the creative sensibility echoes the words of
artists through the ages in conflict with prevailing ideology,
political censorship, or any authority except their own
perceptions. James Joyce's situation as an Irish writer in exile
offers an obvious parallel: "When the soul of a man is born in
this country there are nets flung at it to hold it back from flight.
You talk to me of nationality, language, religion. I shall try to fly
by those nets." [76] It was an approach that placed Marechera
beyond the pale of the various societies he encountered, resulting
in his isolation and compounding his alienation, as both *The
Black Insider* and *Black Sunlight* were able to demonstrate so
effectively.

3.4 "A postcolonial writer?"

What then of Marechera's status as a "postcolonial" writer?
It was not often that Marechera denied himself the pleasure of
throwing a "spanner in the works" and the omission of the more
traditional features of postcolonial literature seems to have been
deliberate. Thus *The House of Hunger* does not attempt to assert
myths of origin, or explore the themes of collective resistance,
separate national identity and cultural distinctiveness in the way

of Achebe, Ayi Kwei Armah, Ngugi *et al.* Those omissions, coupled with the book's existential nature and obsession with the individual and the "here and now," set it apart from other texts. In addition to this, Marechera's refusal to be labeled a "black writer," his fascination with the individual mind rather than the collective body, and his demand for intellectual freedom from the restrictions of race, class, and nationalism tends to make difficult any comparisons with the school of writers usually categorized as postcolonial.

This approach is particularly important when comparing and contrasting Marechera with other black Zimbabwean writers, as I do in Chapter Six, who tend to be more ideologically purposeful. The various writers react differently to what are current events for some, and history for others; reflecting a changing view of history, certainly, and without any regard for a spurious division at the date of independence. As their writing careers bridged the transition of Rhodesia to Zimbabwe such a division would have been inappropriate in any case. Categorizing Marechera and his work is notoriously difficult, not only because of the unique qualities of the writing, but also because the writer at times appeared to be "against everything." However the rest of this chapter will offer some suggestions of where Marechera's work might be placed among the shifting sands of postcolonial literature and will broach the subject of Marechera's "Africanness" as a writer.

Gerald Gaylard is perhaps understating his case when he suggests ." . . it would seem that an African nationalist reading of Marechera is inadequate." He goes on to say ." . . a postcolonial reading would be more helpful, as he was writing most directly about postcolonial and neo-colonial issues." [77] This claim is, perhaps, more accurate of *The House of Hunger* than the later works. As for *Black Sunlight*, Zimunya argues that it is devoid of any reference to past history:

> . . . you can't run away from your past completely, unless you think of his book *Black Sunlight*. That has nothing to do with the past.

There are no ghouls arising from the ancestral
past, there are no stories or fables at all. It's a
modern state, a human estate which is corrupt,
whether it's African or white – he actually leaves
the setting unidentified, anonymous. [78]

Zimunya's reading however seems to ignore that the factor
of corruption, although a general feature of modern society,
always has a specific basis in historical practices; and also he
appears not to consider the possibilities offered by an allegorical
reading. Of the writer himself Zimunya adds "[Marechera's]
work demands a lot of attention . . . He confuses and bewilders a
lot of readers and I don't think that's a virtue at all." [79] This is a
harsh judgement: Marechera was himself "confused and
bewildered" and his writing reflected that. Zimunya appears to be
taking the stance that the writer should be a "teacher" and that
the "difficult" nature of the text inhibited that role. Undoubtedly
it did, but that is a role Marechera refused in any event. Possibly
Zimunya could have observed that the "confusing" text and the
"confused and bewildered" characters were themselves indicative
of the hybrid nature of the postcolonial condition as experienced
by the individual. And as such are a valuable resource,
instructive and important.

It is perhaps inevitable that Marechera would write, directly
or indirectly, about postcolonial issues – that was after all his
background. But postcolonialism performs the function of a
secondary agenda, which informs the main biographical thrust of
his work; it is not a guiding subtext. Marechera's work also
reflects the hybridized nature of postcolonial culture, not only in
the profusion of references to (mainly) European writers but in
the tacit acceptance of the dialectical process of mutual
transformation which observes that the "transaction of the
postcolonial world is not a one way process in which oppression
obliterates the oppressed or the colonizer silences the colonized
in absolute terms." [80] In short, Marechera's task, as a man and a
writer, was to come to terms with the inevitable and irreversible
hybrid nature of his acculturation. The Marecheran characters,

mostly versions of himself of course, inhabit a world created by a colonial experience to which both parties contributed, however unequally. Chinua Achebe offers an example of this hybridity and refers to the resulting tensions in this memory from his childhood:

> On one arm of the cross we sang hymns and read the bible night and day. On the other my father's brother and his family, blinded by heathenism, offered food to idols. That was how it was supposed to be anyway. But I knew without knowing why it was too simple a way to describe what was going on. Those idols and that food had a strange pull on me in spite of me being such a thorough little Christian . . . [81]

Achebe's adjustment to those opposing forces appears to have been better than Marechera's: "If anyone likes to believe that I was torn by spiritual agonies on the rack of my ambivalence he certainly may suit himself. I do not remember any undue distress." He claims that such exposure was helpful in that it enabled him to see " . . . a canvas steadily and fully." Marechera viewed a similar canvas, not "steadily and fully" but in a distorted and fragmentary way, and yet one with a powerful validity of its own, as, in his words, "At this point the writer ceases to be African or European. He has become the exploding atoms of his searing vision." [82]

On the question of writing style and approach Marechera remarked:

> There are two traditions in African literature: one I will call the traditionalist outlook, whose leader is Chinua Achebe and Ngugi wa Thiong'o also belongs to it; then there is the other, I would call it the modernist group, represented by Wole Soyinka and Ayi Kwei Armah and myself. The three of us are always described as individualists and this word is used in a very insulting way. If people accuse you of individualism, then they are

actually saying you are a reactionary, you are capitalist in your approach to art, you are not a writer of the people. (*SB*, p. 44)

It is significant that this interview took place when, to all intents and purposes, Marechera's writing career was over and the writer appears to be attempting to secure his place in African literature.

There is a certain sadness in this attempt at identification with other African writers which expresses a view contrary to his earlier claim "I think I am the doppelgänger whom, until I appeared, African literature had not yet met. And in this sense, I would question anyone calling me an African writer" (*Dambudzo Marechera 1952-1987*, p. 3). Few critics did call him an African writer, indeed, they had problems in categorizing him at all. As Dan Wylie observed:

> Dambudzo Marechera is the misfit, even the *bête noire*, of African fiction, more scatological than Armah, more "bound to violence" than Ouologuem: a sparkling and disturbing aberration, and a solitary refutation of Claude Wauthier's prediction that African writers were unlikely to "withdraw into some ebony tower, where they can devote themselves to art for art's sake, to the throes of Freudian angst." [83]

Wylie's comments indicate concern about his own inability to "locate" Marechera within the conventions of African fiction. He accommodates that concern by accepting that Marechera had moved the boundaries of the definition of an African writer.

However, whether Marechera earned the distinction of representing the "solitary refutation" of Wauthier's prediction is doubtful. The reference to "Freudian angst" brings to mind Bessie Head, for example, but other African writers (Soyinka and Armah are not the only ones) have taken an approach to writing that owes as much to "art for art's sake" as to any desire to build a new Africa. However, Marechera's work does not offer easy comparison with any other. As a consequence of this, categorization of the writer, or evaluation of, for example, his contribution to postcolonial literature, presents major difficulties. A familiar problem, as Gerald Gaylard observed, is that :

> Marechera did not write according to the political agenda. . . Marechera evades categories with ease and I have had great difficulty in summarizing his viewpoints as "Life is not a plot you know. It does not have one coherent theme but many conflicting ones."[84]

Possibly one category Marechera could not evade – if such as Chinweizu was the one doing the categorizing – is as a writer of "Euro-assimilationist junk."[85] According to Chinweizu, Euro-assimilation "in African literature is the equivalent of the phenomenon in Afro-American music where black artists "cross over" to white audiences by adjusting their musical style, themes and stage manners to suit the prejudices of white audiences, usually to the disapproval of their Afro-American audiences." [86]

Leaving aside the likelihood that musicians, of any creed or color, may well make adjustments to their "art" in the legitimate pursuit of their careers and commercial success, and ignoring the fact that they should, by any standards, have the freedom to change if they want to change, Chinweizu neglects the evolutionary process whereby one thing develops from another. Presumably he would have disapproved of the activities of a small recording company, Sun Records, based in Memphis, Tennessee, in the 1950s, which issued recordings of "black music" by white artists. Plenty of people did disapprove but it was for such racist reasons as "white boys shouldn't sing nigger music," rather than on aesthetic grounds. Those artists, whose records were produced by a white entrepreneur called Sam Philips, included Elvis Presley, Jerry Lee Lewis and Carl Perkins, and they developed a style influenced by Southern blues and gospel music (all black), country music (all white) and rhythm and blues (mainly black). It produced the hybrid that was eventually given the generic of "rock and roll." In a further complication it seems that the elements that made up that particular hybrid were themselves hybridized, as Wilson Harris explained to Alan Riach: ." . . if you go into some so-called black ghetto where you have men beating drums and claiming that they have an independent music, that is not true. They are, *whether they know it or not*, drawing things in from other cultures . . . " [87] (my emphasis).

Just consider for a moment the possibility that some writers can free themselves of "colonial influence" and are able to continue, as though it had never been interrupted, the development of a "purely" African culture, recording it in a "purely" African literature. They are indeed blessed. But surely that does not mean that those who are not so blessed, those who are not able to free themselves of those pernicious influences, should be condemned because their writing shows evidence of those catastrophes? Chinweizu's attack on "Euro-assimilationist junk" assumes that an intellectual choice has been made by the artist to create in a particular style. That may well be so in some cases. But Dambudzo Marechera, I suggest, was not able to make that choice. His writing, and to a similar degree, the man himself, reflected the turbulence of his personal background, history, and upbringing. However much he may have wanted to, he was never able to reconcile that inner turmoil. Marechera's body of work demonstrates quite clearly that he was never able to lay the ghosts that haunted most of his adult life.

Chinweizu's quarrel with writing like Marechera's is that it does not refer to and develop traditional African practices. For Marechera there was nothing coherent there to refer to or to develop. His hybrid nature gives him no coherent and entire body of "African" or black tradition from which to write: "'You hate being black.' she said. My discolored teeth ached. Here we go again, I thought. Can a hollow decayed soul be filled in, the way dentists do it to a mess of teeth?" (*The House of Hunger*, p. 45). Marechera did not hate being black. His acknowledgement that his "blackness" was now "discolored" by the colonial experience did not endear him to the negritudinists or the nationalists. But "discolored" is not necessarily pejorative; it can also be a recognition that irrevocable change has taken place. It is recognition that, for the peace of mind, if not sanity, of the individual, adjustment – *not* acceptance – to the new condition was a fundamental requirement. As for the question about the "hollow decayed soul": the answer is that a decayed soul, whether belonging to an individual or a country, cannot be filled in, cannot be restored. What is lost, is lost forever.

On the simplest level then Marechera can be classified as a postcolonial writer, simply because of his background and subject matter. But this definition is very broad. He did confront issues of "culture conflict" and the "African heritage" but in a narcissistic, undidactic fashion that annoyed some critics. But, although there were many inconsistencies of approach and attitude in his life and work, and much posturing for the sake of maintaining an image, Marechera was never a pseudo-anarchist. He was the real thing. Whether this was out of conviction or perversity, illness even, is a moot point but, as I commented earlier, he did appear to be against almost everything.

Until very late in his life he disowned affinity with race or nation in maintaining his right to his "uniqueness," his individuality. It is precisely that quality that makes his work so very difficult to categorize. His individuality was the desire to be free of all influences and to embrace a universalism that recognized no barriers and acknowledged no preconceived values or standards. Possibly Marechera was aware of the Langston Hughes anecdote about the young negro who wanted to be a poet, not a negro poet, but that apart, Marechera was too widely read and too astute to fall into the trap of "his" universalism being little more than an acceptance of "white orientated aesthetics." [88]

This is not to claim that his escape from such aesthetics was achieved, or even achievable, however much it was desired. The pernicious nature of his education was literally a "death-grip" from which there was no escape, at least for the psychologically fragile Marechera. But contrary to the views of Chinweizu and others, such calamity does not devalue the work. It is authentic in its own right, both as a symbol of the disastrous effects of the colonial legacy on the individual and as a testament to one man's struggle to break free of that legacy.

Europeans speak of a French culture, a Spanish culture, a German culture. Similarly Africa has not one culture but many. In that rich tapestry of cultures the work of the "Euro-assimilationists" forms but a single thread and, as the tapestry grows, the significance of that thread will diminish. But it should not be disowned as it has an integral part in the history of the cultural development of many African countries.

CHAPTER FOUR

The Black Insider and *Black Sunlight*: Neurosis or Art?

4.1 The London Years

On leaving New College in March 1976 Marechera entered a
phase of his life in which he was permanently unemployed and had
no settled home as he lived out the role of the writer-tramp. This
vagrant existence lasted through the London years and continued on
his return to Harare in 1982 until friends provided him with his own
bed-sitter flat, at 8 Sloane Court, in May 1984.

Due to the highly irregular nature of his life it is difficult to be precise about Marechera's movements. However, it is known that he stayed in and around Oxford until October 1977 when he moved to Cardiff, possibly to meet up with a former girlfriend with a view to marriage. Marechera often claimed that he had married while in England but a search of the General Register Office index of marriages (which lists all marriages that have taken place in England and Wales) found no entry for the marriage of a Charles or Dambudzo Marechera. While in Cardiff he was arrested for theft, possession of cannabis, and overstaying his visa. Following the intervention of James Currey and thanks largely to his efforts, Marechera was not deported, although he was jailed for three months. In February 1978, shortly after his release from prison, where, he told Currey, he was repeatedly raped, he moved to London. And there – apart from a short spell in Sheffield between February and April 1979, as writer-in-residence at the University, and a three-week visit to the Berlin International Literature Days (Horizons "79) in June/July, 1979 – he stayed, living in a succession of squats, until he left for Harare in February 1982.

From time to time Robert Fraser met up with Marechera in London, usually at the Africa Center in King Street where, often joined by Ben Okri, they would discuss literature. Combining a comment on the autobiographical nature of Marechera's work and his lifestyle, Fraser suggested, "He [Marechera] couldn't distinguish between literature and life. His life was a story in itself." Occasionally they met accidentally in central London. Fraser describes one such meeting, which was memorable for him, but, one suspects, run of the mill for Marechera:

> It was shortly after he had left Brixton Jail.[89] I was around in central London having just delivered some manuscripts to Heinemann who at that time had their offices in Bedford Square when I saw Dambudzo hurtling towards me, the usual haunted expression on his face. I said "I didn't know you were out of jail" and asked him to join me at a nearby cafe. He talked about being in jail and asked what my plans were. It

was at the time of the strike at the Times and all the supplements had been affected, including the TLS. As a response to this Karl Miller had just set up the *London Review of Books* from offices in Bloomsbury Street. Dambudzo suggested we might try for some reviewing work. I was free-lancing at the time and thought it a good idea.

When we arrived at the offices it was late in the lunch hour, Karl Miller wasn't there but various secretaries and sub-editors were about the place. I thought Dambudzo was about to introduce himself along the lines of "I'm a writer looking for free lance work" and would also introduce me. But as soon as we entered the room Dambudzo was seized with nerves and a kind of self-conscious jittering – he stood looking at his feet, and began mumbling about winning the Guardian Fiction Prize.

This probably seemed very unlikely from the secretaries" point of view because of his behavior and his terribly disreputable appearance. We didn't get as far as asking for reviewing work, as it was quite obvious the secretaries and sub editors thought him a complete nut case. I started then edging toward the door when he suddenly stopped in the middle of this abortive self-explanation and looked at me for a moment before muttering "Let's get out of here."

We ran down the stair well to the landing where his panic turned to anger. He took out a box of matches and struck one while shouting "Burn the place down. Burn the place down." The horrific thought struck me that here I was outside the offices of the London Review of Books with a well known arsonist, apparently about to burn the place down. In the event, he extinguished the match and we ran down the stairs and into the street. He ran in one direction and I ran in another. And that was the last time I saw him. [90]

Fraser offered this story as an example of Marechera in conflict with authority. That may well be so – the incident was certainly typical of Marechera's reaction to having to deal with any sort of "officialdom." However the writer's violent reaction may also be interpreted as frustration at his own personal inadequacies in presenting himself, rather than indicating anarchic or iconoclastic tendencies. Alastair Niven, who, as director of the Africa Center from August 1978 to 1984, had regular contact with Marechera, offers a view of the writer that suggests another possible interpretation of the episode:

> Dambudzo always behaved in a very odd way but there was an element of calculation in it. He knew what he was doing, it wasn't done out of anger. The wildness was either manic, that is he couldn't help himself, or there was a degree of calculation. On balance I think I would vote for calculation. He wanted to create an image, an image of an interesting literary person. Perhaps if he had matured and developed having secured a position for himself [as an established writer] then he may have become a calmer, more reasonable person. But, of course, that never happened . . . he wanted to make a literary mark. Dambudzo Marechera was very young, very innocent and very naïve in some ways. He modeled himself on some European writers who lived a rough, hard life like Dylan Thomas or Brendan Behan. To be the sort of writer he wanted to be he had to live life that way. It was the life he did lead but I suspect there was an intention behind it – perhaps to write a book like *Down and Out in London and Paris*. [91]

Undoubtedly there was an element of image manipulation in Marechera's behavior; equally there is no doubt that the London period was very stressful for him. Veit Wild writes of his stages of serious depression and refers to a story the writer used to tell "…how he wanted to drown himself in the Thames but each time was held back by the dirty water" (*SB*, p. 236). Marechera made reference to this in the unpublished choreodrama *Portrait of a Black Artist in London*: "Ripple softly, dirty Thames, reflect softly our suicide's rain / Clouds of fire loose my millions of blood onto the ebbing tide" (*SB*, p. 268). One memorable night at the Africa Center Marechera read from *Portrait of a Black Artist*. Asked by Niven to read for twenty minutes Marechera, who after a while was accompanied by a saxophonist, went on for more than an hour. Niven recalled (July 1997), "I was usually a strict Chair but I didn't stop him because the audience was enjoying the performance, I was also worried about his reaction if interrupted. Not that one would be personally hurt, but some awful public embarrassment could be caused." A particularly graphic example of such public embarrassment occurred when Marechera disrupted a formal occasion at the Calabash Restaurant at which the British ambassador to Chad was being entertained. Niven recalled "Dambudzo was absolutely at his worst. He stripped of almost all of his clothes and started yelling abuse . . . and upsetting tables."

Wendy Davies, who was education officer at the Africa Center during that time found Marechera to be "charming and infuriating in equal measure," one who was inclined to "prick balloons of pomposity" and a "baiter of authority." She also told me (May 1998) that he could be "generous, warm and responsive" having quite impulsively given her his copy of the *Collected Works of Lewis Carroll*, which she had admired. On checking whether he had written anything in the book she told me "Yes, he has signed it, just above a stamp which states Property of Heinemann Inc."

Portrait of a Black Artist in London was written in 1980 at the Africa Center and his period there, which was during the first two years of his "London exile" (1978–1980), coincided with the most fruitful of his writing career. Since he submitted these particular manuscripts to Heinemann it is certain that it was during this time that he wrote *"The Black Insider," "A Bowl for Shadows," "The Black Heretic,"* and *"Black Sunlight."* The manuscripts of *"A Bowl for Shadows,"* and *"The Black Heretic"* were lost after having been returned to Marechera, and it can only be a matter for speculation how much other work went astray due to his erratic lifestyle.

Davies recalled, "He was often very unhappy and could be outrageously demanding at times but in the middle of a tirade he would suddenly flash a knowing mischievous grin, which was quite disconcerting. Whether it was act or not I do not know. I suspect neither did Dambudzo. My abiding visual memory of him is of a thin, gaunt figure in a big black, wide brimmed hat, hurtling down King Street, bits of paper falling out of various bags and pockets as he strode along."

Alastair Niven met Marechera for the first time in early 1979:

> He was in the bar of the Calabash Restaurant [at the Africa Center], he struck me as a well-dressed young man with a fairly plummy Oxford accent, I had the impression of a rather genteel background. Of course, nothing could have been further from the truth. He seemed a cheery, pleasant and intelligent young man of the sort I wanted to encourage to use the Africa Center. I told him: please make the Africa Center your home, a remark that came to haunt me.

Eventually Marechera's behavior became too much even for the ever-tolerant Niven, and after an episode when he had to be forcibly prevented from sleeping at the Center and then proceeded to cause £700 worth of damage, he was banned. Dr. Niven told me, "The Africa Center gave him a context within which he could operate and I always felt it a terrible defeat that we banned him from it. He was the only person we ever banned and it was in the same week that he was banned from entering the premises of Heinemann, his publishers. I achieved a limited objective in stopping the trouble but I felt it was a defeat. Here was someone who was actually valuable, creative, probably the most able person using the Africa Center, and we were stopping him entering."

This most productive writing period was also the time that his behavior was at its most unpredictable and it is possible that there is a link between the two patterns. Certainly the lack of coherence and continuity in his life at that time is reflected in the fragmentation and discontinuities evident in the structure of his work. In the first part of this chapter I will examine the published London works, *Black Sunlight* and *The Black Insider* and demonstrate how his writing style changed from *The House of Hunger* to become even more autobiographical and "difficult" as his lifestyle increasingly informed both form and content. I will then look very closely at a short story from *The Black Insider*, "Oxford, Black Oxford," a superb example of how well the writer could operate in this demanding discipline. Finally, I will engage briefly with the notion of "neurosis or art" first mentioned in Chapter Two.

4.2 *Black Sunlight* and *The Black Insider*

"Help!"

> He was struggling in every direction, he was the
> center of the writhing and kicking knot of his
> own body. There was no up or down, no light and
> no air. He felt his mouth open of itself and the
> shrieked word burst out. "Help!""
> William Golding, *Pincher Martin* (London: Faber
> & Faber, 1956), p. 7

Marechera's attempts, through his writing, to come to terms with the contradictions generated by his Europeanized education, which began in *The House of Hunger*, continued. But his efforts were hampered by worsening mental health as he tried to follow up the praise engendered by his first published work and to produce the full-length novel sought by James Currey at Heinemann. Marechera wrote *The Black Insider* and "A Bowl for Shadows" in early 1978, closely followed by "The Black Heretic." *Black Sunlight,* the fourth and last version of what started out as *The Black Insider*, was written in mid-1979 and is not a revision but rather a reworking of the same themes and issues after the latter had been rejected by Heinemann for the first time. However, an inspection of the original manuscript reveals that substantial passages had to be edited out of *The Black Insider* before it could be published because they had already appeared in *Black Sunlight*. As it is, many similarities can still be found between the two.

There is no doubt that Marechera struggled to establish a base for himself on leaving the "cloistered calm" of New College. Implying that his time at Oxford had been somehow detached from "real life," he comments in *The Black Insider*, "I was just about to start a journey of discovery in the real United Kingdom" (p. 43). It was to be a struggle in vain and a journey that led him back to Zimbabwe. His lifestyle became increasingly dissolute as he continued to take drugs and drink excessively. This in turn exacerbated his health problems and fed into his writing, as the difficulty he had in creating a coherent narrative leading to appropriate conclusions, which is apparent in *The House of Hunger*, deepened. Subsequent publication of *Black Sunlight* and *The Black Insider* allowed comparisons to be made with the earlier *The House of Hunger* and assumptions formed about the manner in which Marechera's illness had shown itself in his work. The pattern of increasing incoherence and fragmentation, which such comparison reveals, fits remarkably well into the general argument on the effects of schizophrenia on the writer put forward by Geoffrey Grigson in his work on the poet John Clare (*The Poems of John Clare's Madness* [London: Routledge & Keegan Paul, 1949]), who spent the majority of his adult life in an asylum:

> The madness itself, the confirmed psychosis, though it may be difficult enough to say where it begins, does not so much release as destroy. But the preliminaries, the preliminary anxieties and experiences and illuminations, may provide a schizophrenic with a richness of material. To start with, his less impaired normality may incline him to scale down or censor that richness. As his disease extends, the censorship lessens and the poems, or whatever it may be, blossom out like flowers in the night; the experiences no longer cohere, and his sense of form loosens towards the incoherent and the

fragmentary. (pp. 23-24)

The relative coherency of *The House of Hunger* disintegrates in *Black Sunlight* and *The Black Insider* as his deteriorating mental health allowed him to experience the world only in disconnected insights and this fragmented experience is reproduced in narratives lacking direction, cohesion, and continuity. The following example from *Black Sunlight* is a typical diversion. Appropriately enough, it deals with the difficulty of saying what one means (or meaning what one says):

> Keep your shirt on, my dear chap. What does one ever mean? ...It is not what I know that intrigues me now but what I can never know. Imagine it, there are things which our mind and imagination can never think or imagine. And if we are mere puppets to these things then ...Do you see? I don't see. But perhaps you do. I have adjectives to define you. You have nouns to define me. If we do away with the adjectives and the nouns can you imagine the transformation that would take place within you, within me ...? But of course we cling to the adjectives and we stoutly hold on to the nouns. They weave descriptions which are neither lethal nor fatal. Fascinations, complexities that, when inspected under a fine microscope, neither fascinate nor are they complex. You live on the periphery of a centrifugal life – is there not an impossibility there? You live on the outer reaches of a centripetal life – there is also a contradiction there? The head that outpaces its body's marathon, or the body that outruns its head's hundred yards of sprinting, this does not make for clear thinking, clean feelings. Anyway what is clear thinking after all? (*Black Sunlight*, p. 63)

The perceptive reader will discern the subtleties of Marechera's points on language and the management of meaning but, couched in terms of rhetorical terms, his points are not clearly made. However, that observation perhaps only serves to underline the (intentional?) irony of the question "what is clear thinking?" *Black Sunlight* in particular has many such diversions that, although often provocative and interesting in themselves, have the effect of disrupting the progression of the story-line and of breaking the narrative flow.

What little influence remained from the academic conditioning of his university experiences soon disappeared in the indiscipline and impatience that characterized the productive years of 1978 and 1979 as Marechera strove, through his writing, for a clear sense of identity and purpose. As he demonstrates in *Black Sunlight* and *The Black Insider*, he has a sure grasp of the hybrid nature of his identity and his search was not so much for a sense of who he was, but who he might have been, had he not been subjected to the pernicious influences of colonialism. To the outsider his purpose was uncertain and in any event, one suspects, was dominated by factors over which he had no control, the outcome of the liberation war, for example, or the critical reception of his work.

The following extract shows his indiscipline, as the writer is diverted from the main story line to explore a familiar Marecheran theme of the limitations imposed by the structure of meaning attached to language. Also in familiar Marecheran fashion the reader is offered a string of metaphors in an inconclusive series of loosely connected assertions rather than a coherent and cohesive argument.

> The languages of Europe . . . are descended from one parent language which was spoken about 2500 to 200 BC. This Indo-European group of languages – in their modern form – has been carried by colonization to the far corners of the earth. Thus the Indo-European river has quite neatly overflowed its banks and like the flood in the bible has flooded Africa, Asia, America and all the islands. In this case there does not seem to have been any Noah about who built an ark to save even just two words of all the languages and speech, which were drowned.

Literacy today is just the beginning of the story. Words are the waters which power the hydro-electricity of nations. Words are chemicals that H2O human intercourse. Words are the rain of votes which made the harvest possible. Words are the thunderstorm when a nation is divided. Words are the water in a shattering glass when friends break into argument. Words are the acronym of a nuclear test-site. Every single minute the world is deluged by boulders of words crushing down upon us over the cliff of the TV, the telephone, the telex, the post, the satellite, the radio, the advertisement, the bill-poster, the traffic sign, graffiti, etc.. Everywhere you go, some shit word will collide with you on the wrong side of the road. (*The Black Insider* pp. 48-49)

He continues in this vein for several pages, then introduces a "play" that runs for thirteen pages before returning to the central issue of the refuge in the Arts Faculty. This "diversion" (which runs from p. 44 to p. 62) begins reasonably enough as an examination of the narrator's reaction to the war. "The faculty is the last desperate ditch of a state of my mind bred in the tension of war. Black clouds of smoke graze their minutes in the black of the sky, which is still cindered by the shock and concussion of the comet that blasted us in that old twentieth century. The dog-eared history books say so." (p. 44). This elegantly phrased allusion to the traumas of colonization is followed by the ultimately ironic, "A half-digested idea is transformed into an overwhelming description of the world." This is ironic since Marechera then takes a "half-digested idea" (more accurately several such "ideas" on "language," "words" and "attitude") and runs with it for several pages, effectively taking the reader away from the "story" and into a *cul-de-sac* from which Marechera eventually leads the reader using a version of the "Clarence burst his bonds" technique. [92]

The writer's constant striving for a sense of identity and purpose is seen also in the following remarkable passage in which the apparent attack on his mother – although in typically ambiguous form the "fucking bitch" is more probably an allusion to Africa complying in its own rape by the white settlers – and with its air of violent anger, desperation, and self-loathing and its rich mixture of obscenity, blasphemy, humor and poignancy, is a prime example of Marechera's writing. The extract also indicates that he could handle diversions without losing continuity or direction.

> As I swung gently by my heels in the thick fat fucking breeze of sheer humidity, I had a clear view of the court and could see and hear all that went on there. So this is humankind. Swinging. Backwards and forwards. Swinging through history. These are my people. I am their people too. Crucified upside down by my heels. My Golgotha a chicken yard. Father! Father! Why the fucking shit did you conceive me? You have no meaning. I have no meaning. The meaning is in the swinging. And that is ridiculous. Absurd. Ha! That fucking bitch, my mother, why did you open up to receive him? After that annunciation, that lecherous gleam in his single glittering eye. Did you writhe and shake our history's shirtfront? As now I grind my teething people in a cocoon. Swinging. Swinging in a cocoon of chickenshit. Europe was in my head, crammed together with Africa, Asia and America. Squashed and jammed together in my dustbin head. There is no rubbish dump big enough to relieve me of my load. Swinging upside down, threatening to burst the thin roof of my brains. Those years of my travels. Years of innocence and experience. Motherfucking months of twiddling my thumbs with insecurity. In search of my true people. Yes, in search of my true people. But wherever I went I did not find people but caricatures of people who insisted on being taken seriously as people. Perhaps I was on the wrong planet.
> In the wrong skin.
> Sometimes.
> And sometimes all the time. You know. In the

wrong skin.
This black skin. (*Black Sunlight*, pp. 3-4)

The passionate and shocking corruption of the Crucifixion and the brutal parody of Christ's cry from the cross are powerfully wrought, as Marechera conflates the death of Christ both with his own wish not to-be-born, and the despoliation of Africa. Marechera identifies with the fate of the African, "These are my people. I am their people," but only insofar as they represent his beginnings. His central concern here is the effect of the colonial experience on him as an individual. In search of his "true people" he finds only "caricatures" who, tragically, do not realize they are "caricatures" and so, as they do not share his concern, they see no reason to search for "truth." His conclusion is simple; he cannot find his "true people" because, as a result of the colonial experience, he is the "wrong" person in the "wrong" place. The solution, however, is far from simple. As this reading of *Black Sunlight* makes clear, to find the "right" person he must rid himself of his hybridity. And to do that he must go back to his beginnings.

The quest for a sense of self so evident here pervades the London work.

> "Can you prove that I exist?"
> "Yes if you tell me who is speaking."
> "That is the point of these many words." (*Black Sunlight* p. 115)

This exchange is an inner monologue as the narrator recognizes he speaks with many voices, has many identities. The question "Can you prove that I exist?" is not about existence, *per se*, but it is about multiple identities and the likelihood, or otherwise, of being able to identify which of them is asking the question. In effect the narrator is asking, "Who am I?" Therefore the point of "these many words" is not to prove existence but to consider the inevitably hybrid nature of identity itself. The (impossible) solution is to destroy the layers of influence, socialization, politicization, call it what you will, until only the unadulterated core remains.

Both *Black Sunlight* and *The Black Insider* are explorations of the self. However, this is not a narcissistic exercise nor is it a search for self in the way of a Rogerian self-awareness or knowledge of self gained in relation to others. Nor, in view of its disintegrative intent, is it quite a Jungian process of individuation, since it lacks the emphasis Jung placed on integration and wholeness. It is rather a search for the self or knowledge of the self as I in primordial form, a knowledge of self gained prior to that gained by identification with the other. In this way Marechera is seeking to discover the true, the unalloyed self, free of contaminating influences, particularly, as he makes clear, of the colonial experience but also before the dialectic of identification with the other has begun the irreversible process of encoding identity. The search for self as primordial I is a quite compelling philosophical exercise, but it is an impossible quest. The important feature of the search is the process itself, a quest for understanding of "self-as-is." If a coming to terms (*not* a blind acceptance) with that condition follows then something better than mere coexistence may be possible. It should be possible, for instance, to achieve a Rogerian congruence between "self-as-is" and "self-as-would-like-to-be" thus securing an end to personal dissonance and inner turmoil. All the evidence suggests Dambudzo Marechera never reached that state of mind. Rogers suggests that reconciliation of self-image with that of "self-as-others-see-us" is reached by having an "unconditional positive regard" for others. Marechera was unable to form lasting relationships with things or persons outside himself and was often judgmental, thus denying himself access to helpful feedback. As a result, the search for self-actualization, which *is* realizable, also became an impossible quest.

To achieve "knowledge of self" Marechera has to explore his past and both *Black Sunlight* and *The Black Insider* incorporate the classic form of the journey. *Black Sunlight* has the excursion to and then through the Devil's End, headquarters of the Black Sunlight terrorist group. *The Black Insider*, although the action never leaves the Arts Faculty, presents Marechera's travels from Rhodesia to Zimbabwe via England, from colonialism to neo-colonialism, from non-combatant to combatant.

Marechera's search for the unalloyed self can also be viewed as the search for the id. The id "contains everything that is present at birth," it is the individual, primitive, unorganized and emotional, before the rational realities of the ego become a shaping force. Such a search may well be the inevitable result of colonization, Fanon argued: "Because it is a systematic negation of the other person and a furious determination to deny the other person all attributes of humanity, colonialism forces the people it dominates to ask themselves the question constantly: 'In reality who am I?'"[93] Fanon's comments have particular relevance for black Zimbabweans who, due to the activities of the boycotted Smith government' found themselves isolated not only from the white minority but also from the rest of black Africa. In effect, black Zimbabweans suffered a double isolation. On top of this Marechera was also faced with the debilitating effects of a hazardous lifestyle and a mental illness.

Lacan viewed the formation of the I as a "fortress" or "stadium" containing within itself, "a remote inner castle whose form represents the id." Exactly this type of symbol is prominent in Marechera's work; he describes the Devil's End of *Black Sunlight* as a type of fortress and the Arts Faculty in *The Black Insider* becomes a fortress. In turn the opposed fields of contest are represented on the grand scale by the black/white dichotomy of colonialism and on a personal scale by the attempt to reconcile the "multiplicity of our singleness" as Marechera "flounders" in the attempt to return to his beginnings. Additionally, Devil's End is "a network of caves and interlocking tunnels, natural and man made" (*Black Sunlight*, p. 52), and the Arts Faculty is " . . . small when seen from outside; but inside it is stupendously labyrinthine with its infinite ramifications of little nooks of rooms, some of which are bricked up forever to isolate forever the rotting corpses within" (*The Black Insider*, p. 35).

The Devil's End of *Black Sunlight* and the Arts Faculty of *The Black Insider* must on some level be considered representations of Marechera's psyche. The activities within the structures, that is, within Marechera's psyche, are a search for the unconscious self, the id and the characters he encounters are versions of Marechera himself engaging in debates with Marechera the narrator. The reader is presented with the prospect of Marechera talking to Marechera about Marechera. This need not be seen as interminable navel gazing but is rather the agony of a tortured psyche trying to break free of unwanted influences. It is also a psyche exploring the possibilities of alternative scenarios. Thus Owen in *The Black Insider* and Nick in *Black Sunlight* are versions of Marechera who did not emigrate but who stayed, not only to write but also to join the armed struggle. However, before I look at those roles and others, it will be useful to examine the specific section in *Black Sunlight* featuring the "great cunt."

One complete chapter in *Black Sunlight* is devoted to the journey through Devil's End, which places it at the center of the novel, both in an organizational and a philosophical sense. At the center of that chapter and therefore at the heart of the novel are several pages in which "Franz's brother" (Franz is presumably Franz Fanon, in which case "Franz's brother" seems to be Marechera himself) delivers a polemic on the nature of the "great cunt." His use of the word "cunt" has various significations. I have already commented that Marechera was working under extreme difficulties to fulfill the demands and expectations of the readers, publishers, and critics of *House of Hunger*. In its pejorative sense the "great cunt" is aimed at those whom he saw as being responsible for his physical and psychological deracination and those people and forces who he imagined were preventing him from producing the expected work. It is not difficult to imagine the bleak despair of Marechera who, with the vision before him of producing a definitive work on his own beginnings, realized the impossibility of the task he had set himself. His passions, the combinations of qualities that made him unique, he had either inherited from others or they had been given to him ready made and second-hand. This includes the influence of his voracious reading, which showed itself in his work in the extensive references to other writers. (In her essay *Difficult Joys,* Helene Cixous offers an interesting hypothesis when suggesting that it is authors who give birth to the author. Parents, she writes " . . . belong to two different species . . . the real biological parents . . . the others are texts, other writers, other books.")[94]

Responding to the question "Are you an illusion" Franz replies:
> . . . I am I suppose the sum of all the thoughts and
> delusions and feelings which I hold. In a sense I am
> the fiction I choose to be. At the same time I am the
> ghoul or the harmless young man others take me for.
> I am what the rock dropping on my head makes me. I
> am my lungs breathing. My memory remembering.
> My desires reaching . . . I am all of those things. Are
> they illusions? I do not know. And that I think is the
> point. That we never do know for certain. (p. 68)

This is quintessential Marechera as the reader is presented with
the options of Marechera being his own fictive creation or the fictive
creation of others. The only certainty on offer is the impossibility of
being certain who, or what, is on offer. In other words, the only thing
we can be certain of, according to Marechera, is that we can't be
certain what is real and what is an illusion, a theme he explores to
brilliant effect in "First Street Tumult (*Scrapiron Blues*).

In denigrating all humanity he apparently denigrates himself
most of all: "We are the great cunt. Whatever you do, whatever you
think, whatever you feel, whatever you aspire to, it's dictated by the
great cunt. In fact it's the DNA in us, that great cunt" (p. 70). But this
self-denigration is misleading. He refers to the DNA in us as being
the "great cunt"; some of his DNA he inherited from his mother;
because she had a tainted inheritance she was advised by the *n'anga*
to pass it on to him; as a result he became doubly cursed

The "great cunt" is also, perhaps, a metaphor for the Jungian
collective unconscious, that is, a "psychic disposition shaped by the
forces of heredity." The "great cunt" is inside Devil's End, which is in
turn Marechera's psyche; the connections with the collective
unconscious are made quite plain. First, Marechera confronts the
notion, promoted by, among others, R. D. Laing, that madness is less
a state of mind than a comparative and judgmental "diagnosis"
passed by others. Marechera claims, "You're only mad when there
are other people around you, but never when you are on your own"

(p. 71). He then makes reference to Fanon's work on the mental illnesses induced in black Africans by the processes of colonialism. Bringing together the ideas of Fanon, Laing, and Jung, Marechera argues:

> "It's people who manufacture all kinds of crazinesses, like you and me and Christian here." "Franz was really mad about it in the catacombs, these miles of burial ground, these passageways of the great cunt . . . " "You don't know the history of these caves I suppose? Nobody really does. But they are pre-human. All kinds of monstrous beings used to roam in and all around here, beings long extinct, . . . Anthropoids hung around shivering, begetting, dying. There is a lovely collection of remains and artefacts to attest to the fact." (p. 71)

This imaginative writing not only presents a picture of the complexity of the human mind, it is also a pointed comment, in terms of poetic symbol, on a lost history and an eloquent lament for a lost culture.

The "great cunt" is the totality of experience that gave Dambudzo Marechera the insight to see what he wanted to do at the same time as it convinced him of the impossibility of realizing his vision – that of resurrecting the primordial I. "It's inside you. It's everything you are. It's the soul that's inside you looking out into the world. It's everything outside your self that looks inside you. That's the great cunt. That's the great whore" (p. 70). The whore could possibly be taken as a reference to Marechera's mother, as he so describes her in *The House of Hunger*. However, it has a wider resonance than that. The whore is not only the whore in the traditional sense of selling services (connecting perhaps with the idea of Marechera being asked, in his terms anyway, to prostitute his art), but in the deeper sense of despoiler, as one who taints and contaminates. He continues, "You see things and you think it's you seeing the things but all the time it's the great cunt seeing through you. You touch things and you think it's you touching things but it's the whore touching things through you" (p. 70).

Marechera was constantly struggling with the specific effects on his psyche of growing up in Rhodesia. The "great cunt" can therefore be read as colonization. Marechera makes clear that he knew what action he should take: "I knew what to do. But even the knowing what to do wasn't my own and even right now I am what the great cunt wants me to be. A kind of one-slogan agitator whose very obsession is the proof of his tolerated madness" (p. 70). Marechera emphasizes his desperate situation by suggesting that even his madness is hardly noteworthy as it is greeted with a kind of benign paternalism and resigned inevitability-of-it-all that undermines his individuality still further. Here is bleak despair and hopelessness as the writer explores his Catch-22 situation. He wants to escape from the person he has become but he can only want that because he is that particular person; he is bitterly critical of his environment but part of the conditioning of that environment is that he should be critical of it. Thus, by not conforming, he inevitably conforms.

There is an escape, and that is to destroy the version of Marechera that is so contaminated. Psychologically he has been consumed by the many versions of the "great cunt"; to reflect this in *Black Sunlight* Christian is swallowed: "The rough slimy tongue waddled me onto the huge molars and as they came to chew me, the power of their coming ripped out all screaming from my deepest phosphorescence. . . . Swallowed alive by the great cunt" (p. 73). He is swallowed in order that he may be reborn. Reborn into a silent world. "The silence was the first person singular. A small noise in a long thin tunnel. A single bright eye blazing at me" (p. 73). Marechera presents a view from the womb (the "head of the stream" as it were): his rebirth is a success as he is reborn free of all nurturing influence, reborn in the first person singular. The search for the primordial I, the id, is over and a new journey can begin.

How deeply Marechera felt about the implacable historical and ideological influences that contaminated his writing is indicated by his plaintive "I have been an outsider in my own biography."[95] He goes on to comment "A writer is no longer a person, he has to die in order to become a writer." The narrative thread in *Black Sunlight* is guided by a journey in which the narrator meets his doppelganger, who is a writer, and *The Black Insider* also features a journey, a journey in which several versions of Marechera die so that the remainder, which is the essence of Marechera, can survive and become a writer.

The Black Insider is an allegory of ideas in which the sense of the primary signification, the prose fiction, is undermined by the secondary level of meaning as Marechera explores his experiences, antecedents, and influences. It is a deceptively simple story in which a disparate group of people threatened by an unnamed plague gathers in an unspecified city and take shelter in the Arts faculty of a ruined university. There they discuss a range of philosophical issues as an enemy army approaches. On one level it is just that, a work of fiction and perhaps a pointed comment on the activities of intellectuals whose inclination is for talk rather than action. As a work of fiction it is also a metafiction in which the author intrusively introduces personal experiences that may or may not be true. It may also be an allegory in which the reader chooses the time and place, a post-war, possibly post-holocaust, fiction, in which the Arts faculty represents precolonial Africa, postcolonial Zimbabwe, or is located somewhere in Europe. Or it is an allegory in which Marechera himself stands at the center of the novel not only as narrator but symbolically as the crumbling Arts Faculty with the various characters being versions of the author himself exploring his own experiences.

All of these implications are organized within the overarching symbol of the Marecheran psyche as metanarrative, " . . . stupendously labyrinthine with its infinite ramifications of little nooks of rooms, some of which are bricked up forever to isolate forever the rotting corpses within." At the time of writing *The Black Insider* Marechera gave every indication of being very ill; his behavior was often paranoid, highly erratic, and irrational; the labyrinthine faculty with its rotting corpses and bricked up rooms is a terrifying portrayal of the writer's psyche at this point of crisis.

If this interpretation of the Arts Faculty holds good then the individual who wrote *The Black Insider* was in deep psychological trouble. The plague is inside, the advancing armies are outside and an unexploded bomb sits menacingly on the roof. Clearly the Arts Faculty – inside Marechera's psyche – is a dangerous and unhealthy place. Identifying himself with the Faculty by his reference to "*my* roof" (my emphasis) and revealing his paranoia and sense of alienation by referring to attacks on him from both sides engaged in the war, he writes, "They also had fighter planes on each side which occasionally strafed my roof because some fucking joker had painted a bull's-eye on it" (p. 34). Possibly the bull's-eye symbolizes the transference to him of the "family illness," in which case his mother is the "fucking joker." But, more reasonably perhaps, the incident is symbolic of the experiences of being a black Zimbabwean with a value system subjected to a European education. In this instance the "fucking joker," like the earlier "fucking bitch," is the African colonial experience itself.

The plague is, among other things, the alienating effects of a European colonial education: "The plague has taken its toll of those like myself who have sought refuge under its dark wing" (p. 141); in order to destroy the plague he has to destroy himself. The unidentified army, which is neither black nor white but both with "blackened faces," represent the difficulties a paranoid Marechera perceived had dogged his life and the bomb represents both an uncertain future and the fear of the unknown.

As for the different characters in the Faculty, the versions of Marechera, Holland refers to this technique as "splitting," [96] arguing that a "simple" story can be elaborated into a "complex, multi-faceted work" by the "doubling or splitting of characters." The writer is then able to adopt different psychological positions with different characters. In his essay *Creative Writers and Day Dreaming* Freud referred to " . . . the inclination of the modern writer to split up his ego, by self observation, into many part-egos, and, in consequence, to personify the conflicting currents of his own mental life in several heroes." [97] Marechera's conflation of himself with his characters was probably more an unconscious act than that suggested by Freud's comments but the insight offered by those comments is still valid. The concept of "splitting" and "part-egos" certainly has resonance in

The Black Insider where in one sense the various characters are false selves created to explore false realities.

It is not difficult, for example, to imagine Marechera seeing himself as Cicero, the brilliant orator and castigator of corruption, or as the tragic, haunted figure of Hamlet, or as Owen, the Marechera who stayed to fight. In another sense, the fact that they have different degrees of blackness (Otilith is "coal black" (p. 75), the African Schweik has "dark skin" (p. 99). Helen, who is "paler than the whitest ghost" [p. 39]) is clearly symbolic and represents the writer's awareness of his own mental colonization as he presents himself not as one of these types but as all of them. The use of male and female characters as versions of the writer is not surprising. The id in its primitive form, prior to the influence of the ego, is asexual, thus in the elemental writing of Marechera the unconscious takes either male or female form. The writer can be either or both, the creation has a biological determination but is gender free. So it is that Helen, a fourteen-year-old white girl, who is introduced in the early pages of *The Black Insider*, symbolizes the white colonial experience in the Marecheran psyche. It is also significant that she is isolated, as the author allows her no dialogue with the other characters, and that she plays a major part in preparing the narrator to take up arms. Such a reading may seem forced. But it answers surprisingly well the actual experience of reading this self-involved novel.

The writer makes it clear in *The Black Insider* that his education and educators had infected him with the "plague of intellectualism," which had placed him outside the armed struggle and out of reach of the people: "I had seen how our education had given us too early the veneer of experience which our elders mistook for mature and solid knowledge of a world that had rapidly ceased to be ours" (p. 141). Marechera appears to be suggesting that an inappropriate European education gave a false impression of political sophistication. He is also suggesting that such education moved those so educated away from a "grass-roots" understanding of the African people, and towards a European society from which they were excluded. Isolated by his education, Marechera portrays himself in *The Black Insider* as belonging neither to Europe nor to Africa. In this way his status as non-combatant is justified; he could not take up arms as an African until his "intellectualism," his European education, had been purged. Similarly he could not act against the forces of colonialism and neocolonialism until his mental colonization had been expunged.

In thrall to such forces the writer, as writer, is impotent. Appropriately then, the shells that destroy the Arts Faculty and kill Otilith and the others, thereby removing both the education system and the results of that system in Marechera, also kill Helen, at one and the same time destroying the colonial experience. Thus the narrator attains a sort of freedom and a sort of psychic unity and moves closer in his search for the primordial I.

That he is not yet wholly free is evident from the fact that the novel closes as he prepares to confront those unidentified fears that still haunt his psyche in the form of the approaching army. John Wyllie, a Heinemann reader, commented that the unpublished *Bowl for Shadows* was "in R. D. Laing territory." The violent end of *The Black Insider* and my earlier comments about Marechera's possible schizoid state call to mind Laing's *The Divided Self*:

> Destructiveness in phantasy goes on without the wish
> to make compensatory reparation, for the guilt that
> prompts towards preserving and making amends
> loses its urgency. Destructiveness in phantasy can
> thus rage on, unchecked, until the world and the self
> are reduced, in phantasy, to dust and ashes. In the
> schizophrenic state the world is in ruins, and the self
> is (apparently) dead. (p. 85)

Black Sunlight and *The Black Insider* were written while Marechera was living in a squat in Tolmers Square in London, effectively homeless and penniless, drinking excessively, experimenting with drugs, unemployed and unemployable, and suffering from a psychological illness that had been diagnosed as an untreatable personality disorder. Little wonder perhaps that there is evidence in *The Black Insider* that apart from the many problems he could give name to, Marechera suffered from the ultimate terror, an unnamed and unnamable dread, a fear of being here, of being anywhere. In the circumstances of his existence in London it is reasonable to presume that his life was without form or direction, a danger in itself, as Kristeva argues: "For the speaking being life is a meaningful life: life is even the apogee of meaning. Hence if the meaning of life is lost, life can easily be lost: when meaning shatters, life no longer matters." [98]

The option of suicide discussed earlier appears to be behind the cryptic comment "The other side of the world is only a drop of blood away" (*The Black Insider*, p. 100 and p. 144 and *Black Sunlight*, p. 112), the blunt "I was drunk and tried to end it all with the large kitchen knife" (*The Black Insider*, p. 171), and an awareness of his own parlous condition indicated in the bleakly poetic "There is nowhere to hide on the road to suicide" (p. 52). There is abundant testimony from those who knew Dambudzo Marechera personally that his chosen lifestyle was very dangerous for his physical and psychological health and one can only speculate how close that lifestyle was to a death wish.

Although he wrote compulsively about madness, often with telling insight – for example, "It is not sanity or insanity that I fear but the power that consciously shapes these in others" (p. 72) – Marechera reacted violently to any suggestion that he had any form of mental illness, claiming that it was not him but his environment that was sick. In this he is at least partly supported by R. D. Laing who argued that the schizophrenic sees things others do not see, not always in a delusory manner: " . . . the cracked mind of the schizophrenic may *let in* light which does not enter the intact minds of many sane people whose minds are closed." [99] Arguably it was this heightened perception, this acute awareness, rather than drink or drugs, that led Marechera to produce his brilliant writing and extraordinary images. It may also have generated what Benedetti has called a " . . . deformed world, which is not only a world of logical nonsense but is also a world of erroneous sensory evidence, of hallucinations." [100] Such criticism is not aimed at undermining Marechera's achievements as a writer. On the contrary, Benedetti's view enables a better understanding of the nature of those achievements by offering a structure within which to frame the extraordinary world of Dambudzo Marechera.

Both *Black Sunlight* and *The Black Insider* demonstrate that Dambudzo Marechera was a writer of exceptional vision and talent, possessed by an unattainable ambition and driven by the desperate need to escape his predicament and his illness. I argued above that the striving for knowledge of self as the primordial I, that is without reference to the other, is an impossible quest. According to Sartre, "The other appears as being able to effect the synthesis between the conscious thesis and the unconscious antithesis. I can know myself only through the mediation of the other, which means that I stand in relation to my id in the position of the other." [101] But if the other is destroyed, which is precisely what happens in *The Black Insider,* then only the id remains. However, it is not self-knowledge that is gained by this action, quite the reverse. It is a destruction of all the others –"the versions of me that did not come out of the womb with me" – (p. 144) thereby destroying all accumulated knowledge and self-knowledge in order to start again with a *tabula rasa.*

Here is the key to the work that followed *House of Hunger* and came out of London. Quite simply, Dambudzo Marechera did not want to be where he was or to be who, or what, he had become. He wanted to go back to his birth and to start again. Whether the complete rejection of all around him and his desire to start with a clean slate indicates intellectual anarchy or artistic posturing is part of the polarized argument mentioned above; both can be demonstrated sporadically but neither with the consistency of the all-pervading nihilism that was evident to a lesser degree in *House of Hunger* but took center stage during his London period. It is very apparent that Dambudzo Marechera did not settle at New College. Unfortunately, the "cure" of leaving Oxford was worse (for Marechera) than the "disease" as his always fragile grip on his mental health was loosened by his erratic lifestyle. *Black Sunlight* and *The Black Insider* stand as eloquent testimony to an outstanding talent trying valiantly to establish himself as a writer and struggling to develop a sense of identity – a struggle frustrated by an unclear perception of who he was, and what his role was, and complicated by his ongoing battle with a debilitating illness.

4.3 The Other Stories:

" . . . something intensely personal. . . "

Apart from the eponymous story in *The Black Insider* there are five other works, three short stories and two poems making up the collection. The stories had been published earlier in *West Africa*: "Night on my Harmonica" in May 1981; "Oxford, Black Oxford" in June 1981; and "The Sound of Snapping Wires" in March 1983. Both "Night on my Harmonica" and "The Sound of Snapping Wires" were written in 1980/1981 when Marechera was living in Clerkenwell Road, London, and feature his drinking habits, his attempts to write, and his relationships with women. Both are very short and feature the narrator musing on recent experiences. They are episodic and somewhat undeveloped although both have memorable passages:

> Outside, the thunder of trucks, cars, loud heavy metal music. Screams as some prostitute was being beaten up. My neighbors were mostly squatters, dossers, derelicts, single parents who had given up. Young old men who passed themselves off as sculptors and painters. These were now my people. I was one of them. A down and out drifter who happened to write books. Something inside me tore. Two days ago it happened again. I was drunk and tried to end it all with the large kitchen knife. There was all this blood everywhere. I was more or less seeing the inside of my own ravings. "Night On My Harmonica," *The Black Insider*, (p. 171)

There is a film-like quality about the pace and direction of this short sequence as the reader is presented with an external view of the apartment block, moving in to focus on the tenants before settling on the isolated figure of the writer. Marechera takes the reader further by extending the journey into the writer's psyche. And yet in "The Sound Of Snapping Wires" he decries such an approach: "When he pared this down to the bone of his own personal experience, the anaemic imagery of self-analysis soon revolted him" (p. 165). It may have revolted him but it was a technique he used himself. One successful example of a controlled use of self-analysis is the story "Oxford, Black Oxford," which I examine in detail below. In that story rain seems to be employed as a metaphor for the hostility Marechera experienced at Oxford. Marechera's use of rain as a metaphor is not confined to hostility as he demonstrates in "The Sound of Snapping Wires." Here rain is inspirational, it has a cleansing, almost purging effect, as it dispels "some of the night's bitterness":

> It was raining when he came out clutching his box of chips and spare ribs. The chill gusts blew hither and thither, billowing out his coat, hitting his face with the liquid globules of yet another indecisive London rain. He liked it.
> The fresh and cold blast of sanity, soaking him already with its attendant sense of rootlessness, blew into his lungs and dragged out of him some of the night's bitterness. He drank every last drop of it. Before him was the tall YMCA building: immediately to his right was the illuminated fountain, the blue- green water sparkling upwards like a long-drawn-out yearning only to fall back to be recycled upwards once more. Like his own expectations. His own ambition – what had it been so long ago in high school and then at university? What was it? It had started in Africa and now found him here in London. Mooching his way in the small hours towards Clerkenwell Road. "The Sound Of Snapping Wires," *The Black Insider*, pp. 166-7

No doubt some license has been exercised by the writer in this romantic presentation of a few moments in his life. Whether the event happened or was partly or wholly imagined is impossible to know; and is, in any event, of no real consequence. In this very short extract Marechera captures the essence of his erratic life and grounds that in the mundane experience of visiting a fast food store. There is a heart-breaking beauty in the image of the slightly intoxicated writer, battered and blood-stained, eating chips and spare ribs while standing in the rain admiring the rise and fall of a fountain which he compares to his expectations of life. There is tragedy in that the expectations, the ambitions, are now nothing more than an imperfect recollection.

Of course a major factor in the "failure" of his ambitions at university was his sending down from New College, an issue that is central to the third piece, "Oxford, Black Oxford." This story, rather longer than the other two in this short sequence, has a formal structure of a beginning, a middle, and an end, three developed characters, and, like "First Street Tumult (*Scrapiron Blues*), demonstrates Marechera's considerable talent as a short story writer. "Oxford, Black Oxford" presents a central character, clearly Marechera himself, as a diligent and gifted student but one whose very survival as a student is placed at risk by his alternative existence as a violent drunk. The disjunction within the characterization, gifted student or drunk, is matched by a disjunction in the story as, with dramatic effect, the portraits of Oxford and Africa presented in the opening paragraphs are superseded by a foregrounding of the protagonist and a shift in narrative style and tone.

The story was probably written shortly after he had left New College in 1978, and the title "Oxford, Black Oxford" contains several nuances. With the obvious echoes of William Henley's "England, my England" [102] it can be read as a bitterly ironic comment on Marechera's experience of exclusion at Oxford. Such a reading suggests that Marechera may have felt an enormous sense of loss at leaving Oxford. "Oxford, Black Oxford" is also black in the sense that Marechera was black and a mocking acknowledgement that although Oxford accepts black students it is, the story suggests, underpinned by white values. The title can also be seen as a direct reference to the bouts of depression and paranoia that caused the writer such grave problems during his time at New College. Here black has the same correlation with mental illness as it has when applied to Churchill's "black dog"[103] or Kristeva's "black sun."

The opening paragraph concludes with the sentence "My mind an essay in itself." and the first two paragraphs can be read as a typical student essay with Marechera as the ideal student. The first paragraph presenting a collage of Oxford images and the second a collage of African images juxtaposed to draw vivid comparisons. The imaginative link connecting the paragraphs of the "slow calm walk to a tutorial in All Souls" reflecting Marechera's actual journey from Africa to Oxford.

> A few rusty spears of sunlight had pierced through the overhead drizzling clouds. Behind the gloom of rain and mist, I could see a wizened but fearfully blood-shot sun. And everywhere, the sweet clangor of bells pushed in clear tones what secret rites had evolved with this city. Narrow cobbled streets, ancient warren of diverse architecture all backed up into itself, with here there and everywhere the massive masonry of college after college. ("Oxford, Black Oxford," *The Black Insider*, p. 158)

With its colorful combination of a stereotypical African icon (a spear) and a stereotypical English icon (rain) the opening sentences – "A few rusty spears of sunlight had pierced through the overhead drizzling clouds. Behind the gloom of rain and mist, I could see a wizened but fearfully blood-shot sun." – offer a memorable image. In view of what ensues it is worthy of note that the spear (the African?) has been damaged by the action of the rain (the English?). The "wizened but fearfully blood-shot sun" can be seen as a vision of the future under threat but more reasonably represents Africa, and the "spears of sunlight" represent Africans leaving Africa. Thus, it can be argued that "spears of sunlight" is an implicit metaphor for the black Africans at Oxford and the "drizzling clouds . . . the gloom of rain and mist" likewise a metaphor for the hostile environment that greeted them.

In the opening paragraph the language teems with images of

exclusion: "secret rites" and "ancient warren"; the almost incestuous "backed up into itself"; "close-packed little shops"; "crowded pavements"; leading us to the agencies which had directed Marechera to Oxford, agencies of faith, hope, and charity, given cynical expression here as "Myth, illusion, reality." It is perhaps not too far-fetched to see the faith he had placed in the education system destroyed because it was based on the myth of equality for all, his hopes therefore an illusion and his dependence on charity a reality. Of course Marechera rejected any notion of charity but, that rejection apart, the reality is that his very existence became dependent on the charitable actions of sundry others, his presence at New College the result of a Junior Common Room Scholarship partly funded by the fees of other undergraduates. [104]

"Myth, illusion, reality were all consumed by the dull gold, inwardness, narrowness." That "Myth, illusion, reality" should be consumed by an "inwardness" a "narrowness" is in keeping with the tone of the paragraph, but why "dull gold"? An oxymoron, "dull gold" signifies the welcome and unwelcome experienced by Marechera at Oxford. It also represents a tarnishing of the prize he had "won" with his scholarship to Oxford. The "sheer and brilliant" extent of his achievement and its potential seem now an "impossibility . . . as the raindrops splashed and the castanets of stray sunlight beams clapped against the slate roofs, walls and doorways." Notably the raindrops act together but the sunlight acts in "stray" beams and is denied access at all points as the psychological and cultural barriers opposing the black African are given physical, if metaphorical, form.

The reference to Zuleika Dobson – " . . . did Zuleika Dobson ride past, her carriage horses striking up sparks from the flint of the road?" – is more than a mere example of wide reading. By implication it inserts the black narrator, intertextually, into the earlier work by Max Beerbohm (1911).

> As the landau rolled into "the Corn," another youth –
> a pedestrian, and very different – saluted the
> Warden. He wore a black jacket, rusty and

amorphous. His trousers were too short: almost a dwarf. His face was as plain as his gait was undistinguished. He squinted behind spectacles.

"And who is that?" asked Zuleika.

A deep flush overspread the cheek of the Warden. "That," he said, "is also a member of Judas. His name I believe is Noaks."

"Is he dining with us tonight?" asked Zuleika.

"Certainly not," said the Warden. "Most decidedly not."

(Zuleika Dobson, p. 3)

The resemblances to Marechera himself – the unusual appearance, the squint, the spectacles, the implied difficult relationship with the Warden – are too strong to have been chosen accidentally. In "Oxford, Black Oxford" Marechera "watches" the carriage pass by, as in Zuleika Dobson the passengers in the carriage look out and see his equivalent from the turn of the century. In this way Marechera indicates that his experience of prejudice and exclusion are not unique; they are, he appears to be suggesting, endemic in Oxford.

A key word linking the opening paragraphs is the adjective sweet, as in "sweet clangor of bells" which pervades Oxford, in contrast with "the evil-sweet fumes of the ever-open beer halls" of the townships. However, the main link is between the closing and opening sentences of the respective paragraphs as the "mind" in which the initial essay was written or imagined becomes a vantage point through which various stereotypical images of Africa are presented.

The clear and specific references to Oxford are abandoned here in favor of generalizations aimed not at a locality or even a country but at the continent of Africa itself.

Drawing apart the curtains, opening the windows, to let in . . . the hail of memories. The reek and ruin of heat and mud-huts through which a people of gnarled and knotty face could not even dream of

education, good food, even dignity. Their lifetime
was one long day of grim and degrading toil,
unappeasable hunger whose child's eyes
unflinchingly accused the adults of some gross
betrayal. (p. 158)

Thus the "people of gnarled and knotty face" is, metaphorically
speaking, the African nation, and "the child's eyes" is probably
intentionally reminiscent of the haunting images of starving Biafran
children, which in themselves became symbolic of Africa in the
1970s. In this context "child's eyes" is a trope for the 1970s
generation of Africans whose unattainable dreams and plight of
"grim and degrading toil, unappeasable hunger" – intellectual and
physical hunger, that is – are blamed on the alleged complicity of
earlier generations.

In counterpoint to the "Narrow, cobbled streets, ancient
warren of diverse architecture . . . with here there and everywhere
the massive masonry of college after college," township life is
described in a single graphic sentence.

The foul smells of the pit latrines and the evil-sweet
fumes of the ever-open beer halls, these infiltrated
everything, from the smarter whitewashed hovels of
the aspirant middle class to the wretched squalor of
the tin and mud-huts that slimily coiled and uncoiled
together like hideous worms in a bottomless hell.

Marechera emphasizes the all-pervasive extent of horror and
filth by using the simile of "hideous worms" to describe the "smells"
and "fumes" and stresses the reptilian unpleasantness by describing
the fumes as "slimily" coiling and uncoiling in "a bottomless hell,"
the latter a metaphor not only for the township but also for life in the
township. The final sentence returns to images of the African in
Oxford before a "sudden downpour" (the hostile environment of
Oxford) drives away thoughts of Africa as "the blood-shot mind . . .
[the blood-shot sun of the first paragraph now figuratively the
African collective unconscious, saturated with bloodstained
memories] was completely shrouded by the heavy clouds."

To a certain extent the opening paragraphs admit their fictionality as the author intrudes to admit that he is writing an essay. The rest of the story, in contrast, is in a realistic mode. The tone shifts from that of a detached observer to one of intimate involvement as the narrator relates his experiences. In a series of exchanges with Stephen, a fellow student and a tutor, Dr. Martins-Botha, Marechera confronts the issues of class distinction and prejudice, using the different voices to disseminate different points of view and different perspectives. The name, Martins-Botha, is of course a bitter cross-cultural joke. Dr. Martins is the name for the footwear worn almost exclusively (in the 1970s) by National Front skinheads. Pieter Botha was a National Party MP in the Verwoerd government renowned for his extremist support of apartheid and for his views on the purity and supremacy of the Afrikaner. In fairly direct fashion Marechera is, through the made-up name of a college lecturer, linking the supporters of the UK-based National Front and the Afrikaner supporters of apartheid. By placing that link in a position of some authority he is suggesting that racial prejudice can be found at Oxford.

Inevitably the voice in the story has an ideological dimension and the various exchanges highlight that Stephen and Dr Martins-Botha share a value system from which the narrator is excluded. In the following extract the tutor has asked the narrator a question but before waiting for an answer turns to address Stephen:

"Had a good shoot?"
Stephen actually blushed with pride as he said, "I bagged seven. Two are on the way to your house right now."
"Ah, a decent meal for once."

In addition to the idiomatic "Englishness" of the language, for example, "good shoot" and "bagged seven," the exclusive intimacy implied in this exchange by the revelations that Dr. Botha knew Stephen had been shooting, Stephen knew Dr. Botha's address and that he would accept a gift, is confirmed when the narrator observes, "Dr. Martins-Botha's right hand was between Stephen's thighs." This homosexual encounter could be hallucinatory. It certainly has a surreal air, and shockingly emphasizes the narrator's isolation. On the other hand it could be realistic and a comment on the impotence of the black student in that he is of so little significance that he is allowed to witness behavior that, if reported, could have severe consequences for the perpetrators. The narrator is of course unable to make such a report because, apart from the obvious barriers of class and status, his own reputation is such that it is unlikely that anyone would give credibility to his complaints about the "bad" behavior of others.

In the following example the themes of drinking – the reason for his precarious situation – and exclusion are combined and when he says he is "dying for a drink" and Stephen "produced his hip flask, a silver and leather thing" in response, drink is clearly in the text and exclusion, equally clearly, in the subtext. Earlier the "sweet clangor of bells" in Oxford was contrasted with the "evil-sweet fumes of the ever-open beer halls" of the unnamed township. The gulf between the students is again driven home. The taking of alcohol, in the case of the white student, involves a silver and leather flask and in the case of the black student, it is a stinking experience in a crowded beer hall. In addition, perhaps, as silver is an epithet often used to describe the tone or color of bells, it is suggested that those who drink from such flasks are more familiar, and therefore have more in common, with an environment ringing with the "sweet clangor of bells" than those who frequent beer halls in a "bottomless hell."

In typical contradictory Marecheran fashion the characterization in this very short story is stronger than in the longer works. Stephen is cast firmly as middle class or even, perhaps, aristocratic. He is on familiar social terms with his tutors, he hunts, he uses a hip flask. When he is first introduced he is presented in the classical pose of the indolent though confident student. "He leaned back against a wall, hands in his pockets, ankle over ankle." Marechera's choice of language for Stephen shows him to be patronizing, as the following demonstrates:

> Always wanted to know where you learned your
> English, old boy. Excellent. Even better than most of

the natives in my own hedge. You know. Wales.

At the time of the writing of this story the Welsh nationalists were deep into their campaign of English-holiday-home-cottage-burning and the restoration of the Welsh language was a major issue. Marechera, who had lived in Wales, would have been aware of those activities and this apparently banal exchange is deep with meaning as he exposes the venal attitude of the colonizer. The exchange continues:

> "It's the national lingo in my country."
> "It's not bambazonka like Uganda?"
> "Actually yes, your distant cousins are butchering the whole lot of us."
> "Mercenaries, eh. Sorry old man. Money. Nothing personal."

The use of "bambazonka" is confusing – it serves as an arrogant neologism but the absence of a clear meaning obscures the apparent link to genocide made by the author. One possibility is that by using a neologism Marechera was indicating the complete disregard of the European for the African language and, by extension, African culture and the African people.

A key phrase here is "Nothing personal" as it is used again when the narrator in an ironic reference to identity confusion, cannot distinguish between Stephen and Dr. Martins-Botha:

> I picked up my essay from the floor and began to read. I was halfway through it when Dr. Martins-Botha laughed quite scornfully. I stopped. I did not look up. I waited until he had finished. I was about to resume when he suddenly – or was it Stephen's voice? – said, "Nothing personal. You know."

There is of course a heavy irony in Marechera's use of the phrase "Nothing personal." The action of the colonizer had disastrous effects on the individual, and the scorn of the tutor is clearly aimed at the narrator – by linking the two denials Marechera suggests that such acts are justified by the perpetrator by the simple expedient of denying the individuality of the other. Significantly, Marechera closes his story with a reference to "something intensely personal [which] was flying towards me."

Of particular interest in this short piece is Marechera's reference to "The language of power." Although apparently aimed at the mocking "Language, dear boy. Language." it actually refers to the summons from the warden and appears to acknowledge that power is inevitably associated with status. The exchange that precedes this bleak statement is notable for two things. One is the carefully affected tone of the students' dialogue, in which both observe a student's script in playing their parts. The other is the contrast between the narrator's utterances and his thoughts.

> Shit. I had forgotten to check my mail. There was probably a summons to the dean in it. Not again, for Chrissake. But I said in an off-hand way, "Bloody uppity these porters, if you ask me. When a bloke is quietly sneaking back into his rooms, they make a fuss."

Here, perhaps, is the nub of the story. The desperation of the unspoken thoughts is very evident in the appeal "Not again, for Chrissake.", but his observable reaction is very different. The character created by Marechera cannot show concern for such matters – both in this story and in his own life, it could be argued – and responds "Bloody uppity, these porters . . . " His use of "uppity" to describe the porters may hint at its common association with "uppity nigger," deliberately reversing the stereotype. In this way, by contrasting the content of the spoken with the unspoken, Marechera is able to highlight the dilemma of his narrator who apparently cares deeply about an issue but, because it would contradict the image of the hard-drinking, anarchic student, is unable to admit that is the case. His reaction confirms the image he has presented, and the result is another step away from his role as "ideal student."

Almost inevitably the story closes with the narrator drinking triple whiskies as he contemplates an uncertain future: "At last something – not much – but something intensely personal was flying towards me like the flight of a burning sparrow." "Intensely personal" is a repudiation of the earlier "Nothing personal" protestations of Stephen and Dr. Martins-Botha and the "burning sparrow" a nightmare vision, or a deliberate Spoonerism of spear and arrow? As so often happens with Marechera's work the reader is left with uncertainty – is the ending a carefully crafted surreal image, or a flashy meaningless gesture of a writer suddenly bored with the exercise? Unfortunately for the reader looking for certainty, the complexity of the man and the writer is such that either alternative could be true.

4.4 "From the heart and mind of the artist"

This is not the place to seek a deep engagement with the "art *versus* neurosis" debate and I intend to do so only briefly in order to state my position. I am aware of the accusation that *Black Sunlight* and *The Black Insider* are essentially self indulgent; indeed some would see that this disqualifies them from any consideration as "works of art." I take a broader view. In *Black Sunlight* and *The Black Insider* Marechera engages with the difficulties of being a black African, both in white minority ruled Rhodesia, and in England, and he does so in a highly individual way by confronting the issues raised *for him* and exploring the possible solutions to *his own personal dilemma.* As a record of a writer who lived through the most dynamic period in the history of Zimbabwe the works offer a unique opportunity to examine one man's struggle to come to terms with those turbulent times.

But, are they "works of art"? Or, being predominantly personal, do they simply deserve to be treated as symptoms of neurosis and no more? These questions raise two basic issues to address: first, that for all the mess in his life Marechera's art *is* nevertheless a detached and objectively realized self-expression; though there are such examples – "Oxford, Black Oxford," "First Street Tumult," and "The Skin of Time" come to mind, this would be difficult to maintain with any degree of conviction. Second, that, although at times defective in objectivity, messy and confused by personal complications,

Marechera's work is nevertheless interesting and should be valued in human, as well as artistic terms. This latter point, which if anything is understated, is surely indisputable.

Anthony Storr argued that "The creative person is constantly seeking to discover himself, to remodel his own identity, and to find meaning in the universe through what he creates." [105] Not unreasonably Storr is implying that a successful (in terms of understanding, that is) search by the "creative person" will also provide meaning for the reader. Marechera's search for the primordial I was not (could not be) successful. But the journey, as destination in itself, and the reasons for undertaking that journey were successful in terms of exploration and understanding of self. I am not implying that Marechera's psychological journey was successful in personal terms, but rather that the recording of that journey was successful in artistic terms.

As discussed above both *The Black Insider* and *Black Sunlight* represent not only a search for the primordial I and a sense of self but also a journey, Marechera's journey to become a writer. Lacan argues that " . . . psychoanalysis may accompany the patient to the ecstatic limit of *"Thou that art,"* in which is revealed to him the cipher of his mortal destiny, but it is not in our power as practitioners to bring him to the point where the real journey begins." [106] The continual self-examination by the writer is a form of psychoanalysis in which the search for self, *"Thou that art,"* is revealed as fruitless and, as a consequence of that, Marechera does not reach the point where his "real journey" can begin.

If Marechera had been able to start his "real journey," to become established as a writer in the new Zimbabwe, the outcome is impossible to know. But it must include at least the possibility of the eventual emergence of a "great writer." Schneiderman presents both sides of the "art or neurosis" debate:

> It could be argued . . . that great writing transcends the sufferings and confusions of the author and represents the achievements of new heights, where craftsmanship and inspiration overshadow the

personal factor. In the same vein, it could be said that great writing replaces the personal and idiosyncratic with universal symbols and meanings. Inferior writing. . . could be characterized as showing all the seams that went into its composition, including the psychic scars of the author. But these arguments in favor of the essential normality of great writing are the result of wishful thinking, rather than being based on a careful study of the relationship between biography and literary creativity. Such a study reveals that great literary art is a synthesis of technical skill with tremendous fear, rage, or other powerful emotions, and that the fundamental character of great writers reveals significant failure along developmental lines, that is, a basic lack of maturity. [107]

Schneiderman's is an interesting, if rather unorthodox, argument. He is saying more than that great writers are not of the common herd. His argument that technical ability when allied to a series of powerful emotions may produce "great literary art" has something to commend it. The ability to focus on an issue(s) or theme(s) and to reveal all the subtleties and nuances, and to express them succinctly and creatively, is certainly a basic requirement.

Marechera's work and career appears to offer some support for elements of Schneiderman's argument. Along with his "obsessive behavior" and possible "lack of maturity" there was no "essential normality" to Marechera's life. His writing, often undisciplined, occasionally fragmented and rambling, is also memorable, full of great passion, fear and rage. He could, with justification, be described as obsessively concerned with his own personal problems. Additionally, his personality was such that he was unable to form working relationships with, among others, his fellow writers, his publishers, and the Zimbabwean nation builders. As a result of this there was "significant failure" if not along developmental lines, then certainly in the quantity of work the writer actually managed to finish and present to his publishers

If Marechera had been able to complete his first journey, to rid himself of his demons and to become established as a writer in Zimbabwe, and to start out on his "real journey" towards a more consistent and substantial body of work, then, possibly, that might have led to the early emergence of the "new novel," which, as Salman Rushdie speculated "[is] a postcolonial novel, a decentered, trans-national, inter-lingual, cross-cultural novel." [108] Marechera did not write such a novel although it is possible to discern, particularly in the London works, definite steps in the "new" direction forecast by Rushdie almost twenty years later.

CHAPTER FIVE

Return to Zimbabwe

5.1 " . . . like a bloody tourist"

Marechera returned to Zimbabwe on February 9,1982; on his arrival at Harare he knelt on the airport tarmac and kissed the ground in true returning-exile fashion. He had returned to Zimbabwe, ostensibly for a five-week period, to assist in the making of a television film based on *The House of Hunger*.[109] However, he never left the country again and died in Harare, a little over five years later, in August 1987.

The Zimbabwe to which he returned was in as parlous a

state as the Rhodesia he had left. After the post-independence euphoria, in which the economy had grown at over 12 per cent in each of the first two years, came a rude awakening. As Colin Stoneman comments:

> . . . far from continuing to grow [as projected] . . . the economy contracted; inflation soared, canceling many of the income gains to wage earners, and employment fell; droughts required major feeding programs and imports, and produced a suspension of land settlement; some whites were plainly remaining as South African fifth columnists . . . aid flows slowed, or failed to materialize . . . world markets contracted, and much of the earlier dynamism was seen as a once-and-for-all adjustment following the end of sanctions; South Africa conducted morale-damaging attacks on an airforce base and an ammunition dump and closed off trade routes through Mozambique, forcing more costly and politically vulnerable reliance on South African ports. [110]

In spite of small recoveries in 1984 and 1986, which were no more than false dawns, the economy continued to weaken, unemployment soared, and although education improved, according to Stoneman, fewer than ten percent would obtain the jobs their education had led them to expect. It was against this background of political uncertainty and economic hardship that Marechera spent the final years of his life

Marechera was met at the airport by Chris Austin and the writer Wilson Katiyo, who was hailed enthusiastically by Marechera with a comrade's handshake and the greeting "Ah! A son of the soil." Katiyo had also been in "exile" in London and was a novelist with *A Son of the Soil*. When he met Marechera at the airport Katiyo was working for the Zimbabwean Ministry of Information, which was one of the sponsors of the film, on which Katiyo was employed as assistant director

Within minutes of his arrival, as he was being taken to his hotel Marechera was complaining "Here I am back in Zimbabwe and I'm looking at it like a bloody tourist," and "I can't stay here, I don't belong here anymore." The ebullient mood of his arrival had quickly dissolved into one of disorientation, and the news that *Black Sunlight* had just been banned in Zimbabwe fuelled his sense of paranoia, as he accused Austin of complicity in the banning, and of manipulating his return. Wilson Katiyo did try to explain to Marechera that the censors were still the same people who had operated under Smith and still worked to the same rules, quite simply because the new government hadn't had the time to change them. He explained the banning was not a plot and was not even political but was a throwback to pre-independence routines. In this exchange, which appears in Austin's film, Marechera, possibly in view of Katiyo's position as a government employee, ignores his argument. The interview, filmed a few days after his return, indicates that Marechera was considering staying in Zimbabwe. Under fiercely direct questioning from Katiyo and Zimunya on such practical matters as, what he would do, where would he live, how he would eat, Marechera has no answers to offer. His own personal comfort had never featured very highly to Marechera who appears to be rather taken aback by the pragmatism of his fellow writers.

Austin's plans were soon thrown into complete disarray as the next few days degenerated into a series of violent and drunken arguments. Marechera withdrew his cooperation from the making of the film and unsuccessfully attempted to obtain an injunction stopping Austin from working on it.

There are two particular aims of this chapter: firstly, to assess the works that Marechera produced in the early months following his return to independent Zimbabwe, including *Mindblast*, together with the plays from *Scrapiron Blues* and the drama *The Stimulus of Scholarship*, parts of which were published in the student magazine *Focus* at the University of Zimbabwe in 1983/1984. And, secondly, to consider Marechera's position on the relationship between the artist and society, aesthetics and ideology, contentious issues that have already been considered in Chapter Two. However, it is appropriate to take another brief look at how Marechera dealt with the conflict between the demands of the new establishment and his own individualistic sense of commitment to nation building now that he was face-to-face with the realities of life in postcolonial Zimbabwe.

5.2 *The Stimulus of Scholarship*

Although Marechera appeared to place little importance on his personal comfort and followed a bohemian lifestyle – "I was living [as a] ...Bohemian fulltime writer" (*Mindblast*, p. 125), "...my alienated bourgeois Bohemian lifestyle. (p. 138) – any temptation to stereotype him as simply a woolly-minded idealist should be resisted. As a student at the University of Rhodesia Marechera had involved himself in political activities, though not surprisingly, it was as an individual rather than as a member of a recognized group. Back in Zimbabwe he demonstrated that he was politically aware and outspoken. For example, Richard Mhonyera had this to say after hearing Marechera speak at the University of Zimbabwe: "... at a time when the post-independence mood of the country was on the genial side, he had perhaps more insight and honesty and wouldn't go along with the usual rhetoric. He saw too clearly corruption and double standards and he had this open, unguardedly irreverent tone of voice. There were no sacred cows for him" (*SB*, p. 307). Mhonyera's generous comments have the ring of truth but Marechera wasn't always confrontational. He could broach sensitive issues with great subtlety, as his unperformed play, *The Stimulus of Scholarship*, demonstrates. The play was written in the first weeks of his return when he was staying (illicitly) on the campus at the University of Zimbabwe, having moved there from the hotel into which he had been booked by Austin. Parts of the play were published in *Focus* at the University of Zimbabwe in 1983/1984. Other parts have not been found and it has not been published elsewhere neither has it been performed.

On his return to a highly politicized, socialist Zimbabwe Marechera, the quintessentially individualist aesthete[111] demonstrated his commitment to the construction of a "new" Zimbabwe. In his play *The Stimulus of Scholarship: A Drama by Buddy* he addresses such sensitive issues as racism, power and privilege. The action, which "takes place at the University of Rhodesia in the late 1950s and early sixties," is based on actual events and the characters are thinly disguised figures from the time. For example, "Hudson" is an alias for Terence Ranger (author of *Revolt in Southern Rhodesia 1896-1897*, see above) who was a history lecturer at the University of Rhodesia, a political activist and a renowned anti-color bar campaigner; "Sarah," is Sarah Chavunduka the first black female student to attend the University. The "color bar" of the 50s and 60s on which the play concentrates was a theme still vivid in the memory but was also part of "history" and by focussing on a white liberal hero Marechera avoids a simple post-independence anti-white racism. He is also able to suggest that those who ignore the lessons of history may be condemned to repeat them.

Dramatically very effective, the play also has complex and thought-provoking twists, such as the glee of the racist newspaperman (Wolfe of the *Sunday Mule*) at being able to satirize the blacks and the liberals with his photograph of Hudson being knocked into a swimming pool:

> Wolfe: [*to Citizen One*] Just once more. Yes
> that's it, scowl. [*His camera flashes*] Got it. I'll
> caption it "This is outrageous." Jesus, what a
> day. I think for once we've got the guy tied up
> neatly. There is nothing like apt ridicule to
> fumigate the agitators. (*SB*, p. 101)

The double irony of Wolfe's pronouncements would not have been lost on a post-independence audience. Neither would the patronizing reference to the simple and "pure" native have been lost in this disarming comic song:

Good King Baudouin first looked out
As he courted Farida
  When Lumumba came in sight
  Rigged out in his bowler
  Bring me tanks and bring me guns
  Said Baudouin to his batman:
  I have got some leftwing ranks
  But none as bad as that one
  To pray for your salvation
  If the native's heart be pure
  He won't need education.

A parody of the Christmas carol, Good King Wenceslas (itself a hymn to patronage and popular in the Mission schools) is sung by candle-holding students as part of a Rag Revue. Once more Marechera is using history to draw a parallel with the current situation in Zimbabwe. Here he subtly implies the country is in danger of repeating the catastrophe that followed the creation of Zaire out of the former Belgian Congo. As that catastrophe involved corruption and murder at the highest levels of government this was an audacious attempt at lifting political awareness.

The stage directions to this passage indicate a scene of vitality and color as "Bottles of beer are drunk." Whistles and "obscene jokes" feature in a cabaret and white male students wearing female underwear sing, accompanied by white female majorettes, while floats " . . . as bizarre as the actors think fit . . . figures from cartoon strips, from the history of slavery and colonialism, images from the paranoid white imagination," cross the stage. The scene closes on a bitter note as a black student approaches Citizen One: "Black student: Will you give something for charity, sir? Citizen One: Willingly. [He spits in the student's face. The student retreats.]" (*SB*, p. 103). It is tragic that this promising work should have been published only in a student magazine. Such work seems to suggest that had circumstances been different, had Marechera been handled with more sensitivity by colleagues and the authorities, then perhaps he could have contributed to the "struggle," he could have been "a useful citizen" (*Mindblast*, p. 45).

Marechera did try to contribute on a wider scale than just through his writing but circumstances were against him. He stood for Secretary – General of the Writers Union in 1984 only to be beaten by the narrow margin of four votes by Musa Zimunya – unfortunately his behavior after the defeat so angered the union that they refused to offer him assistance when he was arrested at the Book Fair later that year. Relationships with his contemporaries deteriorated until meaningful communication was impossible:

> The few other writers in the city also seem paralyzed by the ungainly atmosphere; we eye each other with the oblique glance of mistrust, competitiveness, and when we are not busy pontificating to tired reporters, we casually stab each other in the back. It all seems hopeless.
> (*Scrapiron Blues*, p. 26)

In an intelligent and practical attempt to use his expertise for the benefit of his emerging society he attempted to set up a literary agency. As he recounts in the "Journal" section of *Mindblast* (pp. 133-4) this was a disaster, partly due to the enormous and unmanageable amount of interest it attracted, and partly because of police harassment.

However, what may eventually be recognized as a dramatic *tour de force* did emerge from this difficult period. If *The Stimulus of Scholarship: a Drama by Buddy* showed Marechera's potential as a dramatist then *Mindblast Part One, The Skin of Time: Plays by Buddy* is a revelation.

5.3 Mindblast

"A very, very personal conflict."
When I walk down the street, those wide, paved

streets of the hot City, I feel in my bones that it
is no longer a theoretical battle between different
ideas of Africanness but a very, very personal
conflict between Harare and I. *Mindblast* (p.
132)

Within a year of his arrival back in Zimbabwe Marechera
had written the pieces that were collected and published in 1984
as *Mindblast*. In an interview with Fiona Lloyd in May 1986
Marechera said:

Mindblast is based on contemporary Harare . . .
There is no particular Harare psyche or
mentality. That is why the book consists of many
voices. I divided it into different sections trying
to use at once a fictional or Orwellian style
mixed with a kind of iconoclastic technique; and
mixing poetry with drama and with the diary
form. (*SB*, p. 311)

His comments on the structure of the book have the flavor
of intellectualized afterthought and there is more than a hint of
self-justification. The work he generated on his return to Harare
and published as *Mindblast* is a miscellany written over a period
of time and brought together for the purposes of publication. The
collection confirms his qualities as a writer of memorable prose;
it also shows him to be an accomplished and sensitive lyric poet
and a dramatist with a fine sense of theater.

Mindblast is representative of a time and place, and can be
seen as a metaphor for contemporary Harare at a time when the
newly independent Zimbabwe was experimenting with new
directions and encountering new experiences. However, it is,
perhaps, on analysis, more representative of the writer and of his
state of mind. Quite possibly Marechera's comments to Lloyd
represent his own analysis of the published work rather than his
original intention as he intimates. On the other hand, being back
in Harare gave an external focus to his work which, in *Mindblast*
unlike the London works, is recognisably operating within the

three spheres of person, place, and time.

5.3.1   *Mindblast* **Part One**

The Skin of Time: Plays by Buddy

Though as lucid and accessible as *The Stimulus of Scholarship*, *The Skin of Time* is not based on historical "facts" and, as a later work reflecting his own experiences of the "new" Zimbabwe, is understandably less "public-spirited" in theme and approach. In view of the political climate of the Eighties it had no chance of being performed. Marechera would certainly have been aware of this, intensifying his alienation still further.

Effectively the "plays" constitute a single drama in three acts. Act One – The Coup – sets the scene with a neat satirical point though the coup has been transferred from political history to a business transaction. The action takes place "Any [where] in the Third World." Act Two – "The Gap" – is in "Zimbabwe" and Act Three – "Blitzkrieg" – is set in "Norman Drake's house in Harare, Zimbabwe. The immediate vicinity of the toilet." Significantly, as the focus tightens to become specifically Hararean, the time of the action in Act Three is "Zimbabwean Party Time."

Characterization is dependent on caricature rather than being fully developed. However, it works successfully through the farce stereotype (particularly in Act Three), in some ways reminiscent of the work of Joe Orton, and Marechera is able to demonstrate his sure hand with crisp and pithy dialogue, clean, incisive and full of life.

> Manager: There's such a thing as Justice, Drake. [*Ominously*] And Prison. The disgrace. I could never look even a skunk straight in the eye.
> Drake: Justice, Spotty? It doesn't exist. There is only the Law and that's fuck all to do with Justice. (*Mindblast*, p. 11)

The Manager (Spotty) and Drake (who is accused of theft) are "white" and the first act explores the relationship between the two, one a conventional conformist, the other a rakish amoralist:

> Manager: You've been leaning on me all your crooked life, Drake. I allowed it, positively enjoyed it. It made the likes of me – the spotty nonentity called the silent majority – feel at least useful. If I could not aspire to greatness I could at least cheer greatness. You've been my hero for a long time, Drake, something I knew I could never be ...I forgot that those above us seldom look down to see where they put their feet. (p. 11)

Drake reminds him that he used to protect Spotty from the bullies at school, and provide him with girls. But the Manager argues this was only "when it suited your image" (p. 12) and goes on to give a symbolic vision of the social structure based on their relationship:

> Manager: ...Insults from one's personal hero are not the same as insults from nonentities. I treasured your casual insolence, your unthinking cruelty. That is how the spotty silent majority becomes the compost heap upon which criminal tyranny flourishes. (p. 12)

The warning note implicit in Spotty's remarks, in which white berates white, would not have been lost on a post-independence audience contemplating the actions of the first black administration. That warning is made even more pointed by Drake's response, which is initially personal but develops a larger symbolic dimension:

> Drake: ... All these years I have had nothing but pure hatred for you, Spotty. A voluptuous contempt for you and your ilk who think life is merely following others. And when for some reason you lose track of the leader's manner, you

sneak out of liquorice-stained pockets slimy half-baked notions of justice and morality and sit there and enjoy like a cat with a mouse playing with me before you fire me and call the police. [*Spits*] Spotty, you will never change your spots. [*Silence*]. (p. 14)

Dynamic action is maintained on the stage as the Manager places "so-called Shona sculptures from Zimbabwe" (apparently stolen by Drake) around the office. The act closes with a flurry of action as Drake effects his coup by assaulting the Manager, taking over his position, and proposing a toast heavy with cynicism " . . . May the spots on the earth of silent majorities increase and multiply" (p. 17). As a final act a Japanese accomplice throws the Manager out of the office.

The first act is then a witty allegory of the white role in the transition to Independence; Spotty represents the ideological muddle of the typical white "silent majority." Drake is the cynical manipulator who makes corrupt deals (with Japanese help) with members of the incoming black government to oust him. The style is expressionist farce but with a conventional political thrust.

In Act Two Spotty has decided to "take the gap" (that is, go to South Africa) in style, and is busy with explosives preparing to destroy his house. A running theme is the failure of Spotty and his son, Dick, to communicate clearly (the generation "gap"?).

Spotty: You know, Dick, there was a time when we were all really happy.
Dick: Would that be the night I was conceived?
Spotty: [*Slowly*] I guess I've brought you up all wrong. (p. 22)

Dick is asked to bring the "Castor Oil" which is "under the bed by the bedpan" (p. 23) and with surreal stupidity consistently brings the wrong thing until finally in a moment of high farce he brings the bed itself. As the curtain falls, he collapses in tears at his inability to please his father.

The action and dialogue move at a cracking pace and the characters are witty and articulate, sacrificing realism in Wildean fashion to heighten the satiric comedy. This adds to the virtuoso theatrical effect of the basic situation, with Spotty holding a grenade (and on occasions threatening to pull the pin) while engaged in angry telephone conversations with Drake and Jane, and actual conversations with Dick and Arabella.

Symbolically, Act Three takes place outside the toilet in Norman Drake's house:

> 3rd Man: . . . See what I mean about the country going to the dogs? All these shortages of essential things! We are queuing for cooking oil, we're queuing for matches, we're queuing for bread, and NOW WE ARE QUEUING FOR LAVATORIES! And for what?
> 5th Man: To shit decently, of course. (p. 41)

One can readily suppose that this exchange would have been well received by a contemporary audience. As in this theatrical work he is writing only dialogue Marechera reveals a lighter touch than that evident in the longer works with their descriptive and reflective approach. In *The Skin of Time* he avoids the philosophical excesses of his prose; as a result his "message" is much clearer and the impact more apparent. However, the following extract with its vivid evocation of post-independence disillusion is redolent of the prose fiction. It is at the center of a two-page speech, eight times longer than anything else in the play and the only example of the familiar confessional outpourings of the prose, which in production would surely have required severe pruning. There is reference to, among others, traditional African values, street life in Harare, CND demonstrations in London, the Brixton riots, Hamlet, Linton Kwesi Johnson, and the National Front in typically frenetic Marecheran fashion. With that in mind this clear and unequivocal statement is all the more refreshing:

. . . I was discovering that there are many shades
of black but the only true one is that of the have-
nots. Don't mean to sound bitter—yes I do mean
to sound bitter, but it seems to me for all the
ideals our independence is supposed to represent,
it's still the same old ox-wagon of the rich
getting richer and the poor getting poorer.
There's even an attempt to make poverty a holy
and acceptable condition. You say you're hungry,
and the shef peers over his three chins down at
you and says Comrade, you're the backbone of
the revolution as if your life's ambition is to be
thin and lean as a mosquito's backbone. And you
try to say "Shef, I don't want to be the backbone,
I want to be the big belly of the struggle against
neo-colonialism like the one you got there under
that Castro beard." And before you even finish
what you are saying he's got the CIO and the
police and you are being marched at gunpoint to
the interrogation barracks. I'm not saying that
there's such a thing as an absence of free speech.
Rather there's an excess of it to feed the
numerous ears that have been unleashed "for
security reasons." (*Mindblast*, pp. 37/38)
Here the medium does not obscure the message.

Stanley Nyamfukudza had to do battle with the College
Press to get *Mindblast* published as they considered the book
anti-government. Surprisingly, in view of the above passage,
when the book appeared Nyamfukudza was able to claim "not a
murmur of protest was heard." This is not strictly true:
Marechera was badly beaten by a "colonel in the Zimbabwean
army" who accused him of "filthy writings" that defamed his
country and his government." On the other hand Veit-Wild noted
that the book was well received "...especially among the young
Zimbabwean readership" (*SB*, pp. 335/339).

The dialogue in *The Skin of Time* is powerful but so also is the sense of stagecraft. Marechera handles his characters with great skill from the relatively restrained movement of the sculptures scene in Act One, the "bed, bedpan, castor oil" running joke in Act Two, through to the mass fight in Act Three. The action is unrelenting. It would work brilliantly on stage.

The Skin of Time is a satirical farce in which, significantly, a cynical white is in control, abetted by a Japanese entrepreneur, bribing the black politician and being pursued by the politician's would-be sophisticated wife. The satire is even-handed throughout. Everyone, men and women, black and white, young and old, is contemptible. As moral therapy and a cathartic antidote to official jargon it is superb: "When I say a thing it means exactly what I want it to mean, no more, and no less" (*Mindblast*, p. 15). In view of the attention that his published work has attracted it is ironic that an unperformed drama may well be Marechera's most lasting achievement. It will certainly take its place as a pioneer work in any Zimbabwean dramatic tradition, which may eventually unfold.

Described as a sequel to "The Toilet" and published in *Scrapiron Blues* in both English and Shona language versions, "The Servant's Ball" is a one-act play featuring the "below stairs" characters from "The Skin of Time." The drama is more conventional in genre than "The Skin of Time," relying on a keen social realism that explores the relationship between the classes and highlights the divisive effects of the "new order." "The Servant's Ball" is the only known instance of Marechera writing in Shona and may reflect his effort at being "a useful citizen" and, perhaps, an attempt to counter charges of elitism in his writing. In addition to writing in Shona Marechera makes use of work songs and dance, suggesting that "The Servant's Ball" may have been an attempt to recreate folk drama, or at least to introduce a traditional art form within a Western context.

The action takes place in the servant's quarters in Norman Drake's house in Harare. The central theme is the plight of the working class in the newly independent Zimbabwe: "Thomas:

These white people and the chefs have a really good time, but they should think about who clears up the mess after them. Me! (*Scrapiron Blues*, p. 74) – but there is also reference to the strained relations between the generations:

> Granny Mberi: You young people of today are just a load of shit thrown in the way of us older people. We can't even walk without fear of treading on your shit.
> Thomas: You are really talking through your arse, old lady. How can you imagine it's us the youth, who are the future of Zimbabwe? (*Scrapiron Blues*, p. 74)

As employers, black Zimbabweans are compared unfavorably with whites in an exchange that would have appealed to the "povo" in the audience.

> Thomas: It does not matter how these whites behave as long as they give you your money.
> Bonzo: What I don't like are the black chefs. They make you work like an ox in the field.
> Granny Mberi: You have to be careful with them. You may not be paid for three months in a row. And they also bring some of those relatives of theirs who do not know how to use the toilet. (pp. 77-78)

In a clear demonstration that Marechera's sympathies were not with the government Thomas is given beer and cigarettes by Norman Drake as a "reward," which he then sells to his friends, thereby illustrating how black and white combine to exploit the working-class Zimbabwean:

> Granny Mberi: Get off all of you. What harm has my son done? Isn't he the one who is giving you beer and letting you enjoy yourselves here?
> Majazi: It's his neo-colonialism. If he was giving it to us for free I would understand. But he is charging us fifty cents for a packet of Chibuku. Thirty-five cents for a small cup of kachusu.

> Four cents for one cigarette. Thomas, you are
> just as smart as your boss. All the money we
> work for ends up here when we pay for your
> beer. (p. 80)

Significantly the play ends with the proposed marriage of a white man (Dick) and a black woman (Raven) and the toast, "Let us drink some beer to those who love each other and kiss each other – these are what the politicians call the future of Zimbabwe!" (p. 84). The implicit irony is confirmed by the fact that the marriage can take place only because it has been condoned the politicians.

At the curtain the assembled cast gather to shout (in their various languages, Shona, English, Ndebele, Nyanja, and so on) "THE FUTURE OF ZIMBABWE" (p. 84). Here, perhaps, Marechera is satisfying his role as social commentator on the new Zimbabwe by suggesting that the way forward is by a combination of the efforts of all Zimbabweans. At the same time he is able to fulfill his own chosen role as a cosmopolitan artist by the polyglot nature of the closing paean.

If "The Skin of Time" was ever to be produced then "The Servant's Ball" could be introduced as a very effective final act. The use of music – a mbira (a small hand piano, often made from scrap metal) is played throughout – singing and dance would be a rousing finale, particularly as the play closes on a vision of hope for the future. It is a matter of great regret that the play was not produced for a contemporary audience who would surely have left the theater moved and even perhaps inspired by the experience.

Perhaps confirming the ironic reference to the mixed marriage in "The Servant's Ball" Marechera presents an entirely different view of miscegenation in "Alien to the People." Jack, who is black, has married Jane, a white woman, and the play is concerned with the evident culture clash. As one of the characters explains to the couple:

Whitney: The blacks think that you are showing off to them that you are [*leering*] screwing a white woman. And the whites think you are deliberately tweaking their nose and rubbing it in shit. (*Scrapiron Blues*, p. 89)

The play ends in a gun battle in which Jack and Jane's daughter is killed as government forces attempt to rescue the couple. A melodrama, "Alien to the People" is a vicious and harsh expose of the tensions between black and white in Zimbabwe that has none of the humor of "The Gap" and none of the sanguine undertones of "The Servant's Ball." Nevertheless it is a powerful drama written in a straightforward and accessible manner.

Rather less straightforward is "The Alley," an expressionist drama and a blackly sardonic two-hander in which the history of colonialism is seen as an insane mixture of the tragic and the absurd. In this exchange Robin, who is white, is addressing Rhodes, who, with heavy irony, is black, and has just been released from prison:

> Rhodes; Give us a sip man. It's me, Rhodes.
> RHODES.
> Robin [*blindly, groping through a fog of alcohol*]: Never met the bugger. He was in diamonds wasn't he? Got me into all this mess with his Cape to Cairo. [*Peering at Rhodes*] If you're him, you've sure got one hell of a suntan [*Offers bottle, Rhodes drinks, puzzled*] Know where I've come from, friend do you? [*Rhetorical pause*] CHIKURUBI. [a prison in Harare]
> Rhodes: I know. I know. [*He sits with back against the wall*] It's terrible. I've been there myself once or twice. First time we were sentenced together, remember?
> Robin [*half remembering*}: Yes. You and your Cape to Cairo ideas. Painting the whole world

red (*Scrapiron Blues*, p.34).

The drama pursues the classic Brechtian theme of the problems of survival in chaotic, difficult times and there are obvious echoes of Beckett in that the two characters are tramps:

> Rhodes: But we are all brothers now. Comrades Down and Out alias Black and White. Solicitors of the renowned Alley. [*Pause*] I'll drink to your health.
> Robin: And I, yours. [*They toast, exchanging the bottle; wiping his mouth*] Tell me – how did you come to be in this situation? Not that I'm prying, you know. You seem educated and all that.
> Rhodes: Don't know really. Got to the top once but then everything slid from under me. Know what I mean? [*Robin nods*] But maybe it had to happen. There was always something . . . missing.
> Robin: It's God who is always missing. When you really want God-knows want Him, He's never there . . . But Rhodes was always there even when he was not there. Did you know his statue is still lurking around somewhere covered in brambles and weeds in the Botanical Gardens? Honest. [*Thoughtfully*] We'll never be free of the bastard! [*Looks at Rhodes, surprised*] YOU are here – what did I tell you! [*Drinks wildly*] Drink is the only medicine that can drive him from my mind. [*Pause*] Can you tell me where I am?
> Rhodes: Harare. (*Scrapiron Blues*, pp34-35)

The wall of the alley has symbolic significance both as a physical barrier representing the divide between black and white, [Rhodes] "I am your wall, and you are my wall" (*Scrapiron Blues*, p. 46), and as a psychological barrier:

> Rhodes: [*Robin is still staring at the wall*] Oh, quit it, Robin, there's nothing there just a wall.
> Robin [*abstractedly*]: Yes . . . a wall. I'm trying

to remember when I last saw it. [*Thinks*] Know what's behind that wall? It's something that wants me. Something that has always wanted me from the very beginning of human life. It's there and it's not there. [*Hoarsely*] Sometimes I mistook it for my own desires, my own needs. (*Scrapiron Blues*, p. 38)

Marechera's use of sardonic humor (Rhodes is black, and in one scene becomes a black woman, for example) serves to emphasize the overall tone, which is consistently one of despair and bitterness, as this hauntingly beautiful extract indicates:

Rhodes [*He picks up the iron bar and savagely attacks the wall. A very prolonged thin mournful wail, like a fierce wind drawing nearer and nearer, howls as though from a tomb*]: Listen, that's the song that will forever blow like an unsettled spirit from the Zambezi – through Harare, Bulawayo, Mutare, Gweru, down the Limpopo and back again to the Zambezi – from which it will again turn restlessly back searching for you and me so that again and again we can retell their story, which is not our story. Listen to it. How sad, how profound, and yet so heartbreakingly pitiful. (*Scrapiron Blues*, p. 46)

The play closes on a note of reconciliation as the two men leave together. But it is a reconciliation tinged with hopelessness. [Robin] "Rhodes, let's eat. I know one day we'll try to kill each other again but I call it quits for today" (*Scrapiron Blues*, p. 47).

"The Alley" is an intense expression of Marechera's troubled view of human life and human society in contemporary Zimbabwe. In common with the prose fiction the individual in this powerful drama is depicted as being alone in a society that is disintegrating. Unfortunately, in the prevailing political climate of the early 1980s "The Alley" had little chance of public performance.

Veit-Wild confirms that Marechera lost or destroyed many more manuscripts than survived his erratic lifestyle. The few plays that remained, be they farce, folk drama, melodrama, expressionism or social realism, are sufficient evidence of his skill and versatility as a dramatist. However, not for the first time, the overriding emotion on reading Marechera's plays is a painful sense of loss for what might have been. For all their concentration and vivid effects, there is a certain shortwindedness about these works. And because he could not establish a place for himself within the new Zimbabwe his work was largely ignored and his plays remained unperformed. That is as much a tragedy for the development of Zimbabwean theater as it was for the artist.

5.3.2 *Mindblast* Part Two

Grimknife Junior's Story

Mindblast Part Two offers a return to the more wordy and introspective mode characteristic of the writer. Having said that, Marechera did offer a clear, focused and unambiguous explanation of his motivation in writing the book. In an interview with Alle Lansu he commented:

> . . . I don't think our independence so far has made any significant change as far as the working class is concerned, especially for those who became fighters. They joined ZANLA [Zimbabwe African National Liberation Army] or ZIPRA [Zimbabwe People's Revolutionary Army] before they finished their education. Most of them are unemployed and live in the streets. This is what I wrote about in *Mindblast*. (*SB*, p. 35)

As the plays indicate Marechera was certainly capable of dealing with the issue of change in postcolonial Zimbabwe particularly as it affected those at a distance from the locus of power. That issue is implicit throughout *Grimknife Junior's Story* but the story is more notable for the signs of Marechera's growing concern for his own mental health, always fragile but now exacerbated by his harsh lifestyle and the lack of recognition for his work:

> He [Tony] had studied all over Europe under some of the best modern European sculptors. His work was totally cosmopolitan, nothing to do with any particular tradition. After the revolution he had returned only to find his sculptures denounced by critics left and right. His work, they said, is incomprehensible. It has nothing to do with the national historic traditions. And the tourists and dealers of course only wanted to buy "genuine" Shona pieces. It seemed unless Tony joined the numerous "anthropological" Shona sculptors, he would starve or something worse. (*Mindblast*, p. 59)

Here the writer quite clearly confronts the issue of the relation between the artist and society, between aesthetics and ideology. The options appear to be very simple: follow the party line or "starve or something worse." "Something worse," I suggest, hints at Marechera's fear of insanity. It is not difficult to imagine the dilemma of this gifted and sensitive artist torn between his "duty" (as an artist) to the political institutions building a "new" nation and his own sense of commitment as an individual and an artist to nation building. Little wonder perhaps that a recurring theme in *Mindblast* is the writer's preoccupation with the fear of going mad, for example, "boggle the mind right out of your skull" (p. 51), "at the uttermost mercy of his phantoms" (p. 54), "insanity just around the corner" (p. 59), "Buddy dreaded going round the bend" (p. 62), "the donkey work of keeping sane" (p. 63).

Mindblast Part Two comprises a short story, *Grimknife Junior's Story*, which focuses on "Buddy" (Dambudzo) a poet "typing in the square" (p. 51) and "writing poetry in bars, drinking with all and sundry (p. 61). *Grimknife Junior's Story*, like some of the earlier works, is a thinly disguised recounting of Marechera's own experiences in which the characters are not developed beyond the point where they are any more than Marechera's attempts to come to terms with those experiences.

The story opens with a Prologue, an ambitious attempt at an allegorical fantasy in which a "fat giant cat" called "Rix" (p. 45)"[112] is reeducating Grimknife Junior. The purpose of the meeting, which takes place in the bush, is to transform Grimknife Junior into a "useful citizen" (p. 45). The giant cat is a reorientation officer in the pay of the government (significantly Bulgakov's "huge black cat" was in league with the devil). Marechera may also be implying that there are similarities between 1980s Zimbabwe and 1930s Russia as Bulgakov was compelled to write *The Master and Margarita* in secret in order to avoid Stalin's stranglehold on Russian artists and intellectuals. Although comparisons between Mugabe's regime and Stalin are invidious there is no doubt that Marechera was firmly of the opinion that the Central Intelligence Organization had him under constant surveillance. On one tragicomic occasion he was approached by a doting schoolboy who had scoured Harare looking for him, Marechera berated the boy for his approach and accused him of being "a small trainee of a CIO agent" (*SB*, p. 390).

Grimknife cannot understand the official ideological jargon and constantly asserts his own feelings and existential responses: "Something was definitely not too his liking. But he could not put a finger on it. These garish sunsets had it in for him" (p. 45). In the following extract Marechera (as Grimknife) makes a clear statement of the problems he was facing personally, and also alludes to the directing influence of public institutions that tended to prescribe the "duties" of the artist:

> Rix was the Reorientation Officer . . . Grimknife Junior was the mental delinquent who had been dragged here to be reorientated.
> "Well, Grimknife, we are in this together. I'm

here to help you. Help you become a useful citizen,"
"What's that – a useful citizen?"
"Someone who does what he is told. Someone who says exactly what others say. Someone who is the spitting image of Duty, Responsibility, and Patriotism."
Grimknife Junior looked blank,
"You're still talking rot, Officer Rix," he muttered. (p. 45)

Rix and Grimknife continue the dialogue in which Rix demands "Your business should further the aims of the P.E. [Progressive Effort]" (p. 47), and an increasingly desperate Grimknife defends his position. He cannot understand what crime he has committed but is told that his "other" crime is "Using obscene language":
"What have you got against decent language?"
"It's obscenely unnatural," the youth countered.
Decency is unnatural?"
"It is – to natural people."
"Those are dissidents."
"Look, Officer Rix, earlier on you called me a mental delinquent. What's that?"
"You do not think the way everyone else thinks"
The youth, amazed, looked hard at Rix. (p. 46)

The gulf between the two, Grimknife and Rix, the public institution and the private individual, is so wide that Grimknife cannot even agree that two and two equal four when Rix tells him so, "I am trying to find your four but it's not there in my heart." Marechera the writer is here indicating that he would like to follow the dictates of the new government but he cannot offer the blind obedience required. In Kierkegaardian terms, he cannot take a "leap of absurdity" (see below). He must be free to express what is "in his heart" even if it is something so apparently illogical as the refusal to accept two and two equal four. On being told by Rix that unless by midnight he has "experienced the transformation we demand of you then you will be hanged by the neck until you are dead" (p. 49) Grimknife responds by musing: "What exactly would die on the gallows? He had not the faintest idea?" (p. 49). This questioning of his own identity and purpose is followed by a type of transformation as Grimknife's eyes glow (with inspiration?) and blue flashes come from his tongue as he begins to tell his story.

At this point the political satire and the science fiction setting are arbitrarily abandoned and Grimknife's story becomes a series of inner monologues. The first section focuses on Buddy, who is "penniless, homeless and friendless" (p. 51), but driven on by his writing: "He had the writing to look forward to each day – those peaceful mornings in the square. Hungry for poetic inspiration." (p. 51). As in the Prologue, Marechera argues for artistic freedom although there is a clear indication that the writer recognizes this leaves him open to the charge of being no more than a self-indulgent, bourgeois individualist:

> He had tried to publish his poems – and that had produced several laughs. Against him. They had laughed him out of their offices. His poems, they said, were capitalist trash.
> "We want poems that will uplift the people," they said.
> "But…"
> "Know what's wrong with you?" they said.
> He shook his head but in his semiology meaning that he did know.
> "Your education," they said. "You were educated by capitalists and now you write capitalist poems which have nothing to do with our socialist purposes . . . We want simplicity and purpose, something the workers and peasants can understand…" (pp. 51/52)

Interestingly, "workers and peasants" is Ngugi's socialist mantra and it is in the Hararean works that Marechera struggled to move closer to an accord with Ngugi's view of the artist as teacher. The crucial question for both is one of who dictates the content of the teaching. In Ngugi's, case he was exiled, his play *I Will Marry When I Want* was banned because of its political satire, and the theater razed to the ground. As for Marechera, as Veit-Wild argues:

> The book [*Mindblast*] emerged from a complex period in the writer's life; a time of physical and psychological struggle which was richly creative. Marechera was spurred on by his disillusionment; his writing drew energy from his scathing criticism of post-Independence society and his resentment at being marginalized. While others were still intoxicated by the optimism and euphoria of Independence, he named the social diseases he observed around him: materialism, political intolerance, corruption, deceptive socialist rhetoric, growing social inequalities. (*SB* p. 309)

In a sense Marechera's fate of being "exiled" within his own country rather than outside it was a fate worse than Ngugi's. After *Mindblast* he found it impossible to get his work published. Even though he continued to write prolifically there was little chance of his work reaching an audience.

The second section of Grimknife Junior's Story begins with Buddy being knifed by an irate cuckolded husband. After attention at the hospital Buddy ends up phantasmagorically talking in a bar to "the Grimknife" who, somewhat inadvertently, seems to be both the person who knifed him and his own alter ego (the framework in which it is Grimknife who is telling the story seems to have been forgotten by now). In the bar Buddy watches a character called Tony dancing (Tony appears in several of the stories that were later collected in *Scrapiron Blues*). Once more Marechera pursues the dilemma of the artist in a developing society stating, "Tony's sculpture had been found not of the people." Buddy/Tony/Marechera is unable to comply with the desires of the official patrons and institutions and so "would starve or something worse." Buddy sums up the work's overall theme: "This shebeen was the field hospital of the uncompromising artists who refused to be fashioned by the Philistine's hammer and anvil. With insanity just round the corner . . . "(p. 59). Marechera pursues this theme persistently, linking it to the search for self that was a feature of the London novels: "Those in the shebeen clung to that dream, the individual can only find his society by searching to the utmost in himself." This approach served only to increase his alienation: "You suffered the insults of the bureaucrats, the kicks of the police, the puzzled amusement of school mates . . . The malicious gossip of relatives disappointed that you were not interested in using your education to make money" (p. 60).

Ironically, the final scene of the last of the fictional narratives published in his lifetime closes with the words: "With a last insistent shriek of defiance, he tried to rise, with all his strength, to rise, denounce, hurl curses to the sky, but his strength failed. Dr Grimknife, banging the door outside, calling to him, heard the loud sickening thud of the poet's fall." (*Mindblast*, p. 72).

There is an ominous significance about the poet's death at the end of Part Two. Unlike those recorded in his earlier works, it is not a rite of passage. It does not lead to a rebirth. This death is final; the poet is dead and will write no more. Such passages are familiar in all Marechera's works but the difference here is that there is no way forward. It seems that the focus afforded by being back in Harare demonstrated to him that his writing had no place in the newly independent Zimbabwe. Marechera was unpredictable and erratic in his dealings with people but he was, nevertheless, intelligent and perceptive. In spite of his rhetoric and his public stances the politically astute Marechera would have known that he had no future there. He also knew he was unable to leave.

5.3.3 *Mindblast* **Part Three**

Buddy's selected poems

Mindblast Part Three consists of one long poem, "Throne of Bayonets," and forty short poems and fragments. Marechera is a poet of exceptional quality, and the study of his poetry deserves a volume to itself – that is a work for the future. The central focus of this work is on Marechera's prose and plays, so I do not intend to engage with his poetry in any great detail. However it is appropriate to look selectively at some of the work that appears in *Mindblast*. Some of the themes are familiar – "Rather my butchered father/ On a mortuary slab, and I/ All of eleven years old, refusing/ But forced to look." (p. 77) – and the strangely vivid and memorable imagery so strong in the prose is perhaps even more powerfully wrought in the poetry: "The poem screams quietly; / Like flying fish in the oilstrewn burning sea/ The poem is dying alive" (p. 80).

There are indications that the maturing writer was becoming more self-critical. For example, in the "Throne of Bayonets" it appears that he is beginning to question his own experimentalism:

Or so seduce the sense
From the meaning
With experiments random
And indistinct construction
That I resort to the label Post-Modernist?
O for Black Rain to cleanse the blues! (p. 83)

The above could merely represent Marechera's version of the criticisms that had been leveled at his earlier works, but it could also be an indication that he was developing artistically through self-criticism. The same poem offers a powerful and moving evocation of his plight:

How to face alone
This Christian festive dawn?
Nowhere to go: everywhere the slow

> But inevitable approach,
> I live like a folded newspaper
> Abandoned on the front lawn of a deserted dream.
>   "The people as a whole
>   Must come before individuals." (pp. 88-89)

It is Christmas, he is alone and contemplating death, he is unfulfilled, the newspaper, like his potential, hasn't been "unfolded." "Abandoned" he has no role in the creation of the nation which is, in any event, a "deserted dream." At the center of this desolation is the dilemma of the demands of the nation versus the needs of the individual. It was a dilemma he never resolved, as the painfully self-critical "The Footnote To Hamlet" reveals:

> Now or never is here again. Must I
> Look in the face the moon's other side?
> The moment demands decision. My whole
> History is unequal to it – Let me be!
>
> I read all day, walk all night. I have
> No end but this; no resources but books.
>
> Thus again I dawdle and dither. Perhaps
> Th'impatient problem will lose heart at my
> Expert vacillation. (p. 97)

Regret and self doubt are very evident in this poem which, along with others has a clarity rarely found in the prose.

In "Mind in Residence," he once more contemplates death and looks back at his life, perhaps contemplating "what might have been."

> On grey twilit balconies
> In T-shirts and shirt sleeves
> Each shrouded in preoccupied misty thoughts
> The several pasts of my life
> Wait for this and all other days to end.
> Down in the street, antlike thoughts in rags and overalls

Leaning against the derelict buildings
Squatting on the cracked much-stained pavement
All looking up at those looking down
From the grey twilit balconies of hindsight. (p. 116)

The repetition of "grey twilit balconies" in the last line loops back to the first line of the poem to begin again, a circularity matched within the poem as those "looking up" look at those "looking down" who are looking at those looking up. In this way the poet is reflecting on the actions of the past, which he acknowledges are beyond redemption ("shrouded") but which are responsible for his present parlous condition, in "rags and overalls" living in urban squalor. The poignant reference to hindsight suggests a large measure of regret as his future holds nothing more that the prospect of waiting "for this and all other days to end."

5.4   Part Four: Appendix

From the "Journal"

Stanley Nyamfukudza was an editor for the publishers, College Press, and he had to be convinced that the "Journal" should be published as part of *Mindblast*: " . . . he [Marechera] wanted the autobiographical section included and I did not agree. We had a couple of encounters in the Norfolk Bar and elsewhere. I finally conceded" (*SB*, p. 339). The "Journal," which was written by Marechera using a miniature typewriter while sitting on a park bench, appears to cover a period of little more than a week. It is a collection of short pieces, conversational in tone, in which Marechera observes his own behavior as a "cynical bitterbrained and drained novelist . . . sitting in Cecil Square, drinking sour milk in bitter but ingenious mood, homeless but unbroken, having given up people, I was in the wordtrap of the eerie insight born of constantly drunken vision" (*Mindblast* pp. 121-22).

As a recounting of his experiences the "Journal" has distinct echoes of Marechera's previous works. These lines from the second paragraph – "I did not know where I was going. I did not care. I was carrying in a plastic bag all my possessions in the world" (p. 119) – are very similar to the opening sentences of *The House of Hunger*: "I got my things and left. The sun was coming up. I couldn't think where to go" (p. 6). The philosophies expressed here, that of the nomadic free spirit, although separated by some fifteen years, are identical. There is a certain sadness here in that Marechera was still "searching." But such consistency also shows, perhaps, that the writer maintained his integrity in very difficult circumstances. However, it was a consistency that led him into great difficulties as he was unable to reconcile his overwhelming desire for individual freedom with a commitment to the requirements of others. Whether that was his publishers, his friends or his country, his reaction was the same:

> . . . to insist upon . . . Your right to refuse to be labeled and to insist on your right to behave like anything other than anyone expects. Your right to say no for the pleasure of it. To insist on your right to confound all who insist on regimenting human impulses according to theories psychological, religious, historical, political etc...Insist upon your right to insist on the importance, the great importance, of whim. (*The House of Hunger*, p.122)

For the political and cultural nation-builders who became involved with Marechera on his return from exile his, at times infuriating, individualism was a major barrier to any joint enterprise.

In the "Journal" perhaps living out a personal myth in the manner of Dylan Thomas, Brendan Behan or Patrick Kavanagh,[113] he confirms his image as the writer tramp: "I am right now on a park bench typing this story and I am out there in the story" (p. 124). It was an image to which the youth of Harare responded very readily and have subsequently mythologized. Just how much this was so was impressed on me when discussing the writer with a group of young Zimbabweans in Harare in August 1995. This group of young men in their mid-twenties who were attending the first Dambudzo Marechera Symposium and could well represent what has been called the *Mindblast* generation, unfailingly admired the man. But they knew little of his work. They had all read something, usually some of the poetry, but had failed to come to grips with the prose. One student, aged 22, himself a poet, explained to me that when in London Marechera had earned money by giving lectures on the conditions in pre-Independence Zimbabwe. When I asked how he came by this information (which is certainly untrue), he merely smiled and said, "Everybody knows that." The existence of the *Mindblast* generation would have pleased Marechera had he shared Kavanagh's sentiment, "A man is immortal when his ideas are exciting to the young"[114].

The following passage offers insights into Marechera's intentions in writing the book as well as his speculation on how it might be received:

> How to split the atom of the story and in the mindblast survive the theme psychological holocaust. All this dead skin I have to scrape off with literary fingernails. And seed the clouds for the rain to come. Tears that have not been shed for ninety years. I feel cold, like a snake shedding its skin. Is that how the book will go. Firecrackers setting the thick of the night alight. No guidelines but whorls of starbursts, the terrible beauty of walking naked among men like trees to the newly sighted. I have just farted. A small warm explosion. *Mindblast* (p. 144)

The search for the essential self is seen here as the pure energy released by the splitting of the atom, Marechera contemplates surviving the resultant "psychological holocaust." As before, writing (his "literary fingernails") is to be the tool with which he penetrates the layers that have accumulated through the ninety years of colonial rule.

Interestingly, it seems the writer is looking to establish his own place in history, as he sees his work inspiring others to follow his lead, suggesting that his writing will seed the clouds of literary revolution to rain "new" works perhaps. Aware of his isolated position he feels "cold" having shed some of his "skins," that is, having rejected some of the current values and norms of Hararean society. He then fantasizes that his book will be as "a firecracker in the night," a succession of "starbursts" enlightening the partially sighted, the blind and the blinkered, and showing them (other Zimbabwean writers, presumably) the way forward. Aware of the idealistic hopelessness of such fantasy Marechera brutally punctures it with the crude announcement "I have just farted." The writer goes on to describe what is happening in the park:

> The men in green tunics are arguing about who should make their tea – it must be close to ten o'clock. The woman walking always three paces behind her husband, like a haiku. Like a lily. Like a lizard panting in the desert-hot rocks. Like a box of matches full of dead wasps. Like a pen that only writes when full of human blood. (p. 144)

The disjunction of the various images and the rapidity with which Marechera changes tack in this short passage is vivid and arresting if also somewhat disconcerting for the reader. Nevertheless, the sense of the existential moment of the writer's consciousness is brilliantly caught.

Quite obviously Marechera's return to Zimbabwe was not received with the warmth he might have expected. Of his critics he has this to say:

> The ones who have done me most wrong were those who loudly proclaimed the uniqueness of my work and – to my questions – when they could not explain what they meant or even show

that they had read it and I sneered in disbelief,
they became my uttermost critics. (p. 126)

Marechera does not, in the "Journal," that is, offer a reasoned
argument to counter his critics – perhaps he thought that
unnecessary – although he does offer a series of justifications and
explanations of his position:

> I did not care where my future lay, where my
> past was hiding out, where my present course
> would maroon me . . . I had not rejected the
> notion of human brotherhood; I could not
> accommodate its material ends" (p. 120); " . . .
> no longer a theoretical battle between different
> ideas of Africanness but a very, very personal
> conflict...A conflagration I can lose any time.
> Lose my life, lose my mind, or just end up
> maimed or concussed of all the things I do not
> take for granted" (p. 132);"A genuine writer
> must always be prepared to fight for his work. In
> fact he must expect all kinds of trouble from
> every quarter. There is no room for cowardice in
> writing" (p. 134); . . . these doldrums of my
> career – a career which I think will be adversely
> affected by my return to Zimbabwe, a country
> very paranoid about sex and politics. (p. 138)

Marechera was a courageous writer but, as mentioned
above, the running battle to survive increased his fears for his
mental health: "I probably looked burnt out, insane" (p. 119). He
feared the return of the illness that had plagued him in London "I
recognized the mood; once in London the mood of desperation
had lasted five years, punctuating itself with hopeless calls to the
Samaritans" (p. 119). In a chillingly detached manner he
considers killing himself: "The very possibility of suicide
fascinates and repels me. A terrible waste, and yet, an area to
explore" (p. 124).

The original title of the "Journal" was "Journal of the

Damned" and there is evidence to suggest that Marechera remained obsessed with his personal "slings and arrows" of misfortune to the extent that the subject matter of the "Journal" was influenced by that obsession. Many familiar themes are revisited, among others, the reception of his work, the role of the writer, the death of his father, his sense of alienation:

> My father's mysterious death when I was eleven taught me – like nothing would ever have done – that everything, including people, is unreal. That, like Carlos Castenada's Don Juan, I had to weave my own descriptions of reality into the available fantasy we call the world. I describe and live my descriptions. This, in African lore, is akin to witchcraft. My people could never again see me as anything but "strange." . . . I am what I am not because I am an African or whatever but because it is the basic nature of a maker of descriptions, a writer. (p. 123)

Although these themes are reworked and often changed, for example, he has presented several versions of his father's death his position on the aesthetics and ideology dichotomy has never wavered. For Marechera Art is always favored over Politics, individualism should never be sacrificed for the "common good." In the "Journal" he exclaims: "The cliché about the world being what you make it is "true"; weave your descriptions and live in them. Do not ever accept another's description as being your own" (p. 123) to do so would ""violate the treasure of one's uniqueness" (p. 124).

*

As he demonstrated in *The Stimulus of Scholarship* Marechera was capable of producing work with more than a nod in the direction of nation building, but this was however an isolated example. Even when back in Harare and faced with the realities of a heavily politicized situation he remained true to his dictum "If you are a writer for a specific nation, or a specific race, then fuck you" (see above). It is this refusal, or inability, to accept a belief or doctrine blindly – as some would have suggested was his duty – that helps to define Marechera's role as an artist in his society. Because he was unable to take a Kierkegaardian "leap of absurdity" by accepting that commitment blindly and (for him) irrationally, he remained in the darkness of his skepticism in a sort of existential limbo. Other writers, Achebe, Ngugi, and Soyinka, for example faced the same dilemma but still produced very effective political works. Unfortunately Marechera, often homeless, unsupported, alienated, in fear of insanity and in declining physical health, was in no condition to make the sustained effort necessary to establish himself as a force in Zimbabwean literature.

As discussed above, Marechera's early works were an attempt to escape from the effects of the dominant ideology of his colonial upbringing and education. Here it can be argued that his consistent and at times perverse individualism be seen as an attempt to break free from the bleak view of the individual as expressed by Althusser, of an individual as an agent of the system. Marechera's acceptance that he had internalized colonial ideologies seemed to acknowledge that argument when he commented "I have become the skeleton in my own cupboard." However, such astute self-knowledge did not lead to self-realization but rather to the view that self-realization within the superstructure, be it Zimbabwean, Rhodesian or European, was, for Marechera anyway, a contradiction in terms.

I argued above that " part of the conditioning of [his] environment is that he should be critical of it, thus by not conforming, he inevitably conforms." On his return to newly independent Zimbabwe he might have expected to flourish in a more supportive atmosphere, but he found, as with the banning of *Black Sunlight*, that rigid ideas on the role of the writer still prevailed. His reaction was to remain outside of the system where he continued to write " . . . as prolifically as ever but produced nothing that publishers could unequivocally accept. The recurring criticism was that his writings were inconsistent, not marketable and inaccessible to a broad readership" (*SB*, p. 340). Although Marechera could physically refuse to accept the rules and mores of his society and made this plain in his writing and public pronouncements, psychologically he was in thrall to a Foucauldian babel of discourses [115] which, out of his control, made his quest for a sense of self (the primordial I) impossible to achieve.

Mindblast, with its combination of genres, demonstrates Marechera's versatility as a writer of fiction and non-fiction, a poet and a dramatist. For that reason alone it is essential reading. Marechera returned to Zimbabwe as an established writer. As a portrayal of the writer trying to live up to that reputation at the same time as he was trying to adjust to the demands of the political and cultural nation-builders, *Mindblast* is an invaluable resource.

CHAPTER SIX

Scrapiron Blues: A final word

In early 1987 Dambudzo Marechera became seriously ill with pneumonia, and during his treatment it was discovered that he also had AIDS. Later that year he developed pneumonia again, and after three days in hospital died on August 18,1987, at the age of 35. *Scrapiron Blues*, the final volume in the series of posthumously published works, is a *pot-pourri* of prose, poetry, and plays, written by Marechera during the period from 1983 until this early death. The aim of this chapter is to assess that collection (apart from the plays, which were considered in Chapter Five), and to appraise its contribution to Marechera's literary output.

It is evident from this miscellany that Marechera was still searching for his voice. In an interview with Alle Lansu in February 1986 he spoke of using various literary techniques (see below). He was specifically referring to his work on "The Concentration Camp" though evidence of different techniques can be found throughout *Scrapiron Blues*. On one level it is possible to see the tension between such relatively realistic works as "The Servant's Ball" and "Rainwords Spit Fire" and the trial-and-error approach to the "Pub Stories" as one between the desire to become a "useful citizen" within a socialist republic and the desire for self-expression at all costs. Or as Georg Lukacs puts it, "between an aesthetically appealing, but decadent modernism, and a fruitful critical realism."[116]

As the mixture of styles in *Scrapiron Blues* clearly demonstrates, Marechera never achieved Lukac's "fruitful critical realism" in any sustained way, neither did he resolve that dilemma, which might suggest that he was a man of indeterminate principles. However, to accept such an argument would be an error of judgement. What some would see as Marechera's "experimentation" was in fact a search for his authentic voice; it was also a search for a role and a position he could call his own. As was established earlier Marechera's dilemma of "honest artist" or "good citizen" was compounded by his inability to work alongside the socialist nation builders. There is a parallel here with the earlier situation in Europe. Writing of the Stalinist period in Russia Lukacs suggested, "In this atmosphere many critical realist writers stopped writing, or made concessions against their better judgement. And there were some writers whose artistic development was thereby seriously compromised." [117]

Scrapiron Blues has work to admire, but the mixture of short works in a variety of styles confirms that Marechera was still attempting to develop his craft. This posthumous collection indicates that the potential suggested by *The House of Hunger* wasn't fully realized. Undoubtedly Marechera's "development" as an artist was "seriously compromised" by the demands of the socialist system. It would be quite wrong to blame Robert Mugabe's administration for all of the writer's ills, many of which, whether voluntarily or involuntarily, were of his own making. However, it was Marechera's great misfortune to find himself in an environment that, busy with establishing a new country, had neither the time nor the inclination to empathize with one who wanted to march to the tune of a different drum.

The material in *Scrapiron Blues* can, then, be separated between that which is an "aesthetically appealing modernism," and that which is "fruitful critical realism." In "First Street Tumult" for example, Marechera shows himself at his best as a spontaneous, very literary, experiential writer (comparisons can be made, *inter alia*, with Kafka, Joyce and Lawrence) and does similar things with varying degrees of success in "Pub Stories" and "The Concentration Camp." On the other hand, "Rainwords Spit Fire" has a social realist approach in the manner of, for example, Alex La Guma's, *In the Fog of the Season's End*, or Mbulelo Mzamane's, *The Children of Soweto*. The case for social realism is that it renders "art" more accessible to the general populace and Rainwords Spit Fire" shows Marechera in "good citizen" mode. The case against social realism is that it encourages stylistic conformity and though "Rainwords Spit Fire" is often powerfully wrought, it is rather superficial and flat in comparison with his other, more poetic works.

The fact that examples of Marechera's work can be used to satisfy the separate requirements of Lukacs' literary dichotomy is as much a comment on the difficulty of pigeonholing the writer as it is testament to the range of his work. It is a difficulty that is emphasized by the realization that some of *Scrapiron Blues*, "Fuzzy Goo's Stories for Children," for example, do not sit easily on either side of the divide.

6.1 ." . . like a rat in a corner. . . "

The introduction to *Scrapiron Blues* states, "This volume brings together pieces of various literary genres written by Marechera . . . the common theme . . . is urban life. He draws multicolored sketches of the cityscapes of Harare and captures the vibes and psyche of a big urban center in 20th century Africa" (p. ix). Perhaps there is some editorial license here. Marechera does write about "the big urban center," Harare; however, his stories are narrowly focused anecdotes from the bars and shebeens together with autobiographical material and musings on the role of the writer. With the occasional exception, "First Street Tumult," for example (one of the few pieces in the collection to have been published during Marechera's lifetime), they lack the penetrative observation and attention to socially specific detail of, say, Joyce's *Dubliners*, Runyon's *On Broadway*, or even Marechera's own "The Skin of Time" and "The Servant's Ball." Like Marechera's isolated existence at this time, these Hararean tales are often flat, one-dimensional and ephemeral. In the way of some of the poems in Lawrence's *Pansies* [118] they offer little more than reflections as, in Marechera's words, he, " . . . roamed the town in search of stories." and found only "A superfluous time for superfluous characters" (*Scrapiron Blues*, p. 29).

Marechera produced most of the material in the period 1983 to 1985, and wrote " . . . few other manuscripts between 1985 and the time of his death. They were mostly fragments, inconsistent in quality. He did not try to get them published" (*SB*, p. 351). Some of those fragments appear in *Scrapiron Blues* and reflect the disillusion expressed in his interview with the Dutch journalist Alle Lansu in February 1986:

> . . . I no longer have the initial anger I had when I was writing *The House of Hunger* and *Black Sunlight*. I seem to have come to the stage where I think I am ready to sell out my profession. . . . It's that loneliness which is increasingly driving me to all this . . . The isolation is terrible. I'm

> like a rat in a corner, I can only continue
> respecting myself as a writer by living in my
> head, and that can be dangerous sometimes,
> especially if one has also experienced paranoia.
> (*Scrapiron Blues*, p. xi)

It is, of course, very sad that Marechera, at the relatively young age of thirty-three years, should have been expressing such sentiments. Quite obviously his physical isolation had major implications for his mental and physical health. In addition, the resultant lack of intellectual stimulation led to a different type of isolation that had an equally serious effect on the writer. As he explained:

> Sometimes I think it's just that I miss the intense
> literary intrigues of the London journals and
> circles, the nightlong heated arguments about
> what constitutes art, the times when it was easy
> to believe that there was more than 'something'
> in living a life totally devoted to literature. Here
> in Harare all that seems frivolous, trivial,
> nothing to do with 'real' living. . . . There is
> something about this city that is wrong, all
> wrong, for a writer, the way London was not
> wrong. (*Scrapiron Blues*, pp. 26, 28)

There may well be some typical Marecheran hyperbole in his comparisons of Harare and London (which he once scathingly described as "the dandruff and fleas of a balding country").[119] His career in London was in the doldrums whereas his return to Harare revitalized him. His focus was renewed and he soon had a publisher. Unfortunately, this did not last as, unable to compromise with the "nation builders," he failed to establish a permanent place for himself in the new Zimbabwe and gradually withdrew into a decreasing circle of acquaintances. However, it is true that for those "devoted to literature" the two cities are hardly comparable, and it is certain that Marechera missed the intellectual stimulation and companionship of his life in London, particularly when it was based around the Africa

Center. In any event his unhappiness and sense of isolation were real enough.

6.2 "Tony Fights Tonight – Pub Stories"

Of the eleven stories and fragments of stories that constitute "Tony Fights Tonight-Pub Stories" and form the opening sequence of *Scrapiron Blues*, one is less than three quarters of a page and only two are more than two pages long. Some, for example, "The Shining" and "Snakes in Tracksuits" are little more than the reporting of bawdy bar room fantasies of sexual prowess, while others, particularly those involving "Tony" are familiarly autobiographical. Although Veit-Wild refers to the "Pub Stories" as "recording . . . modern urban legends, the new oral literature of contemporary African cities" (p. xii), these fragments have a stronger flavor of unworked notes, perhaps recording an incident with the intention of extending or incorporating into a longer work at a later date. Or they have at the heart a theme or sentiment, which is not developed, like – "Fucking missionaries. Ruined my life." ("The Pinpocketing Roadside Preacher," p. 27). In a way this lack of development and the absence of coherence and continuity also notable in these works is a profile of Marechera's final years, which were marked by the absence of a defining purpose.

Nevertheless, there are instances of fine writing, densely packed with vivid images. The following is the opening paragraph of "Smith in Dead Skin":

> A hard day. Nerves shrieking. The head tight and taut with the facts of heat, crime, lust, power, boredom and food. The ambulance still wailed in the distance. The Air Force had just brutally peeled the enamel from my teeth. The Horse guards were riding by, back to barracks. And there was the Army Ceremonial Band – a controlled din of brass and trumpet, and the uncanny rhythm of stomping feet. Under the

> eyes of cynical, cheerless, drunken, curious,
> fascinated eyes. In navy blue suit and necklace
> of oxtail bones, I watched it all pass by. I had
> looked out of the pub windows. I had come out
> to watch. So this was the Opening of
> Parliament! (p. 2)

The reader is invited to consider two apparently unrelated events. One is in the recent past and involves an ambulance which "still wailed in the distance" and the other, the Opening of Parliament, is happening here and now. The wailing of the ambulance is linked to "hard day" and "nerves shrieking" as with a precise economy Marechera implies that "the facts of heat, crime, lust, power, boredom and food" had caused an unexplained violent incident. He moves from one event to the other via the Air Force fly-by, where sound blends with that of the ambulance, thus transferring the reader's attention from the ambulance (the past) to the Opening of Parliament (the present).

The writer is also moving between the past and the present as he observes that the opening of the Zimbabwean Parliament is celebrated with the all traditions of the former colonial government, hinting at a possible betrayal of the aims of the Second Chimurenga. He emphasizes this apparent contradiction by the deliberate semantic confusion of his "navy blue suit and "necklace of oxtail bones." Here of course his "navy blue suit" could represent either set of rulers, pre- or post-independence, but the "necklace of oxtail bones" is a symbol of the precolonial past that is not featured in his presentation of the pageant. In other words, in Marecheran terms, there is no difference between colonialism and neocolonialism. Both ignore the history of the "people."

The core of the story is one of sexual indulgence featuring the "Opening of the Legs" and an escape in a sack featuring the "Opening of the Sack." These "Openings" lead to a weakly punning closure – "I was thinking of the Opening of Parliament. I was thinking of the Opening of the Legs. I was thinking of the

Opening of the Sack. I rushed to the toilet and was violently sick." – in which the rhythm of the repetition is quite effective but, by comparison with the dense imagery of the opening paragraph, disappointing.

6.2.1 "There's no room for a Norman Mailer in the Third World"

Six of the stories, "Dreams Wash Walls," "The Power," "Babel," "What Available Reality," "A Description of the Universe" and "The Decline and Fall" have a degree of continuity and coherence in that they all explore the role of the writer and feature a character called Tony, the Sculptor/Poet/Artist who, as in *Mindblast,* when he isn't writing, continues to wash imaginary blood off the walls of his flat. This sequence of stories was included in the manuscript "Killwatch or Tony Fights Tonight," which was submitted to, and rejected by, Longman in 1983.

A central theme of the stories is Marechera's difficulty in becoming established as a writer in Harare: "I am trying to grasp the kind of story that will take in the swimming-pool skin of the Harare skies, the slightly mocking darkness that underlies sunset's briefly glowing coals, before the black hand of anxiety clenches its darkness around the city (p. 4). Here the city is a metaphor for his career, which is now "briefly glowing coals," as he contemplates oblivion if he doesn't come to terms with both the demands of being back in Harare and finding the right "kind of story," not only to write but also to live. The uncertainty about his future appeared to be making him withdraw together with the consistent concern for his mental health: "You thought of the future with the self-inflicted risk of unhinging your mind. The future is controlled by people who inflict their dreams on other people…The only little safety left is your own small dream" (p. 15).

As in *Black Sunlight* and *The Black Insider* Marechera

merges with his characters and questions the nature of reality: "Shit, what kind of writer was I? . . . Who was the reality? Fred and Jill? Or Tony and Jane? Was I myself a character in someone's head? (p. 17). The futility of his attempts to become accepted in Harare is summarized by what could well serve as an epitaph for the lonely and embittered writer "There's no room for a Norman Mailer in the Third World" (p. 23).

Significantly, "A Description of the Universe" the final story of the sequence, which opens with a despairing question, "Is it so surprising, I wonder, that everyone is obsessed with the past?" (p. 22)," closes with Marechera abandoned by his own characters as they find places for themselves in the new Harare:

> Tony and Jane are now far from homeless. Tony has bought a house in Brightwood, a quiet suburb on the outskirts of Harare. He has also bought a car. Gone are the days of . . . the tragic washing of the walls. Tony is now something in the Ministry of Information. He still doesn't know exactly what but he has an office, a telephone, a secretary and several big ideas. (p. 26).

The Ministry of Information employed both Wilson Katiyo and Charles Mungoshi so there is a suspicion of a mischievous personal subtext here. The passage expresses Marechera's misgivings about his future role should he join the policy-makers, astutely aware that the trappings of office and "big ideas" are not enough, he "doesn't know exactly" what to do. Marechera never did decide "exactly what to do" and as time passed in Harare his work inevitably became increasingly fragmented.

6.3 "First Street Tumult – More City Stories"

The eponymous story in this second sequence was first published in *The Sunday Mail* of May 29, 1983 and is notable for its detached tone and complete absence of authorial intrusion as the author maintains a third person narrative voice. This aesthetically appealing story, more than any other, is a "multicolored sketch of the cityscape of Harare" (p. xi). The opening paragraph captures a moment when:

> Sunlight stenciled her image in the big gleaming shop-front window. Like a photograph negative held up to the light, her image lingered among the pink harlequins dressed in velvet, silks, corduroy, lingered long and longingly among the latest fashions from London and Paris, a hazy gold-shot silhouette of a tall graceful Afro-crowned single woman, a teacher at Blake High School in Fourth Street, Harare.(p. 108)

The narrator lightly plays with the obvious heavy-handed Fanonesque postcolonial moralism of the richly clad "pink harlequins" (European) contrasted with the "negative" image of the African in favor of a more subtle dialectic between illusion and reality. The writer, in cinematic fashion, then pans around the First Street Mall, describing the scene in order to locate the woman and the moment before he finally returns to her and closes to reveal why he was writing about the woman. But the answer contains a mystery: "And the fierce pulsing rays of the sun could not penetrate to the glittering secret tears coursing one by one down her cheeks" (p. 111). In a curiously jarring shift to the language of an inferior love story, "In just such a way she had thrown all of herself at Dan" (p. 109), part of the secret is revealed. Her lover has left her, she is no longer a virgin – "The freshly mown grass would be the small print on her living contact," – and is pregnant "Green seedlings, suddenly the matter of the morrow" (p. 110). Her flat, to which she is reluctant to return, is now a place of "too many silent and invisible things" (p. 109).

A recurring motif in "First Street Tumult" is a captured image as the writer engages in a debate on the nature of the relationship between illusion and reality. In addition to the "photograph negative" of the opening paragraph Marechera uses as tropes: "the sharp watercolor strokes of pastel-shade people" (p. 108); "A still photograph from a film"; "A hastily scrawled drawing"; "a painting by Monet" (p. 109): "a portrait on the wall" (p. 110). Pursuing the same motif in the actions of his characters he introduces "A young Swede was calmly taking pictures" (p. 110) and "two Norwegian girls carried five canvas paintings" (pp. 110-111). Linking the woman psychologically to his use of artistic terms Marechera reveals she is a teacher, who "taught art: drawing, painting and sculpture" (p. 109). Perhaps for her the illusion of love has become the reality of an unwanted pregnancy.

The closing mystery of the story, the "secret glittering tears," suggests that the image cannot be penetrated. A casual observer will see that the woman is crying but does not know the reason for her tears. As observer, he (or she) can only interpret subjectively what he (or she) sees.

The theme is made clear in surreal fashion by "A group of young university students, dressed in white chef's uniforms cycled into the Mall on a six-seater bicycle; cycled slowly round and round, ringing a Holy communion bell" (p. 111), who read a poem:

> I am what you see, said the cat,
> What you see is in your head.
> Am I in your head, or am I me.

The theme is the familiar Marecheran conundrum of the nature of identity as dialectic between illusion and reality. The images, which are captured in various ways throughout the story, exist in an alternative non-literary medium. But, the writer is asking, how does the captured image relate to the thing itself? Which is the real "I," the one that exists in the minds of others or the "I" that I believe myself to be? In addition to that riddle there is a subtle allegorical link on the nature of illusion, as Zimbabwe moves from the distortions of colonialism to a socialism that is no less distorted. It is a very clever and appropriate allegory that captures the art teacher's unwanted pregnancy and connects it with the notion of the "new" Zimbabwe being little more than the bastard child of colonialism.

In this vividly illustrated and, considering its shortness, powerful and psychologically complex story Marechera has quite clearly taken the route of "an aesthetically appealing modernism" rather than "a fruitful critical realism." However, in spite of the allegedly elitist nature of Marechera's aesthetic the central message of "First Street Tumult" is very simple – whoever is in power, ultimately the people are exploited and suffer.

The final story of the sequence, and possibly the most significant in biographical terms, "Fragments," clearly was written in the last few months of his life. (This assumption is based on his reference in the story to having been in hospital. He was admitted to the hospital for the first time in January 1987, and again in February; he was incurably ill and died in August of the same year.) There is an overwhelming sadness in this story that encapsulates his life as a series of fragments as he raises the familiar issues of the family, his illness, and his relationship with his parents. With heavily ironic humor the iconoclastic Marechera portrays himself as "Harold," a minor functionary in the Ministry of Construction.

In the opening lines of the story he discusses honor and the family name: "Poverty was poverty, but poverty was warm and snug when it could still cover its nakedness with the woolen blanket of honor. Family honor. The family name" (p. 127). Such fond expression is very different from the vilification Marechera heaped on his family on his return to Zimbabwe.[120] There then follows a short nightmare scene in which "Harold" revisits the morgue and encounters his father's corpse whose " . . . battered skull swiveled to face him directly. He scrunched his eyes shut. Refusing. Denying. Shaking his head furiously" (p. 128). The denial theme is repeated later in the story when "Harold" refuses to answer the door and is then himself denied, when "Later, on the phone, he could hear the number ringing repeatedly but no one answered." (p. 128). Thus he denies his past – his father; denies his present – by not answering the door; and his hopes for the future are denied when his telephone call is unanswered. In a final resolution of his role as an artist he denies any responsibility for the "people," "Other people were not his responsibility; they were their own lookout" (p. 130). And he denies his (mental) illness: "Harold was thirty-five but already he conducted himself as an aging invalid whose hold on reality depended on an extreme refusal to acknowledge his sickness"" (p. 130).

Such poignant denials so close to the end of his life have an ineffable sadness. As equally sad is the evidence of the writer circling irresolutely around the same themes and issues he had first introduced in *The House of Hunger*.

6.4 "When Rainwords Spit Fire"

The "aesthetic appeal" of the very short story "First Street Tumult" is exchanged for "a fruitful critical realism" in the rather longer "Rainwords Spit Fire." Described by the author as "a township novella," "When Rainwords Spit Fire" was written in 1984 and describes "one day in the life of Rutendo Township" (p. xiii). With its pervasive air of social realism "When Rainwords Spit Fire" has the flavor of the documentary Marechera apparently tried to avoid when writing "The Concentration Camp" (see below). In familiar fashion the story is a series of brief scenes but, unlike most of his other works, it is written in the third person and is populated by a large number of believable characters.

Another noticeable difference is the change in style and attitude, as Veit-Wild points out: "Where *The House of Hunger* is full of despair, narrative fragmentation and violent images, here the same township life is described . . . in composed, calm and simple language" (p. xiii). Also noticeable is the almost complete absence of images of bodily excretions (blood, sweat, shit, vomit, semen) that are such a notable feature not only of *The House of Hunger* but also of *Black Sunlight* and *The Black Insider*. However, like those earlier works, "Rainwords Spit Fire" is extremely bleak in outlook. In adopting a "new" approach perhaps Marechera was following his own advice, "If you want to write a political treatise, go write a political treatise, but don't try to pretend it's a poem" (*SB*, p. 307, see also below). Arranged in episodic form, the novella explores the actions of a number of people, including children, as they experience life in the township. Using a detached narrative voice Marechera distances himself from his characters in presenting a compelling picture of grinding poverty, unrelieved squalor, heavy drinking, and sex. "On most nights, there would be shrieks and shouts from children playing, men fighting, the wailing of police sirens, the thunderous songs of some obscure religious sect, the hue and cry of "Thief! Stop thief"" (p. 143).

Readers from the townships and frequenters of the beer halls and shebeens will be able to recognize themselves and their predicaments but there is nothing here to aid their understanding of why life is the way it is. Children are portrayed sympathetically but for the adults there is only the existential angst of township life: "Each day death expands the space it occupies in our hearts . . . We are accidents waiting to happen. That was it. You waited and waited but nothing happened" (p. 150).

At the time of writing "Rainwords Spit Fire" (August/September 1985) nothing was happening for Dambudzo Marechera. In the early months of 1985, "Depth of Diamonds," the last piece of work he submitted for publication, although praised, had been rejected by Heinemann and College Press. The grounds were the familiar ones of "difficulty," "too many literary allusions," and "too self-indulgent" and some hopeful advice from a College Press reader: "What I am suggesting would require some drastic rewriting. This is not a question of drawing in loose ends, but of a focusing far more clearly on what is being said" (*SB*, pp. 343-8).

Rainwords Spit Fire" is a brave attempt to avoid those pitfalls and is a lucid and perceptive presentation of township life. In Lukacs" terms Marechera is attempting to choose "the great and progressive literary tradition of realism in preference to formalistic experiment." [121] It again demonstrates that Marechera could produce an effective short story though it is too fragmented to allow his characters space in which to develop. There is an attractive economy about his sparse prose but without Marechera's elaborate poetic rhetoric it fails to develop literary power.

Once again he fails to make best use of his considerable talents. The pattern of his life and his devotion to writing were inextricably linked; in a sense he was writing out his own life. As Robert Fraser suggested (July 1997): "He couldn't distinguish between life and literature. His life was a story." Lukacs asks, "Is man the helpless victim of transcendental and inexplicable forces, or is he a member of a human community in which he can play a part . . . towards its modification or reform?" [122] Marechera did try to play a part in "his" community but, ideologically and artistically, he was unable to stay with the rational choice implied by Lukacs for any length of time.The significance in the stylistic technique, as Lukacs suggested, is not in the form and content of the work but in the ideology underpinning it. Although Marechera's technique changed, the underlying ideology appeared to remain the same.

In spite of its faults, "Rainwords Spit Fire" adds to the belief that had circumstances been different, had Marechera been encouraged to harness his undoubted abilities, then that may have led to his emergence as a short story writer of very high quality with appropriate comparisons to, say, O'Henry, Joyce, and Lawrence. But that was not to be. Now thoroughly disillusioned and disheartened and lacking the mental and physical energy for the effort, Marechera made no attempt to have this, or any subsequent work, published. But he remained a writer and, perhaps simply because he could do nothing else, he continued to write.

6.5 "The Concentration Camp"

In the introduction to *Scrapiron Blues* Veit-Wild refers to
the section called "The Concentration Camp" as:

> ... an unfinished novel-like piece consisting of
> prose, drama and poetry . . . to express his
> horror of the Zimbabwean war of liberation. He
> describes life in the "protected villages," the
> "keeps," in which parts of the rural population
> were kept by the Rhodesian Army during some
> of the wartime, and parallels them with
> concentration camps. (p. xiv)

Marechera began working on the "The Concentration
Camp" during 1985, and it remained unfinished at his death in
1987. Apparently it had been his intention "not to end the
manuscript with Independence . . . it will be about the survivors:
what happened afterwards to all those people" (p. xv). In the
February 1986 interview with Alle Lansu, Marechera
commented on the work in progress:

> I have never written a book like that before for
> which I have to interview people. I have been
> going around Harare interviewing some of the
> people here in Harare who were former inmates,
> prisoners in these protected villages. They told
> me all these horrifying stories. (p. xiv)

And yet it seems this primary source material was not in
itself sufficient for his purpose, as he told Lansu:

> The format of the book is – I am following the
> experiences of two fictional families. The
> problem I am having is the technique, because I
> don't want it to come out as a documentary and
> so I am using a kind of expressionist technique
> and here and there certain surrealist techniques

and here and there straight narrative. (p. xiv)

This experimental approach appears to indicate a change to the views he expressed at what became known as his "farewell lecture" at the University of Zimbabwe on May 6, 1982: "If you want to write a political treatise, go and write a political treatise, but don't try to pretend it is a poem. If you want to scream, scream but don't put your scream on paper and pretend it is a poem" (*SB*, p. 307). Written in a variety of styles, the eight sections offer a loose connection of characters linked by a series of atrocities, as Marechera explores the effects of the war of liberation. Such intentional experimentation raises the awkward question of audience – for whom was "The Concentration Camp" written? Certainly not the street people, nor the povos, nor the ex-combatants, nor the people in the townships who, with their lack of formal education, of which he was well aware, would have made neither head nor tail of it. Some sections, the "straight narrative," for example, are accessible but as an entity complete in itself "The Concentration Camp" is confused in organization.

An alternative view to Veit-Wild's "a novel-like piece," or Marechera's claim that he was writing/had written a book, sees "The Concentration Camp," in similar fashion to *The House of Hunger*, as a series of short pieces ostensibly sharing a central theme. In this reading the different styles reflect the increased fragmentation of the writer's approach rather than a deliberate experiment. On the question of audience, Marechera had no publisher and had stopped trying to get his work published. He wrote because there was nothing else he could do. There is a terrible sadness in this observation which interprets the writer's conversation with Lansu as self-deceptive rationalization tinged with desperate hope. Perhaps Marechera was ready to "sell-out" but was aware that it was too late. The following is from Part Five of "The Concentration Camp," appropriately titled "The Intellectual's Revolt":

> If there is a soul and it is for sale, where is the buyer? And there are all these concentrated possibilities of emotion which find no attainable

confirmation out there, no buyers, no takers.
And the empty honeycomb within the heart-
who or what out there will arrive with the pure
liquid gold and the motor pulse to life again? (p.
180)

Aware that he had failed to become established as a writer
in Zimbabwe Marechera is expressing his despair. He still has
something to offer but now that he is ready to negotiate, no-one
is interested, "where is the buyer? " Worse than that his
inspiration, his drive, has disappeared and he laments the
absence of a person, or a cause, to rouse his muse, "the motor
pulse to life again."

Veit-Wild suggests that "The Concentration Camp"
"employs a children's perspective" (p. xiii). This is true of parts
of the work but Marechera's attempts to preserve the innocence
of children bring about lapses into sentimentality. In this
example he is writing of two children:
> Her eyes in the flames of the cooking fire were
> fully clasped to his and though they did not
> know it, the two were in the crucible of a
> tormenting first love. A love which would not
> declare love but would simply, giddily say; "You
> are alive!" . . . there was something in these
> children which made them resist being changed
> overnight into little cynical adults. Perhaps this
> was the pleasurable pulse rippling through their
> joined hands. It was a terribly sweet thing to live
> for. This realization rushed through them into a
> certainty: the two of them would never die. (p.
> 163)

The sea change in style indicated by a comparison of the
above with his earlier work, for example, the "The Great Cunt"
diatribe in *Black Sunlight*, is quite remarkable. This sad lament
for the lost innocence of childhood is emphasized by the acute
observation of the absolute certainty of purpose children possess;

they *know* what they have will last forever. The writer, and the reader, of course, know different. However, in trying to capture a child-like innocence Marechera has adopted a mawkish tone which is distracting, and a prose style that borders on the banal.

That apart, and although "The Concentration Camp" fails to convince as a single work, there are several examples of quintessential Marecheran style: the Runyonesque portrayal of "Jimmy the Dwarf" and "thin Larry Long" from "City of Anarchists": the bizarre cross-talking double act in the surreal two-handed play which is Part Three, "The Camp," and which also features a pair of talking boots; this vitriolic comment on apartheid from Part Four, "A Cast of Cadres," which is presented entirely in song:

> Apartheid is an ideal
> That twinkles only in the gutters
> Apartheid is an ideal
> To perverts behind closed shutters
> Apartheid is only real
> To faggot Afrikaners
> Who fuck their daughters. (p. 178)

From Part Seven, "Tonderai's Father Reflects," he asks the questions:

> Whose the ghoulish fetid aura in the hold?
> Whose the fiendish despair chained yet bold? (p. 196)

Although he is apparently writing (in a style reminiscent of William Blake) about the "comrades," it is his own "fetid aura" and his own "fiendish despair" with which he is so preoccupied. It is Marechera himself who is in the "hold" (African slaves were of course transported in the hold of a ship). He is despair that he is "chained" by the actions of the authorities, and yet he is "bold" enough to resist them.

Being "bold enough to resist" implies that Marechera made choices. I argued earlier that personality was part nature, part nurture, but was largely determined by hegemonic conditioning. Lukacs" Marxist materialist perspective would maintain that choice and personality are inextricably linked, and that personality is heavily influenced by environmental factors:

> A writer's pattern of choice is a function of his personality. But personality is not in fact timeless and absolute, however it may appear to the individual consciousness. Talent and character may be innate; but the *manner in which they develop, or fail to develop* (my emphasis), depends on the writer's interaction with his environment, on his relationships with other human beings. His life is part of the life of his time; no matter whether he is conscious of this, approves of or disapproves. He is part of a larger social and historical whole.[123]

There is no counter argument to the contention that, for the greater part of his life Marechera was at odds with his environment, and his personal history is littered with shattered relationships. If we accept Lukacs' argument it seems that Marechera's personality was such that it inhibited his artistic development. Of course some writers (I cited Patrick Kavanagh earlier, for example) thrived on such adversity. Unfortunately Marechera was damaged rather than inspired by his lifestyle. How and why Marechera's personality developed as it did is a matter of speculation but for Lukacs such detail is not required – a writer's choices depend on his personality, and that personality is formed by interaction with his environment. Marechera tried to live outside of whatever society (Oxford, London, Harare) he found himself in – that, of course, is impossible. His works are part of the socio-historic milieu he lived through, the fact that he tried so hard to articulate his individual experience of that milieu while hopelessly trying to escape its influence is part of their attraction.

6.6 "Fuzzy Goo's Stories for Children"

According to Stanley Nyamfukudza, "Dambudzo liked children. He was really a very warm and amusing person and he was very good with children, which is something, from his image, you wouldn't expect" (*SB*, p. 341). These children's stories comprise two pieces written in November 1983, "The Magic Cat" and "Baboons of the Rainbow," both rejected as "unsuitable" by the publishers ZPH and Longmans; "Tony and the Rasta" from 1984; and, what was probably Marechera's final work, "Fuzzy Goo's Guide to the Earth," started in July 1987.

Dedicated to "Max and Franz Wild and all the children of Zimbabwe" only "The Magic Cat" with its traditional European theme of the granted wish appears to have been written *for* children. "Baboons of the Rainbow" is a thinly disguised attack on post-independence Zimbabwe in which a coalition of the white baboon and the black baboon destroy the green baboon where green represents the shoots of growth of the new Zimbabwe. The piece, which is in verse form and illustrated by the six-year old Max Wild, includes the lines:

They jumped on Green Baboon
They hit. They bit. They scratched. They beat him up.
They hit him the whole day. It was like thunder.
The rainbow drained of all color.
Black Baboon and White Baboon were eating Green Baboon.
White Baboon liked his Green Baboon with garlic.
Black Baboon liked his Green Baboon with chillies.
"Let us eat him in a civilized way," said White Baboon.
Black Baboon agreed, "Yes, let us eat him in a civilized way."
They carried Green Baboon into the kitchen.
They cut Green Baboon into chops and steaks.

> They cooked Green Baboon with spices and dry
> white wine.
> White Baboon made the salad.
> Black Baboon made the custard. (p. 232)

In typically complex fashion Marechera engages with the tension between European and African influences and muses over which corrupt faction, black or white, will gain ascendancy in the new Zimbabwe from which all hopes have "bolted into the blue"(p. 238). By engaging with current issues in this way Marechera is following the European tradition in which nursery rhymes were often socio-political allegories aimed initially at an adult audience. It was only after the event or issue had declined in importance that the primary level of meaning assumed greater significance than the secondary level.

One can understand Marechera's anxiety to communicate with the younger generations and applaud his efforts as an artist to fulfill that role. However, it is difficult to accept that many Zimbabwean children would have had the intellectual sophistication necessary to appreciate the subtext of "Baboons of the Rainbow." Of course, children would have enjoyed the simple direct story at the primary level (the cannibal activities of the colored baboons) but the obvious political secondary level would have made any publication most unlikely. As a children's writer Marechera was in a double jeopardy: his record shows that he wasn't able to write without engaging with critical political or social issues, but engaging with those issues precluded publication in politically sensitive Zimbabwe.

The other stories are *about* children and may well have been intended for that audience but the intrusion of the cynical narrative voice, subject matter, choice of language and the world-weary tone is disturbing. Of course, even when ostensibly writing for children that may have been Marechera's intention. Eschewing any attempts at escapism Marechera does not create an unrealistic Roald Dahl-like anarchic world in which children triumph. Instead he presents a world township children would recognize and one in which peace of mind and spirit, rather than material possessions, is the desired goal:

> Tony knows everything that goes on in Shantytown. It does not take much imagination. The stealing, fighting, fucking, the incest and rape. It does not take much thought to grasp the disease that is Shantytown. But then Shantytown is the only home Tony has ever had. Tony loves it with great bitterness . . . One day the Rasta teacher drove Tony to Cleveland Dam. It was beautiful and quiet. Tony had been so used to noise and violence in Shantytown that the peaceful silence of Cleveland Dam almost frightened him. The Rasta squeezed Tony's hand and said, "Do not be afraid of peace."
> Tony knows many shanty people who are afraid of peace because they have never known it. Never, never known it. (from "Tony and the Rasta, p. 216)

"Tony" is almost certainly the younger version of "Tony" who features in the pub stories and is Marechera himself, of course. Quite possibly the visit to Cleveland Dam actually happened to the young and impressionable Marechera, providing a vivid contrast against which to place in context his day-by-day experience of life in Vengere Township.

"Fuzzy Goo's Guide (to the earth)" is divided into three small sections, "Blah," "Pebble" and "Gah." As with "Fragments," which was also written in the weeks immediately preceding his own death, the impact of his father's death some 24 years earlier is still very evident: "When my father died I just wanted to be on my own but my mother made me see the body" (p. 242). Apparent also is the still strong desire to rationalize his mental illness: "Paranoid means seeing all the things which big humans have been taught not to see" (p. 241). In a way reminiscent of Huxley and Orwell he warns about the insidious control exercised by the state:

Television really tortures little humans. It makes them think of BMX bicycles and goodies. It makes them prototypes of the blah adults they will grow into with time. It makes them enjoy watching (on TV) the destruction of things so that they are too tired to destroy the society that is actually a lunatic asylum. A lunatic is someone who knows there is something wrong somewhere but does not know exactly *what*. An asylum is where they are going to put me when they catch you reading all this I am writing. (p. 245)

In all probability the above is the final Marecheran tilt at the role of the artist in society as he implies that his views and beliefs have secured his exclusion from those with power and authority in Zimbabwe. The odd venture as a "good citizen" is abandoned as he affirms his consistent view of his role as an individual with a responsibility only to himself and to his art as a writer. As he commented during his lecture in Harare in October 1986, "The writer has no duty, no responsibility, other than to his art." It is a responsibility and an approach that he accepts have defined him as an outsider. In a more obvious attack on the role of the state, he advises potential young readers to ask of themselves "whether African socialism means you can be as nasty, dirty, savage, native, murderous as Jack and his hunters in William Golding's book *Lord of the Flies*" (p. 246). If this is the last piece of work Marechera produced, it is a testament to the consistency of his philosophy of individualism that was first introduced in *The House of Hunger*.

Some of the works in *Scrapiron Blues* sit easily with *Mindblast*, the plays and the "Tony" stories, for example. Others: – the children's stories, "Rainwords Spit Fire" and "The Concentration Camp" – confirm that, although his work had a consistency of theme, he was inconsistent stylistically. That he could write effectively in a variety of styles is a tribute to his talent. However, his failure to stay with a particular genre long enough to develop his talent to its full potential is a matter for considerable regret. The publication of *Scrapiron Blues* completed the work of the Dambudzo Marechera Trust. By including some of the last works written by Marechera, the trust ensured that, given the writer's erratic lifestyle, a reasonably comprehensive representation of his output has now been published.

6.7 "Then that's how it is."

As he made clear in The *House of Hunger* Marechera did have some happy memories of childhood. He still held those memories when writing *Scrapiron Blues* although now seasoned with a weary resignation:

> The trick was to convince yourself (and accept) that this was all there was, all there was ever going to be . . . You got on with it – the rest was without enchantment, without that enticing rubescence which for some is the aura of childhood, the tug of those salad days. Salad days? Or mere digression down Oxbridge lanes? Mentally, a down and out Gatsby in a rundown apartment, making do with tortured vision rather than a beguiling tenacious beauty. In Harare. (p. 187)

It is evident from this passage that Marechera had become disillusioned. By casting himself as Scott Fitzgerald's Jay Gatsby he is at once romanticizing his own position and also acknowledging that his fight has been won and lost. In this intertextual link, it can be argued, the "tortured vision" of his present situation is represented by the doomed Myrtle Wilson and the "beguiling tenacious beauty" of his childhood dreams by Daisy Buchanan who he (Gatsby/Marechera) had possessed briefly, then lost. On the other hand there is the tortured vision of the young "Tony's" experience of living in Shantytown – "The stealing, fighting, fucking, the incest and rape" – to set against the beauty of the "enticing rubescence . . . the aura of childhood."

The different presentations are not contradictory, Marechera was aware of the ability of children to withdraw into a world of their own construction, "the aura of childhood," to escape the sheer awfulness of everyday life. Unfortunately the loss of childhood dreams served only to emphasize the dreadful predicament of the township dwellers.

It is not without irony that, now that Marechera was seriously ill, he had developed a tactic for surviving adult life: "He has stopped asking himself what's wrong. If this is how it is. Then that's how it is" (p. 181). More than a weary fatalism is indicated by these words which also signal that his pursuit was over. There is of course the search for a sense of his own identity that pervades the longer works, but if he was pursuing other goals they never became clear. Perhaps that is because the majority of his work was produced looking over his shoulder at where he had been rather than where he was going. His tendency was to revisit and to rewrite his experiences, a restless search for understanding as he explored different levels of meaning in a particular experience.

Irene Staunton, a publisher with Baobab Books in Harare, knew Marechera in London and saw him infrequently on his return to Zimbabwe. In a telephone conversation (August 1, 1997) she confirmed that Marechera was a solitary figure but according to her "no more in Harare than in London." Believing he had more potential as a critic she did find him a project producing a primer on literary criticism for use in schools but this was turned down by Zimbabwean publishers because of his reputation and image. Radius Books in England eventually accepted the project, but Marechera died before Staunton could get the news to him. In his interview with Lansu Marechera admitted, "My contacts with other writers are on a superficial level" Marechera suggested that isolation was intentional: "Rather loneliness experienced deliberately, intensely; an experiment into the hazards of being yourself" (p. 188).

Staunton confirmed that, in her experience, there was little interaction between Marechera and his fellow Zimbabwean writers. On Marechera's apparent ostracizing, Veit-Wild comments: "Those in charge of Zimbabwean culture rejected him as an outsider and did nothing to encourage him to live in Zimbabwe and contribute to its literary life. With very few exceptions, government officials, university lecturers, publishers and fellow writers were unable to deal with his "heretical" views and provocative personality" (p. 337).

Musa Zimunya was a fierce critic who believed Marechera should change his lifestyle and writing style and accept the responsibility of a role model for new Zimbabweans. But he was also a good friend who assisted in the unbanning of *Black Sunlight* and allowed the writer to use his office and typewriter. For his own reasons Zimunya has refused to talk about his experiences with Marechera. While conceding that Marechera's behavior often placed him on the fringes of literary society in Zimbabwe, one can only speculate on Zimunya's role in keeping Marechera out of the mainstream of Zimbabwean literary affairs. I am not specifically referring to Zimunya's defeat of Marechera for the post of Secretary General of the Writer's Union in 1984 but to his earlier comments on the role of the writer in *Those Years of Drought and Hunger* and his corrosive attack on Marechera's *The House of Hunger* which he effectively placed outside his definition of the requirements of the Zimbabwean literary canon.

In the months before he died Marechera cooperated in the making of a film, *After the Drought and Hunger*, by Moonlight Productions, Zimbabwe. The film is a "portrait of the Zimbabwean literary scene" and features interviews with, among others, Stanlake Samkange, Charles Mungoshi, Stanley Nyamfukudza, Wilson Katiyo, Musaemura Zimunya, and Marechera. Marechera was, by that time, living in his own flat and acknowledged that, in comparison with the masses, and although a "declassified person," he led a "comfortably privileged life." Nevertheless, he still complained that "In

Zimbabwe I am not treated with respect but treated as one would treat a snake that you do not know whether it is poisonous or not." He also complained of being depressed by his solitary life, adding "I am treated as an eccentric growth on the skin of Zimbabwe." The interview was clearly filmed at different times and in different places. One short and painful scene shows a very distressed Marechera, clearly in a state of deep depression, explaining his role as a writer. Struggling to control his voice and with tears streaming down his face he claimed his purpose was "to recapitulate all the suffering and pain that my people have suffered and will continue to suffer."

Although this statement is similar in sentiment to that expressed in *The House of Hunger* – "I found the idea of humanity, the concept of a mankind, more attractive than human beings" (p. 7) – it would be unwise to take his subsequent assertion at face value as a rebuttal of his earlier denial that he wrote for a "specific nation" or a "specific race." However, it is very apparent that it was something he desperately wanted to believe, perhaps even did believe, at the time he was saying it.

Earlier declarations apart, the texts themselves, with the exclusion of some of the plays and shorter stories, confirm the notion that his writing was very often little more than a highly personal record, a record in which Marechera wrote of his own suffering and his own pain. And, as can be judged from the film, that suffering and pain were very real indeed. Whether his comments indicate that he hoped that his works would eventually be read as representative of "his people," or whether towards the end of his life he deluded himself that his work was always intended to be representative of "his people," remains open to debate.

There is an unsurprising similarity between *The House of Hunger*, *Black Sunlight* and *The Black Insider*. All were written within a thirty-month period in similar circumstances and have strong thematic links to each other. *Black Sunlight* was a revision of *The Black Insider* and both were written in an attempt to repeat the success of *The House of Hunger*. On his return to Zimbabwe in 1982 Marechera was inspired to produce some of his most vivid work, published in *Mindblast* and *Scrapiron Blues*. Unfortunately he was unable to find a place for himself among the policy makers and decision takers as he was unwilling to join the "deliberate campaign to promote Zimbabwean culture" (*SB*, p. 39) and gradually withdrew. Staunton's comment suggests that Marechera's career may have been about to be revived but the attack on African socialism written in the weeks before his death (see above) suggest that although his lifestyle had changed his views on the respective roles of the state and the individual were as uncompromising as ever.

*

In a relatively small body of work that comprises plays, prose, and poetry Marechera wrote in a variety of styles. From the existential angst of his longer works, the absurd realism (and more) of his plays, to his lyric poems and the occasional critical work, Marechera is extremely difficult to pigeonhole as a writer. To apply a label that defines his style as a writer, or identifies him as a particular genre writer in any meaningful way, is impossible. When Marechera commented "I have been an outsider in my own biography" [124] he was acknowledging his hegemonic conditioning, and, in spite of the caustic protestation "If you are a writer for a specific race or a specific nation, then fuck you", he was ineluctably a Zimbabwean writer. Of course Zimbabwe is a relatively young country and that definition remains fluid. Without doubt, however, Marechera's work helps to establish the parameters of what it means to be a Zimbabwean writer. With that in mind, in my final chapter I will consider the contribution made to the Zimbabwean literary canon by this eclectic body of work.

CHAPTER SEVEN

Marechera and the Zimbabwean literary scene

7.1 "Quarrying for literary treasures"`

In his obituary of the writer, Robert Fraser said:
> Marechera's existence was one restless odyssey
> of risk. From the University of Rhodesia where
> he devoured Homer and outfaced Ian Smith's
> bully boys, to New College Oxford where his
> eccentricity provoked puzzlement, to Sheffield
> where as writer-in -residence he banged out the
> hundred odd pages of *House of Hunger*,[125] he

carried the torch of his quixotic, delectable revolt.
(*Dambudzo Marechera 1952-1987*, p. 15)

Fraser's obituary is typical of many in that it offers selective memories of a remarkable man and comments on his lifestyle, rather than memories of a notable writer or an assessment of his literary achievements. It seems that many of those who met Marechera can testify to his erudition and his capacity for intellectual debate, or can offer vivid anecdotes of his occasionally outlandish behavior. In some cases, indeed, such comments often outweigh evaluations of his writing.

Writing in *Parade* in December 1995 Musaemura Zimunya, in an article which is ostensibly about Marechera, but is in fact little more than a withering attack on Flora Veit-Wild,[126] offers the comment, "I am amused no end when I see university professors and their quislings who wouldn't touch Dambudzo's hand with gloves while he was alive now carrying his torch and quarrying for literary treasures in his grave." Exactly which of his fellow countrymen Zimunya consider to be quislings is far from clear. In the main, research interest in Marechera has been maintained from outside Zimbabwe. With the notable exceptions of Chennells and McLoughlin, there has been little input from Zimbabwean academics and writers. The reasons for this are complex and, I suspect, vary between individuals, but include self-interest, lack of interest, a lack of development in the literary infrastructure, and a simple lack of resources.

Zimunya's scornful comment "quarrying for literary treasures" is ill-advised. The work of the Dambudzo Marechera Trust should be surely be seen as a valuable effort in making available a much wider range of Marechera's work than looked likely at the time of his early death. Together with her colleagues on the Dambudzo Marechera Trust Veit-Wild acted as Marechera's literary executor and, in addition to the posthumous publications, created a Marechera archive at the University of Zimbabwe. Zimunya apart, Veit-Wild has her critics,[127] but her immense contribution helped place work in the public domain that otherwise would have been lost forever.

I suggested earlier that some of the over-lavish praise given to *The House of Hunger* was, at least in some measure, due to the desire to "find" a Zimbabwean Achebe. Another possibility is that Veit-Wild, and, among others, James Currey and Doris Lessing, saw vitality and intellectual anarchism when there was "only" immature or undeveloped, undisciplined writing. In an interview with Ahmed Rashid, [128] V S Naipaul comments:

> It is very easy for people now to feel that Asian imaginative writing is immensely vital . . . However, the vitality comes from the fact that the form is borrowed and this new material is poured into it. When enough of that new material has been poured into this particular borrowed form the vitality will also appear to go.

In answer to the question, "Are you dismissing the huge explosion and popularity of postcolonial literature?" he replied "I am not dismissing it. I am just saying that we should not be seeing vitality where there is only first-time writing." Naipaul's comments, although concerned with Asian literature can be applied with equal appropriateness to Zimbabwean literature (and elsewhere of course) and his warning about confusing vitality with "first time" writing can, with reservations, be applied to Marechera.

Although, as a body of work, Marechera's writing lacks a sense of substantial completeness, he did write three unique novellas, some excellent short stories, two extraordinary plays, and some fine lyric poetry, which will survive and become part of the Zimbabwean canon.

7.2 "Most unforgettable is the tormented figure of Marechera"

The "Zimbabwean literary canon" to which I refer is that

represented by black Zimbabweans writing in English. These are few in number and of relatively recent origin. (The first work in English by a black Zimbabwean, Stanlake Samkange's *On Trial for my Country*, was published in 1966. The second and third, Mungoshi's short stories, *Coming of the Dry Season*, and Sithole's *The Polygamist*, appeared six years later in 1972. It was to be another three years before black Zimbabweans began publishing with any regularity, for example, Samkange and Mungoshi (1975), Katiyo (1976), Sithole (1977), Samkange, Mutswairo and Marechera (all 1978)). A clear definition of the canon, with its implications of substance and hierarchy, has yet to emerge. Until a definitive and substantial body of work does emerge, from an individual or group of individuals, against which others may be compared, the canon will remain somewhat ephemeral and ill defined. Associated with this difficulty, as I explored above, is the tendency of some critics to discuss "African writing" and "African writers." This may be understandable, but it can be rendered illegitimate when it is used to deny the authenticity and appropriateness of a national voice. A work, or body of works, may achieve universal acceptance but they remain anchored forever in the social and historical space in which they were created. The development of a national, rather than continental, literature will accompany the evolution of a separate cultural identity. The process may take decades but it is under way. It is a slow process; the war and its effects is still a major pre-occupation with writers, as Chapman comments: "Zimbabwean literature has . . . remained marked by the warts of experiential living." [129]

Writing the blurb for the film *After the Hunger and the Drought* (Moonlight Productions, Harare, 1988), Kenneth Harrow, Professor of Humanities, Michigan State University, says:

> A powerful case for a national literature as an emergent reality in Africa is made by *After the Hunger and the Drought*. The presence of older writers like Stanlake Samkange and younger rebels like Dambudzo Marechera permit us to

grasp the scope and distance this literature has traveled since colonial times. Samkange's memories combined with the visuals of colonial Rhodesia evoke striking images of the difficult circumstances under which the African writers had to labor. The fruits of independence are marked by the personal vision and testimony of Charles Mungoshi, Bertha Musora, and others who recount their own personal experiences as well as giving testimony to current issues. Most unforgettable is the tormented figure of Marechera whose anguish burns on the screen with all the directness of his prose. All in all, an indispensable portrait of the Zimbabwean literary scene.

In taking this highly focused, genre-specific, approach the film follows the precedent established by Kahari (1980) and Zimunya (1982). The only fully comprehensive surveys of Zimbabwean literature, that is, including work written in Shona and Ndebele as well as English, have been produced by Flora Veit-Wild. *Survey of Zimbabwean Writers* (1992) was based on a list established by Veit-Wild in 1987 containing the names of 212 black Zimbabwean writers. The criteria for inclusion was:

> . . . publication of "creative writing" in any of the three languages, Shona, Ndebele or English. Authors were considered if they had: published or co-published books of at least twenty pages: published more than five poems or more than two short stories in literary anthologies or magazines." [130]

Veit-Wild built on the survey to produce *Teachers, Preachers, Non-Believers* (1992) which is subtitled *A Social History of Zimbabwean Literature*, it is an extremely valuable resource, capturing the background to literary development in Zimbabwe.[131] It is, however, too wide-ranging and includes too much work of a peripheral nature to be regarded as defining the

Zimbabwean canon.

The shorter, more closely defined, works produced by
Kahari and Zimunya do set out to define the canon and
concentrate exclusively on the output of black Zimbabweans
writing in English. The writers named by Kahari and Zimunya
(all of whom were also featured by Veit-Wild) together with
writers who emerged after publication, such as Chencherai Hove,
Shimmer Chinodya, Stanley Nyamfukudza, and Tsitsi
Dangarembga (featured in the later Veit-Wild work), and those
who have recently appeared [132], such as Yvonne Vera, Alexander
Kanengoni, and Nevanji Madanhire, form the basis on which the
Zimbabwean literary canon will eventually rest. They also offer a
frame of reference within which to evaluate and place the prose
fiction of Dambudzo Marechera. It is worth pointing out that in a
survey carried out in 1986 on the literature syllabi at twenty-six
universities in fourteen anglophone Africa countries, Bernth
Lindfors found that Marechera's work was included on ten
courses at four universities in four (unnamed) countries.[133] No
other black Zimbabweans feature in the survey. Other than the
bare statistics no details are offered, nevertheless it is possible to
speculate that in some universities and with some academics at
least, Zimbabwean literature is represented solely by Dambudzo
Marechera.

In order to place Marechera's work in context within
Zimbabwean literature I will begin with some comments on the
earlier writers, Samkange, Vambe, Sithole, and Mutswairo. I will
then compare and contrast his writing with other significant
voices of his generation, such as Katiyo, Mungoshi, and
Nyamfukudza, before moving on to a comparison with later
writers, to determine whether his contribution had any
discernible effect on writers such as Hove, Chinodya,
Dangarembga, and Vera. My intention is to comment only on
major themes and issues and, apart from an occasional
illustrative extract, I shall not enter into a detailed exposition of
the work of each writer. My final comments will address the
question of the impact of the writer on Zimbabwean literature as

a whole.

7.3 A Utopian Vision

The initial wave of black Zimbabweans writing in English produced fiction as a secondary occupation. For example, Samkange was first and foremost a historian and university lecturer, Vambe a teacher and journalist, Mutswairo a teacher and university lecturer, and Sithole a politician. Their genre was historical fiction, or more accurately half fiction, a mixture of truths and part truths, folk stories and historical "facts." Presented in realistic, if sometimes idealistic, style, the works were authoritative in tone and didactic in intent. Samkange admits when interviewed for the film *After the Hunger and the Drought*, "I wanted to reach people who wouldn't be caught dead reading history books, so I wrote fiction by sugar coating my history." This approach occasionally left his work uncomfortably between fact and fiction and open to criticism. As Michael Chapman observes: "A mythologizing tendency in his [Samkange's] work . . . undermines historical causality."[134] This is a good point, but one that may well have been lost on an unsophisticated audience who, unable to differentiate between myth and historical fact, would not have questioned the authenticity of the work. In oblique fashion Marechera questions Samkange's credibility in *The Black Insider* when the "Bishop" gloats: "And I have the best of advisers; that professor who wrote *On Trial For My Country*" (p. 55). The "Bishop" is Bishop Abel Muzorewa, party to the ill-fated "internal settlement" between the minority whites and those allegedly representing black Rhodesians. Muzorewa became Prime Minister of Zimbabwe/Rhodesia as a result of winning the dubious 1979 elections. By casting Samkange as his "adviser" Marechera is attempting to impugn Samkange's reputation by association.

Vambe and Samkange in particular took much of their information from Terence Ranger's book, *Revolt in Southern Rhodesia 1896-1897*, which as I established in Chapter Two was subsequently discredited. By endorsing the version of a great and glorious past (the First Chimurenga), Vambe, Samkange, and Mutswairo encouraged the perception of the liberation struggle as a Second Chimurenga by presenting a utopian vision of the restoration of the empire that apparently had existed before the whites had arrived. As McLoughlin points out[135] these earlier writers, particularly Samkange, wrote novels with " . . . a veneer of historical accuracy" but with the emphasis on " . . . historical processes rather than historicity." Of the same three writers (Samkange, Vambe and Mutswairo) Veit-Wild observes: "These books, [which are] representative of Zimbabwean historical fiction . . . mythologize the uprisings of 1896-97 in order to support the ongoing war of liberation. . . . by establishing the pride and dignity of their people the three authors try to prove to the whites that they were wrong to betray the concept of partnership and destroy the achievements of Federation" (*Teachers*, p. 109).

Of course those most directly involved in the struggle were largely illiterate and those who could read had little access to books and would have been presented with a world purporting to be theirs but unrecognizable and of little relevance.[136] So, at what audience were Samkange and his contemporaries directing themselves? It seems that they were aiming at a small intellectual elite within Zimbabwe, but mainly for consumption by a growing number of readers of "African literature" in Europe and the United States. Apart from the very unspecific "writing about Zimbabwe," this may be the only point of reference between Marechera and his predecessors, that is, writing for an audience outside of Zimbabwe. (Marechera did, of course, write "The Servant's Ball" and "The Skin of Time, Plays by Buddy," which, if they had been produced would most probably have been very well received by Zimbabwean audiences.) By most standards of critical comparison, style, form and content, use of language and so forth, there is nothing to indicate a shared literary heritage.

However, it was against this literature of false historicity and extravagant ideas about nationhood and national identity that Marechera attempted to express his own experiences of growing up in a country isolated from the rest of Africa by the activities of the Smith government, and a country in which power, wealth and status was firmly in the grasp of the white minority. Little wonder perhaps that he did not share the rosy view of the earlier writers who only began to write, often from self imposed exile, when their own positions protected them from the dreadful hardships experienced by the vast majority of black Zimbabweans. That he did not share that view is evident from his fiction; there is no evidence, apart from rumor, the odd scurrilous anecdote, asides such as the Samkange reference, and his brief comments to Lansu (see below), on what he thought of the writers themselves. As he had so much to say about the role of the writer and quoted other writers so extensively in his own work, it is remarkable that as far as can be traced he never referred directly to, or quoted from, other Zimbabwean writers.

7.4 "From sickness to death"

In a study of the black Zimbabweans who were writing in the years around Independence, Ranga Zinyemba observes, " . . . to move from Nyamfukudza to Marechera is to move from cynicism to oblivion, from sickness to death, to nothingness." [137] In the same vein Zimunya observed, "From Mungoshi to Marechera is a season away," [138] whereas McLoughlin commented "[Marechera] has long been regarded as the iconoclastic outsider in Zimbabwean writing. The posthumous publication of his novella *The Black Insider* may well add to the case for keeping him on the fringes." [139]

Marechera's own view of his fellow writers was unequivocal, as he remarked to the Dutch journalist Alle Lansu: "Zimbabwean writers – my own contemporaries – will never dare to write something like *Mindblast*, precisely because there is this heavy emphasis on developing our traditional values" (*SB*, p. 38). Whether he meant the same "traditional values" as those espoused by the Literature Bureau or something different is not clear, but other writers did tackle similar themes to Marechera's, albeit in vastly different styles. For example, in *Going to Heaven*, the sequel to *Son of the Soil,* Wilson Katiyo explores the difficulties of a Zimbabwean exile adjusting to life in London after escaping from pre-independence Zimbabwe.

Writing at the same time as *The Black Insider* Katiyo uses a straightforward linear structure unified by the perspective of the third person omniscient narrator to examine the inner conflict of Alexio Shonga as he encounters the culture shock of leaving his homeland and of becoming a student in London. Although *Going to Heaven* raises the same basic issues as *The Black Insider,* – the problems facing the terrorist sympathizer in Rhodesia, and subsequently, the black exile in London – comparisons are difficult to draw. *Going to Heaven*, with its accessibility, simple and direct narrative, its detached tone, the absence of the author's voice and the complete lack of existential angst, is fundamentally different from *The Black Insider.* On reading *Going to Heaven* one gets the sense of Katiyo consulting his *London A-Z* in order to locate his characters whereas with Marechera the reader is left in no doubt that he had actually walked the streets of "that vast and anonymous London" (*The Black Insider*, p. 94).

And yet, those obvious differences are concerned with style and form. The basic content, the main themes and issues, although handled very differently, have equally obvious similarities. Some of Marechera's fellow writers did confront the major issues of the day, but chose to do so in a different form. Herein lies the essence of Marechera's contribution to the Zimbabwean literary scene. His very uniqueness serves to redefine the canon from within its "borders," which have to be moved to accommodate his "difference," and are inevitably extended by his presence.

Although Marechera often reacted to his experiences and recorded them in a way that was unique to him, the experiences themselves were not unique. For example, at least two of his contemporaries shared his experience of expulsion from the University of Rhodesia in 1973; Nyamfukudza and Zimunya were also expelled, and also gained scholarships to read English at Oxford (Nyamfukudza) and English and History at Canterbury (Zimunya). Both completed their degree courses, and Zimunya went on to study for an MA in modern literature. Zimunya's MA thesis became *Those Years of Drought and Hunger*, and although his poetry has been distributed quite widely, he has not published any prose fiction, apart from the occasional short story. Nyamfukudza has published works of fiction but none makes reference to his experiences in England. His first, and to date, only full-length novel, *The Non-Believer's Journey*, is firmly grounded in Zimbabwe and set in the final years of the war. His other published work is a collections of short stories (*If God was a Woman*, College Press, 1991) about the struggles of the individual to adjust to the new life after independence.

Due no doubt to his shy and retiring personality Charles Mungoshi has not attracted the fervent personal following of Marechera. However, for his achievements, in both Shona and in English, in 1976 he won the top prizes in two sections of the PEN International Book Center Award for the best work in an African language and in English with his novels *Ndiko kupindana kwamazuva* (*How Time Passes*) and *Waiting for the Rain*. That suggests he is a better role model than Marechera for the would-be writer, and the consistently high quality of his prose fiction and poetry assures his central position in any assessment of Zimbabwean literature. Writing steadily throughout the 1970s and 1980s, he published ten books between 1970 and 1989. He met with international recognition when a collection of the stories from *Coming of the Dry Season* and *Some Kinds of Wounds* published as *The Setting Sun and the Rolling World*, won the Commonwealth Literature Prize in 1988 (*Teachers*, p. 268). In comparing the two writers, McLoughlin observed, "With the independence of Zimbabwe in 1980 and the conclusion of the war, fiction is less likely to take Marechera as an example than Mungoshi whose work offers a more feasible mode of analyzing the one area of experience that has so closely touched millions of lives in Zimbabwe for so long, the war." [140] In spite of his eminence as a Zimbabwean writer Mungoshi, in common with Marechera, saw his experience as redolent of the human condition on the grand scale, as he remarked to an interviewer in 1988: "What I had to say was universal. There is no English fire or African fire, human experience is human experience" (*Teachers* p. 297).

Wilson Katiyo, whose novel *Son of the Soil* closes with the stereotypical metaphor of the birth of a healthy child and the implication that the struggle was worthwhile and productive, offers a view that is not shared by Mungoshi, Marechera or Nyamfukudza. Instead, they confront the socio-psychological traumas left by both colonialism and the struggle for independence: recognizing the reconstruction of the lost precolonial society to be an impossible dream they search instead for the location of the inner self, the key characters strangers in their own land. The writers who preceded them, notably, Samkange, Vambe, and Mutswairo, fused historical matter with fiction, looking back to and beyond the first meeting with white settlers, in an attempt to recover an ethnic identity and to create a national image with which to greet a hopeful future. This line is also followed to some extent by Katiyo but rejected by his contemporaries who concerned themselves with the "here and now" cataclysmic effect on the individual of past and recent history. Of those contemporaries none explored that direction with greater determination and dramatic effect than Marechera.

7.5 A Dystopian Vision

The utopianism of Samkange and his contemporaries was replaced by the existential angst of Mungoshi, Marechera, and Nyamfukudza, which in its turn has given way to the dystopian view of their successors. In his article "Land, War and Literature in Zimbabwe," Eldred Jones argues: "For these Zimbabwean writers victory and liberation have a hollow ring. The war has not solved even the problem of the land; it remains to be divided up, fought over, worked and suffered with, all over again."[141]

Jones points to a consistency in the development of a Zimbabwean literature written in English. The themes and issues remain the same as thirty years ago and it is possible to discern a line linking the historical realism of Samkange *et al.* through the social realism of Mungoshi and Nyamfukudza to a similar approach adopted by the more recent writers such as Hove, Chinodya, Dangarembga, and Vera. Chapman comments, "In replying to a concern that writers should look to the civil society rather than back to the destruction, Chinodya says he believes that "writers shouldn't rush to deal with current affairs, but let time give perspective to their vision.""[142]

The sentiment has a certain Marecheran resonance about it; however it is difficult to maintain that he had anything other than an implicit influence on other writers, and that probably owes more to the man, his lifestyle and his reputation, rather than to the writer, in that, without exception, the standard conventions of form and content are observed by his contemporaries.

Shimmer Chinodya's *Harvest of Thorns* explores the pre- and postliberation period subjectively rather than in a quasi-historical fashion and includes biographical material but there the similarities end. Of Marechera's "experimentation" there is no trace. This complete absence of any sense of experimentation is common to the work of all the other Zimbabwean writers with the minor exceptions perhaps of Hove's mystical, almost surreal, evocation of the First Chimurenga in *Bones* or Tsitsi Dangarembga's exploration of new ground in *Nervous Conditions* (which won the African section of the Commonwealth Writers Prize in 1989) by discussing such issues as anorexia and the exploitation of Zimbabwean women. Because of her strongly feminist stance Dangarembga has attracted a great deal of attention although it should be pointed out that Hove's *Bones* deals very powerfully with the plight of Zimbabwean women as does Barbara Makhalisa, whose collection of short stories, *The Underdog* was published in 1984 and whose first work (in Ndebele) was published in 1969. Although Dangarembga's novel received critical acclaim nine years have passed since publication as the writer has been exploring other areas, as indicated by her award at Africa's film festival FESPACO 1997 for *Everyone's Child*, a film she wrote and directed. Referred to as "one of the most consistent and inspired of writers to emerge during this decade," Yvonne Vera has produced a volume of short stories *Why don't you carve other animals?* (1992), and two novels *Nehanda* (1993) and *Without a Name* (1994). Born in Bulawayo, Vera (who read for a doctorate at York University, Toronto, and is now the regional director of the National Gallery in Bulawayo) writes of the experience of women in the war of liberation but also evokes a sense of history by confronting the issues aroused by opposing cultures; for example, of a treaty offered by the white men, Ibwe, a chief and a central character in *Nehanda*, has this to say:

> Our people know the power of words. It is because of this that they desire to have words continuously spoken and kept alive. We do not believe that words can become independent of the speech that bore them, of the humans who controlled and gave birth to them. Can words exchanged today on this clearing surrounded by waving grass become like a child brought up by strangers? Words surrendered to the stranger, like the abandoned child, will become alien – a stranger to our tongues. (pp. 39-40)

There is a similarity here with Marechera's work in that he too was fascinated by language and what he saw as its traps: "You can bind a man with long ropes of words" (*Black Sunlight*, p.3), for example, (see also Chapter Two). It seems the similarity is not accidental; in our conversation (May 1998) Vera spoke of Marechera "luxuriating in language." She also referred to her desire to develop her characters psychologically while dealing with current themes such as incest and the exploitation of women. Vera's work has a direct simplicity of approach and has a relevance and importance in modern Zimbabwe. On

Marechera's current relevance, Vera said: "Marechera is still very trendy among the young. I don't think people write because of him. I think it is fair to say that he inspired an attitude to literature, which was more a love of reading, rather than the practice of writing." A less sanguine view was expressed by Nyamfukudza (June 1998) who, although he agreed that young Zimbabweans still admire Marechera it is an admiration "based on the figure he [Marechera] presented rather than on his writing. Zimbabweans," he added, "are not great readers of books."

7.6 A "wizard of the written word"?

Dambudzo Marechera's place in Zimbabwean literature is secure and permanent. Although it would not be accurate to describe Marechera as a "moulder of his nation," Yeats' words have a certain appropriateness: "We call certain minds creative because they are among the moulders of their nation and are not made upon its mould, and they resemble one another in this only – they have never been foreknown or fulfilled an expectation." [143] Certainly one "who had never been foreknown or fulfilled an expectation," Marechera in his body of work offers a unique account suspended in the social and historical space and time of the most turbulent period in Zimbabwe's history. Much of his work is grounded in his own biography, and the many "flaws" have an integral part in contributing to an understanding of the writer. Marechera's work is a moving expression of the impact on him of the strictures of colonialism and the excesses of white minority rule. The traumas of the struggle for liberation and the straitjacket of the socialist expectations of the nation builders in the false dawn which followed independence closely followed these experiences. It is here that Marechera's contribution to Zimbabwean literature is located as he confronts those issues and reveals the devastating effect they had on him.

The sense of loss at his death is captured in Ray Mawerera's obituary which appeared in *Parade* (Harare) in October 1987:

> Dambudzo Marechera is dead . . . With his death,
> Zimbabwe has lost one of its most prolific and
> ingenious writers, an international wizard of the
> written word. Hate him or love him, hate his
> ideas or his lifestyle even, but he was a fact of
> life that couldn't be ignored. His books are now
> part of the country's literary treasure.

Now that more than a decade has elapsed since Marechera's
death how do we view such extravagant statements? It is still a
fact that he can't be ignored, but part of the country's "literary
treasure"? Most certainly, in the range of his work, prose fiction,
plays, poetry, and criticism, and his exploration of different
styles, Dambudzo Marechera's contribution to the Zimbabwean
literary canon is immense.   With the possible exception of
Charles Mungoshi he is the most talented black writer to emerge
from Zimbabwe. Although an accomplished poet, playwright,
novelist, and critic it is inevitable that his novels have attracted
most attention as his plays have not been performed and his
poetry, until *Cemetery of Mind*, was not widely available.

Concerning Mawerera's comments an important point to
make is that the "treasure house" of Zimbabwean literature does
not enjoy an embarrassment of riches – Yvonne Vera, for
example, spoke of a "very small handful" of "serious writers"
and Stanley Nyamfukudza said: "Independence seemed to act as
a release. But after that initial surge things slowed down and the
literary scene is much quieter now." Of the most recent writers to
emerge it is possible to identify two types. Firstly, the writers
who have lived and studied outside of Zimbabwe, for example,
Dangarembga and Vera, who explore major issues in a
sophisticated manner, aiming at an international audience; and,
secondly, those writers who have stayed in Zimbabwe, and
explore the same or similar issues in a less sophisticated manner,
in some ways reminiscent of the folkloric tales authorized by the
Literary Bureau but updated to allow a political content. For
example, Violet Kala's heroine, Loveness, in *Waste Not Your
Tears,* is an illiterate girl from a rural background who, after

being seduced and deliberately infected with the AIDS virus, becomes an international emissary, addressing conferences on the traumas of being HIV positive.

Another example: of the hero, Musiiwa, of *Goatsmell*, Eldred Jones observes, "It is scarcely credible that the young man [Musiiwa] could be a great artist, a brilliant academic, could research, write and publish a book, spearhead and execute an artistic project . . . and build an arts center while managing an undergraduate course as well as a drink problem." [144] I should emphasize that I do not intend a comparison here with Marechera's work, I merely wish to indicate that an unsophisticated audience will encourage unsophisticated writing. Undoubtedly the next Zimbabwean writer of Marechera's stature will come from somewhere unexpected and do something quite unprecedented, as all good writers do.

The current position of literature in Zimbabwe seems to indicate only a very steady rate of progress, which may well be expected from a newly developing literate society in which the first novels written in English appeared barely thirty years ago. It also seems to indicate that the expected impetus toward raising the overall standard of Zimbabwean literature (which was forecast after the attention commanded by Marechera's work and the publicity attracted by his death and the activities of the Dambudzo Marechera Trust) has yet to yield any tangible results. That may yet happen; the Budding Writers Association of Zimbabwe formed in 1990, with admiration of Marechera as one of its basic principles, appears to be flourishing – at least in Bulawayo from where I have had reports of reports of "enthusiastic meetings."

Following his comments about writing that has concentrated solely on "experiential living" Chapman goes on to argue that the development of a coherent Zimbabwean literature is inhibited by the absence of a "single direction or style that could be discerned as Zimbabwean" [145] Perhaps giving unconscious voice to his desire for wider recognition one of

Marechera's *alter-egos* in *Mindblast* and *Scrapiron Blues* is
Tony, a sculptor. Zimbabwean stone carving, with its unique
"Zimbabwean style", is easily recognizable and highly praised
and, unlike Zimbabwean literature, it is well established, long
standing, and held in high regard throughout the world. An
activity that has its roots in the ancient history of Zimbabwe
stone carving has evolved to its present position over centuries.
Black writing in English in Zimbabwe is barely thirty years on
from the first publication and the first faltering steps towards a
"Zimbabwean style" are still being made. Marechera was an
integral part of the beginning; whether or not he affected the
direction of the Zimbabwean literary movement or will have a
long-term influence on its style remains a moot point awaiting a
longer historical perspective.

It is of course impossible to know for certain but it is
interesting to speculate that the development of black
Zimbabwean writing in English would not be any different if
Marechera had never emerged. This is not to argue that his
writing has not made a contribution to such a development. It has
of course made an enormous contribution. But it does recognize
that in attempting to break the mold that he saw constraining
black writers he reached for different standards in ways others
had not, and have not since, attempted. Stanley Nyamfukudza
suggested (June 1998) that "other writers in other literatures had
experimented more successfully" than Marechera, adding "that is
not a criticism Dambudzo was the first Zimbabwean to take such
an adventurous approach. It is a pity that Zimbabwe and
Zimbabwean literature wasn't ready for him."

Reference is made above to McLoughlin's suggestion that
Marechera was "on the fringes" of Zimbabwean writing; there is
a pejorative implication to this that is inappropriate for a writer
who has international status. All the work published by
Heinemann – *House of Hunger, Black Sunlight* and *The Black
Insider* – is on current worldwide distribution. *Mindblast,
Cemetery of Mind*, and *Scrapiron Blues* are still available in
Zimbabwe. Marechera was on the fringes only in the sense that

his treatment of his subject matter was different from that of any other Zimbabwean writer. One contribution to Zimbabwean literature is then clear – Marechera's work has promoted the notion of a Zimbabwean literature to a worldwide audience. His "experimental" style, whether it is classed as "intellectual anarchism," "pretentious rubbish" or somewhere in between, continues to attract comment. Another contribution is not yet quite so clear: Dambudzo Marechera was a very charismatic figure and even after his death he has a large following; whether that will lead to an increase in reading and eventually to an increase in writing is difficult to determine and dependent, in no small degree, on the activities of the Mugabe government (and whatever follows) and a much increased investment in the education system throughout Zimbabwe, from the primary sector through to the universities.

Dambudzo Marechera may or may not inspire others to write; to an extent, investment in education apart, that fate will be decided by the whim of what is in vogue. What is certain is that his corpus of work will grow in stature as time allows memories of the man and the myth to fade and those who would know Marechera and want to understand him, or quite simply want to know what it was like to be "black in a too white world,"[146] turn to his novels, his plays, and his poems.

Notes

[1] See Flora Veit-Wild, *Dambudzo Marechera: A Source Book on his Life and Work* (London: Hans Zell, 1992), p. 53. (Hereafter *SB.*). Apart from myself Flora Veit-Wild is the only person to have written extensively on Marechera.

[2] The Dambudzo Marechera Trust was established in 1988 with Michael Marechera (the late writer's brother), Flora Veit-Wild and Hugh Lewin as founder trustees. However, as Michael Marechera died in 1995, Veit-Wild accepted a permanent post in Germany in the same year and Hugh Lewin has also left Zimbabwe, the trust has an uncertain future.

[3] *The Black Insider* was published in Harare by Baobab Books (1990) and in London by Lawrence and Wishart (1992). Throughout this work references have been taken from the 1992 edition.

[4] Camus, Albert. "Hope and the Absurd in the Work of Franz Kafka," Ronald Gray (ed.) *Kafka* (New Jersey: Prentice Hall, 1962), p. 147.

[5] According to Heinemann's files, three novellas, *The Black Insider, A Bowl For Shadows* and *The Black Heretic*, were offered to them by Marechera before he submitted *Black Sunlight,* which was following a request to him to rewrite the manuscript that was eventually published as *The Black Insider.* In spite of intensive efforts by the Dambudzo Marechera Trust and others *A Bowl For Shadows* and *The Black Heretic* have not been traced.

[6] Two branches of the Bantu peoples form the indigenous population of Zimbabwe; the Shona (Mashona) have about 80 percent and the Ndebele (or Matabele) about 20 percent, Europeans and Asians account for between 1 percent and 2 percent (1991 estimates). Dambudzo Marechera was of the Shona people.

[7] The writers were: Wilson Katiyo, *A Son Of the Soil* (London: Rex Collins, 1976); Charles Mungoshi, *Waiting for the Rain* (London: Heinemann, 1975); Solomon Mutswairo, *Feso* (Cape Town: OUP, 1957) and *Mapondera* (Washington D.C.: Three

Continents Press, 1974); Stanlake Samkange, *On Trial for My Country* (London: Heinemann, 1966), *The Mourned One* (London: Heinemann, 1975) and *Year of the Uprising* (London: Heinemann, 1978); Ndabiningi Sithole, *The Polygamist* (London: Holder & Stoughton, 1972).

[8] Apart from *The House of Hunger* the only works considered by Zimunya and not included by Kahari were Charles Mungoshi, *Coming of the Dry Season* (Nairobi: OUP, 1973), and Geoffrey Ndhlala, *Jikinya* (London: Macmillan, 1979).

[9] Kevin Foster, "Soul-Food for the Starving: Dambudzo Marechera's *House of Hunger*," *Journal of Commonwealth Literature* (London: Bowker Saur, 1992), p. 58.

[10] Philip Larkin, "The Old Fools," *Collected Poems* (London: Faber and Faber, 1990), p. 196.

[11] In an interview with George Alagiah, "Escape from the House of Hunger," *South*, December 1984, pp. 10-11.

[12] Doris Lessing, "A Cultural Tug of War, "*Books and Bookmen*, Vol. 24.9 (London: June 1979), pp. 62-63.

[13] In his report on *The Black Insider* Heinemann reader John Wyllie has the following, " . . . Marechera . . . could become, in my opinion, as important a writer as Soyinka or, perhaps, a sort of African Dylan Thomas," *The Black Insider,* p. 12.

[14] T. O. McLoughlin "The Past and The Present in African Literature: Examples From Contemporary Zimbabwean Fiction," *Presence Africaine*, Vol 132 (Paris: Societe Nouvelle Presence Africaine, 1984), pp. 93-107.

[15] T. O. McLoughlin, "Black Writing in English From Zimbabwe," *The Writing of East and Central Africa*, G.D. Killam, (ed.) (London: Heinemann, 1984), pp. 100-19.

[16] *ibid* , pp. 100-11.

[17] From an interview with Alle Lansu, February 1986, *Teachers*, p. 5.

[18] T. O. McLoughlin, "Black Writing in English From Zimbabwe," *The Writing of East and Central Africa* G.D. Killam (ed.) (London: Heinemann, 1984), p. 111.

[19] The Zimbabwean novel to which Currey makes reference never materialized. It was Currey's fervent hope that Marechera

would write a novel about Zimbabwe that would establish his reputation as the Zimbabwean Soyinka or Achebe. (Heinemann *Black Sunlight* file.)

[20] In his article "Baby-faced fantasist who aspired to be damned," *Independent On Sunday* January 12, 1992, Caute refers to *Portrait* as a "verse choreodrama . . . complementary to the prose work [*The Black Insider*], a brilliant (but typically uneven) satire on racist Britain."

[21] Landeg White was director of Southern African Studies at the University of York until 1995. These comments were extracted from an unpublished piece written (circa 1991) in support of Dambudzo Marechera for the Noma Award.

[22] In 1996 *Frankfurter Rundschau* together with other European newspapers asked ten authors to select their "Book of the Year." Soyinka chose *Scrapiron Blues*. The newspaper published a Soyinka essay on December 10, 1996 which was reproduced in *Emerging Perspectives on Dambudzo Marechera* (New York: Africa World Press, 1999) pp. 251-2.

[23] Max J. Friedlander, quoted by E H Gombrich in *Art and Illusion* (Oxford: Phaidon Press,1960), Oxford, p. 3.

[24] C. G. Jung, *Modern Man in Search of a Soul* (London: Ark Routledge, 1984), p. 175.

[25] Lionel Trilling, "Freud and Literature," *Critical Theory since Plato*, H. Adams, (ed.) (London: Harcourt Brace Jovanovitch, 1971), p. 949.

[26] R. D. Laing, *The Divided Self* (Harmondsworth: Penguin Books, 1959), p. 19.

[27] Jean Paul Sartre, *Existentialism and Humanism* (London: Eyre Methuen, 1948), p. 42.

[28] Dr Hoare and Professor Gelder examined Marechera and recommended that he undergo a course of counseling. He rejected their advice.

[29] Jacques Lacan, *Ecrits – A Selection* (London: Tavistock/Routledge, 1977), p. 5.

[30] C. G. Jung, *Dreams* (London: Ark Routledge, 1985), p. 260.

[31] Howard P. Kainz, *Hegel's Philosophy of Right, with Marx's*

Commentary (The Hague: Martinus Nijhoff, 1974), pp. 6-15.
[32]   Buuck, David.   "Hybridity and Identity in the Work of Dambudzo Marechera," *Research in African Literatures*, Volume 28, Number 2, Summer 1997, pp. 118-131.
[33]   Raymond Williams, *The Long Revolution*, (London: Chatto & Windus, 1961).
[34] Silvano Arieti, *Understanding and Helping the Schizophrenic*, (Harmondsworth: Pelican, 1981) p. 76.
[35] Aldous Huxley, *The Doors of Perception* (1964) (London: Grafton, 1977), p. 17.
[36] Michel Foucault, *Madness and Civilization* (1961) (London: Tavistock, 1967), p. 85.
[37] From the introduction "From the Author" to *The Brothers Karamazov* (1880), Fyodor Dostoevsky (London: Penguin, 1993).
[38] Michel Foucault, *Madness and Civilization* (1961) (London: Tavistock, 1967), p. 88.
[39] Wilson Harris, *The Radical Imagination*, Alan Riach & Mark Williams (eds.) (Liege: University of Liege, 1992), pp. 14-.15.
[40] R. D. Laing, *Self and Others*, second edition (London: Tavistock, 1969) p. 82.
[41] This argument underpins *Sanity, Madness and the Family* and is referred to specifically by Harriet Stewart in "Fear in the family," *The Guardian* (London: July 26 1996), p. 14.
[42] Anthony Storr, *The Dynamics of Creation* (London: Penguin, 1991), p. 75.
[43] As quoted by Cal McCrystal in "Old boy's class act," *The Observer Review* (London: September 4,1995), p. 8.
[44] Dambudzo Marechera, "The African Writer's Experience of European Literature," *Zambezia*, pp. 99-101.
[45] Simon Dentith, *Bakhtinian Thought* (London: Routledge, 1995), p. 65.
[46] Louis MacNeice, *Selected Poems* (London: Faber & Faber, 1960), p. 10.
[47] Roland Barthes, "The Death of the Author," *Image Music Text* (London: Fontana, 1977), p. 142.
[48] G. Griffiths, *A Double Exile* (London: Boyars, 1978), p. 49.

[49] Chinua Achebe, *Hopes and Impediments – Selected Essays 1965-87*, (London: Heinemann, 1988), p. 30.

[50] Ngugi wa Thiong'o, "On Writing in Gikuyu," *Research in African Literatures*, Vol. 16, Number 2 (Austin: University of Texas Press, 1985).

[51] David Caute, "Marechera and the Colonel," *The Espionage of the Saints* (London: Hamish Hamilton, 1986), p. 15.

[52] In their introduction to *The Radical Imagination* Riach and Williams argue "English is manifestly a globally dispersed and decentered language whose principal connecting legacy is colonialism in all its complexity. Harris invites us to see the historical and contemporary operations of language neither in terms of imperial authority nor in terms of the self-righteous rhetoric of the deprived but rather in terms of continually regenerative hybridization.." p.13.

[53] Michael Dash, "The Way Out of Negritude," *The Postcolonial Studies Reader*, (eds.) Bill Ashcroft *et al.* (London: Routledge, 1995), p. 200.

[54] Wole Soyinka in an interview with Nathan Gardels, "Blood-soaked quilt of Africa," *The Guardian* (London: May 17, 1994), p. 20.

[55] This feature of the work of the Literature Bureau is further developed by Flora Veit- Wild in *Teachers, Preachers, Non-Believers*, pp. 72-4.

[56] Preben Kaarsholm, *Cultural Struggle and Development in Southern Africa* (London: James Currey, 1991), p. 32.

[57] *A History of the Shona* was published in London in 1979. Among others Ranger also cites David Beach, "The Politics of Collaboration," University of Rhodesia, History seminar paper, No 9, 1969, and "The Rising in South Western Mashonaland, 1896-7," doctoral thesis, University of London, 1971.

[58] *The Ndebele under the Khumalos, 1820-1896,* doctoral thesis, University of Lancaster, 1976. Additionally, "The Absent Priesthood: Another Look at the Rhodesian Risings of 1896-97," *Journal of African History*, Vol. 28, No. 1, 1977.

[59] Lewis Nkosi, *Tasks and Masks* (Harlow: Longman, 1981), p. 31.

[60] Julia Kristeva, *The Kristeva Reader* Toril Moi, (ed.) (Oxford: Basil Blackwell, 1986), p. 298.

[61] Julia Kristeva, *Black Sun* (New York: Columbia University Press, 1989), p. 5.

[62] *The Poet Speaks*, Argo Record Company London 1965, PLP 1085. Sylvia Plath recorded her contribution on October 30, 1962.

[63] Quoted by Nicci Gerard in "The crying game," *Observer Review* (London: September 10, 1995), p. 15.

[64] These are the final lines in Robert Frost's poem, "The Road Not Taken," *The Selected Poems,* Ian Hamilton (ed.) (Harmondsworth: Penguin, 1973), p. 77.

[65] Lady Iris Hayter, wife of Sir William Hayter, warden of New College kept a diary of Marechera's activities. The entry for August 10, 1975, reads "W's [William's] day was spent on Charles Marechera who has created havoc in the College, running amok when drunk among conference members . . . W was told of a series of incidents, door beaten down, Mr. Ledwige [a college steward] attacked and so on. Colin Winter was summoned and we hope has taken Charles away." *SB*, p. 163.

[66] Fromm qualifies his comments by pointing out that " . . . truth is the essential medium to transform, respectively, society and the individual; awareness is the key to social and individual therapy" Erich Fromm, *Beyond the Chains of Illusion* (London: Abacus, 1980), p. 16. Marechera was certainly very aware, though for him truth was a negotiable treaty. That said, such a "problem" would not, of course, invalidate *his* transformation.

[67] Carl Rogers, who in turn was quoting Kierkegaard, develops this theme in *On Becoming a Person* (London: Constable, 1967).

[68] From Laing's introduction to *The Politics of Experience* (London: Penguin, 1967).

[69] See David Caute, *Fanon* (London: Fontana, 1970), p. 16.

[70] Carl Rogers, *On Becoming a Person* (London: Constable, 1967), p. 110.

[71] Laurice Taitz and Melissa Levin, "Fictional Autobiographies/Autobiographical Fictions," *Emerging*

Perspectives on Dambudzo Marechera (New York: Africa World Press, 1999) pp. 163-76.

[72] While the ability to merge into the background may appear advantageous, Marechera's reference to a chameleon's properties is to indicate a desire to identify with, rather than to escape from. His use is in a pejorative sense, as he makes clear. See p. 2 and p. 39 for examples.

[73] David Caute, "Baby-faced fantasist who aspired to be damned," *Independent On Sunday*, (London: January 12, 1992).

[74] Philip Larkin, "This Be The Verse," *Collected Poems* (London: Faber & Faber, 1988), p. 180.

[75] A John Wyllie comment about Marechera in his report on *The Black Heretic*.

[76] James Joyce, *A Portrait of the Artist as a Young Man* (London: Paladin, 1988), p. 207.

[77] Gerald Gaylard, "Dambudzo Marechera and Nationalist Criticism," *English in Africa* (Grahamstown: Rhodes University Press, October, 1993), p. 90.

[78] Jane Wilkinson, *Talking with African Writers* (London: James Currey, 1992), p. 211.

[79] *ibid*, p. 203.

[80] Bill Ashcroft, *The Postcolonial Studies Reader* (London: Routledge, 1995), p. 183.

[81] Chinua Achebe, "Named for Victoria, Queen of England," *The Postcolonial Studies Reader*, Bill Ashcroft *et al.* (eds.) (London: Routledge, 1995), p. 190.

[82] Dambudzo Marechera, "Soyinka, Dostoevsky: The Writer on Trial for his Time," *Zambezia*, XIV (ii) (Harare: University of Zimbabwe, 1987), p. 107.

[83] Dan Wylie "Language Thieves," *English in Africa*, Vol 18, No 2 (Grahamstown: Rhodes University Press, October, 1991), p. 43.

[84] Gerard Gaylard, "Dambudzo Marechera and Nationalist Criticism," *English in Africa*, Vol. 20, No. 2 (Grahamstown: Rhodes University Press, October, 1993), p. 90.

[85] Chinweizu, *Voices From Twentieth-Century Africa* (London: Faber & Faber, 1988.), p. xix.

[86] *ibid,* p. xxi.

[87] Wilson Harris, *The Radical Imagination* (Liege: University of Liege, 1992), p. 41.

[88] The story goes, "One of the most promising of the young negro poets said to me [Langston Hughes] once, "I want to be a poet, not a negro poet," meaning, I believe, "I want to write like a white poet," meaning subconsciously, "I would like to be a white poet," meaning behind that, "I would like to be white" *Voices of Negritude* (London: Quartet Books, 1988) p. 186.

[89] As far as can be determined Marechera was arrested several times for being drunk and disorderly or using threatening behavior. He may have been detained in the cells overnight occasionally but the only time he was charged and sentenced was the Cardiff episode.

[90] A critic of African literature and a free lance writer, Fraser was also poetry editor of *West Africa* at the time of his friendship with Marechera. I met him and recorded an interview in London on June 30, 1997.

[91] Dr Niven is now director of the Literature Department at the British Council This material is from an interview recorded on July 1, 1997 at Dr Niven's London. office.

[92] This reference alludes to a story (possibly apocryphal) about a writer of a weekly serial for a London newspaper in the 1930s. The writer considered himself to be underpaid, but before asking for an increase he took the precaution of leaving his hero (Clarence) chained hand and foot at the bottom of a deep, water-filled well. As no other writer could think of a way of releasing Clarence in time for the next edition, the editor, in order to secure the next instalment had no alternative other than to pay up. The next instalment began, "With a superhuman effort, Clarence burst his bonds . . ."

[93] Franz Fanon, *The Wretched of the Earth* (London: Penguin, 1990), p. 200.

[94] Helene Cixous, "Difficult Joys," *The Body and the Text* (Hemel Hempstead: Harvester, 1990), p. 14. Also, for a development of this argument see David Pattison, "Call No Man Happy," *Journal of Southern African Studies*, Vol. 20, No. 2

(Abingdon: Carfax Publishing, 1994), pp229-30.

[95] Dambudzo Marechera, "The African Writer's Experience of European Literature," *Zambezia*, XIV (ii) (Harare: University of Zimbabwe, 1987), p. 102.

[96] Norman Holland, *The Dynamics of Literary Response* (New York: Columbia University Press, 1989), p. 56.

[97] Sigmund Freud, *Creative Writers and Day Dreaming*, standard edition Volume 10 (London: Hogarth, 1959), p. 143.

[98] Julia Kristeva, *Black Sun* (New York: Columbia University Press, 1989), p. 6.

[99] R. D. Laing, *The Divided Self* (Harmondsworth: Penguin Books, 1959), p. 27.

[100] Gaetano Benedetti, *Psychotherapy of Schizophrenia* (New York: New York University Press, 1987), p. 110.

[101] Jean-Paul Sartre, *Being and Nothingness* (London: Methuen, 1943), p. 222.

[102] William Henley, *For England's Sake*: "What have I done for you, England, my England? / What is there I would not do, England, my own?"

[103] Winston Churchill, British Prime Minister in the 1940s, suffered from lifelong depression. He likened it to being followed everywhere by a very large black dog.

[104] Professor Barton's letter to me dated July 5, 1997 casts an interesting light on Marechera's relationships with his fellow students:

Charles was a small man, but he could and did inflict a good deal of physical damage on the other undergraduates when (as was pretty often the case) he was drunk and spoiling for a fight. They were sympathetic to him, but understandably found it hard to be regularly beaten up by someone they had themselves brought to the college and wanted – without any condescension whatever – to make friends with.

Marechera's behavior had dire implications for other would-be-students as Barton points out, "The JCR experiment, I believe, has never in consequence been repeated."

[105] Anthony Storr, *Solitude* (London: Flamingo, 1989), p. xiv.

[106] Jacques Lacan, *Ecrits - A Selection* (London:

Tavistock/Routledge, 1977), p. 7.
[107] Leo Schneiderman, *The Literary Mind* (New York: Insight Books, 1988), pp. 206/207.
[108] Salman Rushdie, "The novel is not dead. It's just buried," the *Observer Review* (London: August 18, 1996), p. 15.
[109] Details of the contract between Marechera and Chris Austin (director and producer) and Gill Bond of Indigo Productions are given in the *Source Book*, pp. 281-2.
[110] Colin Stoneman, *Zimbabwe's Prospects* (London: Macmillan, 1988), pp. 4-5.
[111] Several of the Zimbabweans in key positions had frequented the Africa Center when in London, so much so that director Alastair Niven said it was known jokily as "Zimbabwe House." He remembers that "Everyone had to declare themselves politically – you were either part of it or you weren't. Dambudzo's independence of mind was brave and perverse. A sense of self-dramatization mixed with a genuine integrity. There was this weird mix of a person who self-dramatized, conscious of the effect he was making and who was at times out of control and at other times acted with integrity because he would have thought it intellectually lazy to accept knee-jerk liberal attitudes (Interview July 1,1997).
[112] The University of Rhodesia lecturer who supplied the reference for Marechera when he applied to Oxford was Len Rix, which may account for the cat's name. Bulgakov also made use of a "giant cat" in *The Master and Margarita*
[113] Comparisons with Kavanagh, who had a love/hate relationship with Dublin and once lived in a park there, are particularly apposite. When Antoinette Quinn (*Patrick Kavanagh: Selected Poems*, Penguin 1996) described Kavanagh as "an embattled writer in a country in which nationalism remained the major collective passion" (p. xxx) and wrote of his "uncompromising hostility towards ethnicity as an aesthetic criterion" (p. xxvii) and "his personalizing of cultural issues . . . a temperamental cussedness...exacerbated by alcohol...an abrasive uncouth persona and a terse barbed wit . . . though he

could be kindly and humorous . . . gallant and charming" (p. xxxi) she could just as readily have been writing of Marechera.

[114] Quoted by Frank Kilfeather in an article commemorating the thirtieth anniversary of Kavanagh's death. "Irishman's Diary," *The Irish Times*, November 17, 1997.

[115] Never straightforward, "a babel of discourses" for such as Marechera is complex. For example, he received treatment at the Warneford Clinic for his "madness" according to western ideas (a western discourse); his mother received treatment for her "madness" from a *n'anga* (an African discourse). In this way, it can be argued not only was Marechera exposed to a babel of discourses, some were in competition with each other.

[116] Georg Lukacs, *The Meaning of Contemporary Realism*, p. 92.

[117] *Ibid*, p. 135.

[118] As Marechera claimed "D. H. Lawrence was the skeleton in my cupboard" ("The African Writer's Experience of European Literature," p. 100) such comparisons are not inappropriate. I have in mind Sagar's criticism of *Pansies* that the "less successful are merely sketches for poems." *D H Lawrence* (Harmondsworth: Penguin, Revised Edition 1986), p. 16.

[119] From *Portrait of a Black Artist in London*, see the *Source Book*, p. 265.

[120] For example, on being told his mother and one of his sisters wanted to see him, he responded "What does she want from me the bitch? Tell her I don't want to see her" (*Source Book*, p. 306).

[121] Georg Lukacs, *The Meaning of Contemporary Realism*, p. 80.

[122] *ibid*, pp. 80-1.

[123] *ibid*, p. 54.

[124] See "The African Writer's Experience of European Literature" published in full in the *Source Book*, pp. 361-68. The above quotation appears on p. 364.

[125] No doubt Marechera was writing at that time but the book was not *The House of Hunger*. He was at Sheffield from February to June in 1979, whereas *The House of Hunger* was submitted to Heinemann two years earlier, in February 1977, and published in 1978.

[126] Musaemura Zimunya, "Flora Veit-Wild: A Black Insider's

Testimony," *Parade* December 1995, p. 29. Zimunya is taking exception to Veit-Wild's allegation (*Parade*, November 1995) that black Zimbabwean writers did little to help Marechera in the final years of his life. He also makes reference to his own interview with Veit-Wild for her book *Patterns of Poetry in Zimbabwe* which he claims presented "an edited version which selectively left out some of the more profound statements . . . creating a distorted impression of me and my poetry."

[127]   For example, Kevin Foster (1994) had this comment on *Teachers* in his review "Regimes of Silence: Untold Zimbabwe," "It [*Teachers*] is impressive in its scope and meticulous in its analysis of the cultural and educational policies that shaped the lives of generations of writers. However, it is marked by the theoretical shortcomings that result in certain striking omissions, not least of which . . . is its failure to substantially engage with the literature."

[128]   Ahmed Rashid, "Death of the novel," the *Observer Review* (London: February 25, 1996), p. 16.

[129]   Michael Chapman, *Southern African Literatures* (London: Longman, 1996), p. 312.

[130]   Flora Veit-Wild, *Survey of Zimbabwean Writers* (Bayreuth: Bayreuth University Press, 1992), p. 9.

[131]   Although Veit-Wild makes several references to the work of the Literature Bureau, very few of the writers published by the Bureau feature in the survey. This (apart from considerations of her stated criteria) may be on the grounds that the Bureau only published ." . . . trivial and folklorist writing" which, argues Veit-Wild, ensured that indigenous writing followed a completely separate development to black writing in English (*Teachers* p. 74). In an information pamphlet published in 1994, the Bureau acknowledges mistakes from the past when [as a result of publishing] " . . . love stories and mediocre historical stories with very little relevance to what was going on at the time . . . The credibility of the Literature Bureau sank very low indeed."

[132]   Progress here appears to be very slow. For example, in the most recent review of Southern African writing, *New Writing From Southern Africa* (London: James Currey, 1996),

Emmanuel Ngara (ed.), Chinodya, Dangarembga, Hove and Zimunya are featured. In addition *Essays on African Writing - Contemporary Literature* (London: Heinemann,1995), Abdulrazak Gurnah (ed.), has essays on Hove, Dangarembga, and Marechera. *The Arnold Anthology of Postcolonial Literatures in English* (London: Arnold,1996), John Thieme (ed.) makes reference only to Dangarembga. Inclusion in works of this nature does suggest that they are, notionally at least, part of the emerging canon. It also appears to confirm that very few new writers are emerging.

[133] Bernth Lindfors, "The Teaching of African Literature in Anglophone African Universities," *Wasafiri* (London: ATCAL, Spring 1990), pp. 13-16.

[134] Michael Chapman, *Southern African Literatures* (London: Longman, 1996), p. 162.

[135] McLoughlin, T. O. "Black Writing in English from Zimbabwe. "*The Writing of East and Central Africa*, G.D. Killam (ed.) (London: Heinemann, 1984), p. 105.

[136] A situation that has changed very little. In an interview for the *Herald* (Harare August 5 1995 "Read more books, urges minister.") the Minister of Higher Education, Dr Ignatius Chombo, said, "If writing is a form of communication, then the communication circuit can only be complete when there is a readership. One of our greatest problems lies in the dearth of a readership. As a nation, we are not doing enough to nurture the readers who are to read what we write.." Supporting this view an unnamed Southern African publisher reported in the Zimbabwe International Book Fair Bulletin (Number 16 March/April 1998) "For me, the greatest benefit at ZIBF was meeting and sharing problems with other small publishers from Africa. Discussion revealed that most of us are struggling in the face of tremendous odds. All of us faced the desperate poverty of our audience and the absence of a reading culture."

[137] Ranga Zinyemba, "Zimbabwe's lost novelists in search of direction," *Moto*, August 1983, pp. 7-10. See also *Teachers*, p. 258.

[138] Musaemura Zimunya, *Those Years of Drought and Hunger*

(Gwelo: Mambo Press, 1982), p. 97.

[139]   T. O. McLoughlin, "Men at War: Writers and Fighters in Recent Zimbabwean Fiction," *Current Writing* (Natal: University of Natal Press, No 3, 1991), p. 152.

[140]   T. O. McLoughlin, "Black Writing in English from Zimbabwe, "*The Writing of East and Central Africa*, G.D. Killam (ed.) (London: Heinemann, 1984), p. 112.

[141]   Jones's article referred specifically to Chencherai Hove, *Bones* (London: Heinemann, 1988), Alexander Kangengoni, *Effortless Tears* (Harare: Baobab Books, 1993), Nevanji Madanhire, *Goatsmell* (Harare: Anvil Press, 1992) and Yvonne Vera, *Nehanda* (Harare: Baobab Books, 1993).

[142]   Michael Chapman, *Southern African Literatures* (London: Longman, 1996), p. 301.

[143]   W. B. Yeats, *Explorations* (London: MacMillan, 1962), pp. 158-9.

[144]   Eldred Jones, "Land, War and Literature in Zimbabwe," *African Literature*, Vol. 20 (London: James Currey, 1996), p. 55.

[145]   Michael Chapman, *Southern African Literatures* (London: Longman, 1996), p. 311.

[146]   Heinemann reader John Wyllie commented on Marechera's " . . . tragic circumstances of being black in a too white world," *SB*, p. 204 (and above).

Bibliography

Marechera, Dambudzo. *The House of Hunger* (London: Heinemann, 1978).

Black Sunlight (London: Heinemann, 1980).

Mindblast (Harare: College Press, 1984).

The Black Insider (Harare: Baobab Books, 1990) and (London: Lawrence and Wishart, 1992). (References taken from the 1992 edition).

Cemetery of Mind (Harare: Baobab Books, 1992).

Scrapiron Blues (Harare: Baobab Books, 1994).

'The African Writer's Experience of European Literature', *Zambezia*, XIV (ii) (Harare: University of Zimbabwe,1987).

'Soyinka, Dostoevsky: The Writer on Trial for his Time', *Zambezia*, XIV (ii) (Harare: University of Zimbabwe,1987).

Appendix

The story that I am going to tell begins around the middle of the last century. It is a story of family betrayal. But I believe Dambudzo would want it recorded because it explains so much about his background and his temperament.

When we buried Tambu (Dambudzo) I was an angry man. For some years I had been aware that there was a family secret that people wanted to keep hidden. I began to ask questions, to put together the pieces. Tambu would appear in my dreams while I was doing this. But as soon as everything was clear to me he stopped. That is how I am sure he would want the story told.

It begins around 1850. My great-grandmother (our mother's grandmother) was a Nyamaropa – they were a powerful family who lived in the Nyanga area. This woman was a dangerous witch, so dangerous that she caused many deaths in the community. Eventually the people decided that they must kill her. They took her into the bush, tied her to a tree and left her to be torn apart by wild animals.

But her spirit powers did not die with her, as I shall explain.

I should also say that the Nyamaropas were

somehow related by marriage to the Marechera family. When my mother was a small girl she actually went to stay with them for a while and it was understood that she would marry into the family when she grew up.

When she returned to the Nyamaropas something happened that was to change her life. When the spirit of a dead person needs to be appeased, a special ceremony is held. Beer is brewed for two days and a young girl is chosen to be the "bride" of the dead person. This is what happened to my mother. When such a girl later marries for real, any children that she bears belong to the dead person – not to her living husband!

When our father, Isaac, later married our mother, his family (the Marecheras) were outraged. He had not properly consulted them and when he brought home his bride they were very angry because they knew her secret. Father did not know about her past because he had grown up elsewhere.

. . . . Towards the end of 1969, Mother became mad. She went to consult a n'anga who told her she could only get rid of the problem by passing it on to one of her children. She did not choose Lovemore because he was her favourite. She did not choose me because I was named after a powerful ancestor whose spirit would protect me from such things. She chose Dambudzo.

In 1971 he began to suffer delusions. He was sure two men were following him everywhere. Only he could see them. He was then writing his 'A' levels and I don't know how he managed because he was taking so many tranquilizers.

Subsequently I felt he must have known what Mother had done. When later he left for England my bones told me he was running away from something. When he returned to Zimbabwe he refused to see Mother – I now understand why.

It is difficult to explain such matters to those who do not know our culture. But I feel this story explains why Dambudzo always said he had no family and why he saw himself as an outcast. (*SB*, pp 53-54)

Index

drinking, 37, 42, 52, 57, 67,
87, 137, 140, 150-3, 176,
183, 204
drugs, 40, 42, 51-5, 65, 122,
137-8,
Drum, 7
The Dynamics of Creation,
45

E

eccentric behavior, 33
Engelhardt, Thomas 23, 41
"England, my England",
142
essential self, 100, 185
Euro-assimilation, 111
Europe, 78, 104, 124, 126,
134, 136, 175, 192, 228
European education, 16, 21,
103, 135, 136
Everyone's Child, 234
exile, 3, 6, 7, 22, 26-7, 75,
78, 119, 157-8, 186, 231-
2
existential, 17, 44, 65, 107,
176, 186, 189, 204, 219,
230, 232
experimental approach, 206
experimentation, 30, 192,
207, 232
expulsion, 67, 90, 104, 231

F

Fanon, Franz 65, 104, 129,
130, 132

father, 48-50, 61, 66, 98,
105, 109, 166, 181, 188,
202, 213
Ferlinghetti, Lawrence 53
FESPACO 1997, 234
"First Street Tumult", 41,
151, 194-203
Focus, 157, 158
"The Footnote To Hamlet",
182
form and content, 30, 38,
121, 205, 228, 233
Foster, Kevin 11, 12
Foucault, Michel 58
"Fragments", 202, 213
Fraser, Robert 88, 104, 116,
118, 205, 221-2
Freud, Sigmund 43-4, 135
Friedlander, Max 42
Fromm, Erich 91
Frost, Robert 82
"Fuzzy Goo's Guide to the
Earth", 211

G

Gadarene swine, 63
Gaylard, Gerald 107, 111
Gelder, Prof. 45, 64
Gikandi, Simon 23
Ginsberg, Allen 53
Goatsmell, 237
Going to Heaven, 230
Golding, William 121, 214
good citizen, 37, 47, 192-3,
214
great cunt, 130-3
Grigson, Geoffrey 122